YOUNG BLOOD

The Inside Story of How Street Gangs Hijacked Britain's Biggest Drugs Cartel

GRAHAM JOHNSON

MAINSTREAM
PUBLISHING

EDINBURGH AND LONDON

This edition, 2014

First published in Great Britain in 2013 by
MAINSTREAM PUBLISHING COMPANY
(EDINBURGH) LTD
7 Albany Street
Edinburgh EH1 3UG

ISBN 9781780576763

This book is a work of non-fiction. In some cases names of people, places, dates and the sequence or details of events have been changed to protect the privacy of others. The author has stated to the publishers that, except in such minor respects, the contents of this book are true.

A catalogue record for this book is available
from the British Library

Printed in Great Britain by
Clays Ltd, St Ives plc

1 3 5 7 9 10 8 6 4 2

To Emma, Sonny, Raya, Connie and Clara

ACKNOWLEDGEMENTS

I would like to thank Jon Elek at AP Watt and Bill Campbell and everyone at Mainstream. Also I would like to thank the following people, who contributed to *Young Blood*: the Analyst, the senior police officer at Merseyside Police who allowed me to interview him and was generous with his time and patient with regard to explaining police procedure, without revealing sensitive or compromising information. I would also like to thank the Analyst for offering his own views on tactics, strategy and performance, which he has formulated over many years of service. I would also like to thank the Dutch police officers who allowed me to interview them. In addition, I would like to thank the Mexican ambassador to the UK, Eduardo Medina-Mora, and his former senior aide Ariel Moutsatsos, who spoke with expertise and authority on the subject of international drug trafficking. I would also like to thank Dylan Porter for his interviews and for allowing me access to his prison diary.

ACKNOWLEDGEMENTS

CONTENTS

PREFACE

Young Blood is the sequel to *The Cartel*, which tells the story of the first 30 years of Britain's biggest drug gang, spanning the period between 1973 and 2003. *Young Blood* brings that story up to date, charting the last decade of the gang, between 2003 and 2013.

The multibillion-pound organisation has gone through important changes, particularly the rise of the foot soldier and the turning point in the police's war on drugs. In recent years, the old godfathers who previously ran the Cartel have largely been usurped by a new generation of teenage street gangs. They are armed to the teeth and refuse to play by the old underworld codes. These US-style gangs, which hit headlines following the murder of schoolboy Rhys Jones in August 2007, would stop at nothing until they were given a piece of the action by the established order of the underworld, blowing them up with car bombs, throwing hand grenades through their windows and spraying up their cars and houses with automatic gunfire. A form of urban terrorism would become the defining characteristic of the new drug dealers, and one that would require an unprecedented counter response by the police. The militarisation of the force, the formation of elite cadres and the widespread use of anti-terror laws and public-order legislation became visible on Britain's streets for the first time. This urban-terrorist phenomenon reached its zenith in Manchester in 2012 when two unarmed policewomen, Nicola Hughes (23) and Fiona Bone (32), were killed by automatic gunfire followed by a grenade attack. According to underworld sources, the murderer, Dale Cregan, was a well-known Cartel debt collector. Before that, more than half of all grenade attacks in the UK occurred in Liverpool. During one thwarted incident, a grenade was left outside the home of former Liverpool manager Kenny Dalglish. On another occasion, a grandmother had a limb blown off after a grenade was launched through her window on the instructions of a senior Cartel enforcer.

The violent power struggle between the older generation and the new led to the assassination of the Cartel's de facto boss of bosses, Colin 'King Cocaine' Smith, in 2007. Numerous other murders followed in Britain, Amsterdam and Spain as the new pretenders, backed by hundreds of fanatical street criminals, formed strategic alliances with members of the old guard who were prepared to adapt.

The upheavals coincided with a new offensive by the police. New law-enforcement policies, better technology and increased national and international cooperation meant that for the first time the police were winning the war against the Cartel. *Young Blood* tells this story from both sides, in the words of both the drug dealers and gangsters who work for the Cartel and the police officers who have dedicated their lives to destroying it.

The Cartel was founded in Liverpool in 1973 by a used-car salesman known as Fred the Rat, who used the illegal proceeds from armed robberies to invest in heroin and cannabis imports. His business model was incredibly successful, and by the 1980s the Cartel was Britain's number-one narcotics supplier. In 1980, Customs and Excise identified the 'Liverpool Mafia' as the country's first and only drugs cartel, as defined by their investigators. A drugs cartel is a loose alliance of crime groups, underworld godfathers and crime families bonded together by shared goals and interests: the import and distribution of controlled drugs.

Later, Fred the Rat handed over partial control to an underworld financier called the Banker, and then to an up-and-coming mixed-race gangster called Curtis Warren. Warren went on to become the richest criminal ever caught in Britain. Warren revolutionised the Cartel, industrialising cocaine-trafficking and flushing its networks with billions of pounds. Opportunities for the criminal classes opened up on a never-before-seen scale. A street dealer called Dylan Porter began peddling £5 deals of cannabis on a suburban road, before graduating to heroin. Within a decade he was a millionaire mid-ranking importer and distributor, shifting a minimum of 20 kilos of heroin a week. But by the turn of the millennium, the opportunities had run out, and he was in jail and facing a 20-year-plus stretch. In *The Cartel*, Dylan Porter explains in detail how he got rich; in *Young Blood*, he reveals the harsh reality of being middle-aged and locked up inside Britain's toughest jails, as well as what it was like to be released into a changed underworld, where ten-year-old gang members talked down to him.

The Cartel tells the story of old-school gangsters who fought to build up their fortunes playing by the 'rules' that the older criminals had taught them. *Young Blood* carries on that theme and reveals how they have fared over the last decade. One such underworld veteran was 60-year-old Yael Feeney, who had made his money from financing drug deals and money laundering. Though Feeney had close associations with drug lords, he refused steadfastly to deal himself. This might have been a self-serving deception, but it allowed Feeney to operate one step removed from the actual drug traffickers. He used the fact to soothe his conscience. Feeney's authority, however, had put him in a unique position within the underworld. During the Cartel's growth years, between 1985 and 2005, he had been brought in by drug dealers to deal with internal disputes as a mediator. In *Young Blood*, Feeney reveals how the situation backfired. He tells how an alliance of cocaine-fuelled street gangs set out to destroy him because his presence threatened their assault on the old godfathers with whom he was allied. Feeney ended up in prison for money laundering, where he was faced with another dilemma. In order to retain his status and power, he would have to engage with the penal economy: he would have to deal drugs for the first time. Feeney reveals the struggle he fought in jail to rebuild his life and retain his position within Britain's most cut-throat criminal network.

Being a young gang member with a reputation for violence

did not guarantee success, however. Bubbley Shalson was a half Persian, half West Indian *pistolero* from the melting pot that was the Toxteth Triangle. Shalson took on rival gangs from the North End of the city and was made to pay a heavy price. He was attacked with guns and bombs and ended up in prison for drug dealing.

But *The Cartel* wasn't only about the criminal's perspective. For the first time, a senior policeman told the inside story of how Britain's police had reacted to burgeoning organised crime. The officer, known as the Analyst, had joined Merseyside Police as a teenage recruit in the 1970s. For most of his career he had watched drug crime grow right before his eyes, as he went from beat copper to custody sergeant to murder-squad detective. In the early 1980s, he encountered a teenager called Colin Smith as he moved on a group of noisy kids from outside a row of shops. For the next 25 years, the Analyst and Smith lived parallel lives on opposing sides. The Analyst investigated Smith as he rose through the rigid hierarchy of the Cartel; Smith tried to outfox the Analyst as he moved up the ranks and the force closed in on him. Smith was integral in setting up drug hubs in Amsterdam, Spain and Portugal, while strengthening the Cartel's ties with suppliers in South America, Turkey and Africa. But eventually he grew too big and was killed by the young bloods in 2007 in an underworld *coup d'état*. The Analyst was called in to investigate his murder, and for the first time was given access to the Cartel's inner workings. The Analyst is Britain's number-one anti-drugs cop, and in *Young Blood* he reveals how he stepped up operations against the dealers – and succeeded.

The Cartel began to tell the story of the young pretenders, the next generation of criminals who would eventually take over the business. They were born in the 1980s and 1990s, often third-generation underclass children whose mums and dads were more often than not drug addicts, offenders or both. Almost all of them were poor and inadequately socialised, and many were raised to be drug dealers. By the time they were growing up, the Cartel was a powerful force within their neighbourhoods. The Cartel offered jobs to the socially excluded, the uneducated, the uncreditworthy and the ambitious. The Cartel was now part of popular culture.

Their brothers were named after famous drug dealers, and the Cartel offered a stable career path that a decade earlier had been the preserve of traditional industries, which were now long gone.

The spiritual leader of the new gang members was a hardcore juvenile killer known as Kallas. *The Cartel* charted Kallas's early years: how he rose from being a pusher on a bike to a feared gang leader, prepared to take on the old-guard hard men such as Yael Feeney. Kallas and his kind wanted into the Cartel badly and, with it, access to instant riches beyond their wildest dreams. For someone who had started off by selling drugs on a BMX bike, Kallas had done well. He'd had no backing. He hadn't come from a big gangster family, nor did he have contacts. But he quickly realised that most of it was an act anyway, and it was possible to strip away the illusion of wealth and power from the leaders, if you were prepared to challenge them. The likes of Kallas, and his underbosses Sidious and Kaim, had nothing, but they saw this as an advantage: their nothingness was powerful. They had no beliefs, no codes, no assets, no organisations, no memberships: that made them nimble and hard to destroy. Kallas began to leap up the rungs of the Cartel's hierarchy and ended up in Spain and Amsterdam, where he and his small gang began to deal drugs on a big scale. In a quiet Spanish urban area popular with Brit expats, they rented a large villa and turned it into an HQ from which they became responsible for selling coke in Marbella and tablets in Ibiza.

The Cartel showed how the drug lords exploited economic and social problems within society to sell more drugs or simply expand their power. Fred the Rat had used the confusion caused by decimalisation and the oil crisis to smuggle heroin during the early 1970s. In the 1980s recession that followed, deindustrialisation provided an army of unemployed foot soldiers, such as Dylan Porter, to swell the Cartel's ranks and extend its reach. In the 1990s, the house-price collapse and subsequent boom provided opportunities to invest the windfall profits from dance drugs into money-laundering property schemes. *Young Blood* tells the story of how the Cartel exploited the next financial crisis: the banking collapse of 2008.

By 2003, the Cartel had gone through 30 years of uninterrupted growth. It had started out as a one-man band, the brainchild of Fred the Rat. Now it had grown into an international business. Thousands of people worked directly for the Cartel in multifarious roles. Thousands more were employed indirectly, or benefited from its economic activity in some other way: for instance, as part-time workers and subcontractors. The Cartel's structure was sophisticated: a rolling, rigid hierarchy that resembled a group of trading partners. In some ways, the Cartel looked like an emerging international business with a basic command structure. Economists call the model an 'international area network'. Over the next decade, the shape of the organisation would change again, solidifying into a pattern normally found in modern global corporations, according to the police. *Young Blood* reveals how the police began keeping a detailed database on the Cartel, with the help of experts like the Analyst, an everyday policeman who had morphed into a kind of crime-fighting James Bond, Britain's number-one asset in the struggle against its most aggressive narcotic group. But he was a hero who stayed in the background and preferred law books to car chases. Scores of Cartel managers and hundreds of employees were identified, meshed together in an extremely complex network of revenue flows and capital assets. Economists would describe the Cartel of having matured into something akin to a 'global matrix structure', a shape that made it possible to optimise the strength of participating units, distributing the pressure of business more evenly, avoiding duplication of functions.

Part true-crime book, part social history, part investigation, *The Cartel* lifted the lid on a crime group that spanned borders and turned the black economy into boom sector, employing thousands of criminals while generating billions in sales. Its economic power distorted businesses, neighbourhoods and even cities, as bad money pushed out the good. In *Young Blood*, the next generation gets their hands on the levers of power. New opportunities open up in places like Mexico and China. The big question is: will they succeed?

WRONG SIDE OF THE TRACKS

1993

The story of the Cartel between 2003 and 2013 really begins a decade earlier, in 1993. Within Britain's biggest drug gang, the time between cause and effect was increasing.

In 1993, Terence Riley was a typical 13-year-old north Liverpool scally. One freezing February morning, Terence and his brother, just a year older than himself, met up with two other mates to go out to play. Like many lads of their age from the local estates, they enjoyed hanging around the railway lines nearby. Terence was tough and liked to take risks: invaluable qualities that would come in handy later on in his life. The disused Walton and Anfield station was still dangerous – the lines remained live in places – but the sidings were one of the few areas where gangs of kids could run wild without being moved on by the police. Even in the days before antisocial behaviour orders (ASBOs), the sight of slow-moving gangs of teenagers being ushered away from shopping parades by community coppers was a familiar one on the streets. Long before curfew orders, Section 60 public-order controls and ultrasonic teen deterrents outside Booze Busters stores, many youths already felt that there were few urban spaces left open to them. It was easier just to get off the street altogether, to hide in one of the city's many post-industrial wastelands. For mischievous boys with an overspill of energy, the railway lines were viewed as a sanctuary, an idyll of freedom in a cityscape wilderness and a place where the lines between

17

safety and harm, boredom and excess, and, on occasion, good and evil blurred into oblivion.

The bonus was that there were always plenty of things to mess around with on the wrong side of the tracks – and no adults to pass judgement. Piles of old fishplates and iron bolts lay next to abandoned dens. The charred remnants of bonfires that had burned black circles into 100-year-old sleepers were a sign of teenage wreckage. Track ballast littered the ground, providing plenty of stones to throw. Sewer water, moss and crackling electrified cables made for a natural adventure playground. Rats scurried around old Victorian tunnels whose scrofulous walls dripped with dirty water. But there was no better space for unfettered graffiti. The giant words 'Liverpool FC' and 'Go Pink Floyd' were scrawled on the walls in white paint, glistening in the darkness. All said, it was an urchins' paradise.

The four boys squeezed through a gap in a fence onto British Rail land. Later that year, in November, Prime Minister John Major's government would pass legislation to pave the way for network privatisation. It was a decision that had come off the back of many state sell-offs during the 1980s. Few experts at the time linked these market reforms to a growth in organised crime, simply because little or no research had been done. But the relationship between the economy and the black market was becoming increasingly interlinked and extraordinarily complicated, mainly because of the effects of an economic doctrine called monetarism, which had been adopted by Margaret Thatcher in the '80s and sought to contol inflation and the country's money supply. However, the associated doctrines of rapacious free markets, large-scale privatisation and concentration of corporate power have been proven to widen the gap between the rich and the poor. Monetarism has also been criticised for relying on enforced unemployment, anti-union legislation, low-paid jobs, outsourcing and deindustrialisation, although supporters claim benefits include economic booms, wealth boosts, easy credit and advances in technology. In addition, similar complexities were emerging as a result of the new links between policing, social problems and poverty, such as the effect of rough public-order policing and riot tactics in poor areas, and the relationship between poor education and reoffending rates, which were only just coming to be understood by social scientists. Few officials were aware that whenever the economy was in trouble, drug supplies and sales boomed. The Cartel had prospered during the recent recession in the early 1990s, the industrial collapse of the early 1980s and the economic shocks of the decade before that, caused by oil shortages and decimalisation in the early 1970s. The evidence was manifest and undeniable, however, it was hard for the experts to get to grips with it, because they tended to study the crime statistics in isolation.

The top of the embankment sloped gently onto the tracks below. There was no need for Terence and the lads to hide: as usual, no one was around. It was a Sunday and, moreover, Valentine's Day made the neighbouring streets seem even quieter. Walton in winter wasn't the most romantic of places, but no doubt there'd be plenty having a lie-in and a cup of tea in bed.

The abandoned sidings were eerily hushed. Across the clearing and behind the boarded-up waiting rooms, there were train tracks that were conspicuously unrusted and they stood out alongside the tired tracks of the unused lines. They were still operational, but there were few trains running today. Slowly, Terence pushed his way through the dewy undergrowth towards the level ground below, darker and dryer than the scrub. The ground was stained black by a hundred years of coal dust, spillover from the steam trains and their hopper wagons fresh from the pit that had once powered the Second Port of Empire, as Liverpool was proudly known during the Industrial Revolution. However, such things were of little interest to a teenager with a penchant for practical jokes and minor acts of vandalism. The young Terence Riley wasn't much of a student of history. In fact, he wasn't much interested in anything at school, according to those who knew him. So much so that his family was getting increasingly worried that he preferred roaming the streets and getting up to no good than getting his head down. But Terence's lack of attention to his lessons was about to become the least of his family's concerns.

What Terence would find at the bottom of the slope would

change his life forever. According to Terence's family, the effects were catastrophic, propelling the teenager on a downward spiral into a life of introversion and low self-esteem. His grandmother was convinced that those few seconds changed his personality completely. There was no going back, and he was beyond reach or repair. Gone, suddenly, was the wisecracking Scouse kid with a cheeky smile and an easy-going nature. In came the outsider who gravitated towards other outsiders, outlaws even: a darker, altogether more sinister individual who began to prefer the company of the same.

The discovery was simultaneously obvious and horrifying. Terence stood glued to the spot, unable to comprehend the magnitude of the chilling sight that lay before him. The dead body of a two-year-old child, mutilated and cut in half, lay across the railway tracks. From that moment on, the victim's name would become known the world over, and the murder of James Bulger would go down in the annals of crime as one of the most heinous killings since records began.

Terence went to his local nick at Walton Road police station to tell the officers what he had discovered. A murder inquiry was set up. Terence's actions in alerting the police led to a hunt for the killers. The investigation discovered that James Bulger had been killed two days earlier on the railway lines – not by an adult but by another couple of local boys. They were not much younger than Terence Riley and his mates. The two ten-year-old boys, Robert Thompson and Jon Venables, were eventually convicted of abducting the toddler, and torturing and murdering him. The details of the attack are hard to read. James Bulger's head was weighed down with stones found on the railway track, so that his body would stay on the line while a train ran over it. The child killers had hoped that once the body had been hit by a passing train, suspicion of foul play would be deflected away from them. It didn't work. CCTV footage of Thompson and Venables emerged, showing them leading James Bulger away from his mother at the New Strand Shopping Centre in nearby Bootle. Later, in court, the pair admitted that they had played truant from school on that fateful day, Friday, 12 February 1993, with the specific intention of abducting a child. No fewer than 38 witnesses saw the boys on their way to the railway lines where James Bulger was brutalised with a troll doll, a tin of Humbrol model paint and several batteries. Two adults had intervened on the boys' journey, but none had thought to stop them, or report the incident to the police, even though the two-year-old was crying and injured on the street. Venables and Thompson had threatened to push him into oncoming traffic and into a canal.

The strange sequence of events that took place as James walked to his death, the age of the murderers and the savagery of the killing were quickly held up as evidence of the breakdown of society. In general, two things seemed true. Adults were growing more fearful of young, violent children. In addition, some of the younger kids, especially the offspring of a new generation of heroin and crack addicts, did seem oddly desensitised to other humans: experts described the phenomenon as the children being 'not properly socialised'. Once again, these were subtle changes that had occurred over a long period, perhaps the previous ten or twenty years. Once again, decisions had been made that had long-term consequences that couldn't be foreseen at the time: these were 'strategic' changes that few professionals fully understood.

Several important questions were raised. How much of this general malaise had been caused by the presence of Britain's biggest drug gang within the community? To what extent had this breakdown been caused, both directly and indirectly, by the increased use of drugs in mainstream society? If it carried on, observers asked, what effect would this have on the next generation of children? People started to talk of 'little monsters' being created who were being bred for a life of crime. Much of the talk was dismissed as reactionary tabloid propaganda meant to demonise poor communities. But a few sharp observers noticed that within the rhetoric there was a poignant shred of shameful accuracy: some of it seemed true.

Terence should have been proud of his contribution, which helped the police trigger one of the most high-profile murder investigations of modern times. But it wasn't black and white, for his visit to Walton Road wasn't the first time Terence had been inside a police station. Aged just 13, he already had a record for petty crimes. And even in the Bulger case, where public anger resulted in 500 protesters turning up outside the youth court where the accused first appeared, not everyone looked favourably on Terence's actions. Some hardened criminals disapproved of any form of cooperation with the police, no matter how tragic the story was. A stultifying criminal culture was seeping into some of Liverpool's youth. Any form of police contact was seen as 'grassing'. Yet it was the subtle repercussions of what happened that day that became vital. The psychological effects of the horrific find upon the young Terence Riley would prove critically important to Britain's biggest drug-dealing gang.

By 1993, the Cartel was 20: just a few years older than Terence himself. It was started in the early 1970s by a former second-hand-car salesman known as Fred the Rat. The Rat had grown incredibly rich, first importing cannabis before moving into Class A drugs. A decade after it was formed, the Cartel went through a second growth phase during the economic recession of the early '80s, mainly by supplying heroin to a mainstream youth market. Ravaged by unemployment, their pain was to be soothed by depressives and analgesics. Heroin was cleverly marketed by the Cartel as a non-addictive choice that was more powerful than cannabis but carried less risk of psychosis than LSD. The launch of heroin by the Cartel netted its drug lords hundreds of millions of pounds. However, the good fortune did not stop there. By 1993, ten years after heroin, the Cartel was experiencing an even more profitable windfall, a third growth phase driven by dance music and Ecstasy.

At 13, Terence Riley was too young to notice acid house, never mind think about cashing in. He was also too young to go clubbing. Terence had missed the boat. But, like many young Liverpudlians, he'd heard the older lads talking about drug dealing. The Quadrant Park nightclub nearby had become infamous as a drug haven. It was a Cartel cash cow. Many of the local scallies made thousands of pounds on Friday and Saturday nights peddling E tablets in there. But there were also much grander role models for an ambitious young criminal to look up to.

That same year, 1993, the richest criminal in British history, Curtis Warren, walked free from charges of importing 1,000 kilos of cocaine and went off to spend the £80 million he'd boasted of getting away with. But before that, Warren returned to his home city to a near ticker-tape parade welcome in his own Toxteth neighbourhood. The Cartel godfather was greeted like a hero. Prostitutes lined up to have sex with the city's latest high-status villain. To celebrate, young mums named their babies 'Curtis'. No surname was required whenever the *Sunday Times* Rich List member was referred to either by police or public. To impressionable young men like Terence Riley, this was the street currency that bought kudos. These were the important lessons that were being learned and discussed. Cartel drug dealers were so powerful, they were above the law. They were celebrated.

In Terence's own neighbourhood, Walton, another example of the Cartel's power was quickly becoming legend. Two 'top-five' drug dealers had just walked away from eighteen-year sentences for mass heroin dealing. John Haase and Paul Bennett provided information that led to the seizure of firearms and were rewarded with a Royal Pardon each. It wasn't discovered until years later that they had set up the weapons find in the first place: they had conned the highest powers in the land. The gangsters celebrated by walking through the local pubs like proud men. Many took what had happened to Haase and Bennett as proof that crime paid. To teenagers, talking about crime became as important as chatting about football and music. It was a rite of passage in a city that had developed a culture of organised drug crime like no other in the UK, to the point where many young men saw drug dealing as a career path in the same way that their grandfathers had looked upon apprenticeships and dock work. Criminality offered the possibilities of success and status that industrial career fulfilment had once given their ancestors. At 13, Terence hadn't started dealing yet, but he was streetwise for his age and he showed promise.

A decade later, in 2003, Terence was well on the way. By then, he was hard and cynical and determined not to miss out on the next Cartel growth phase. The Cartel's number-one business priority was the penetration of cocaine into the mass market, with the specific aim to increase the drug's prevalence in the underclass and in working-class communities. Terence started working for an up-and-coming Cartel gangster called David Hibbs-Turner. Hibbs-Turner was part of a new generation of Cartel leaders who had no respect for the old guard and who saw the police as a force to be destroyed. Hibbs-Turner was viewed as a good all-rounder by the Cartel: he was not only a contract killer and a protection racketeer, but also, best of all, a cocaine-dealing machine of renown.

Hibbs-Turner soon took a shine to Terence. Like him, Terence was dark, and he kept himself to himself. Hibbs-Turner liked him so much that it wasn't long before Terence was running the Dutch side of the gang's massive cocaine operation. Terence developed a simple business model based on a modern British stereotype: the white-van man. The working-class symbol's ubiquity was its simple stroke of genius. The plan was well organised and quickly generated massive profits. Hibbs-Turner's gang bought a fleet of Vauxhall Combo vans, which were adapted to incorporate secret compartments. The inconspicuous vehicles were then driven to Holland and filled with Class A drugs supplied by the Cartel's South American contacts. The vans were then driven back to Liverpool and distributed.

By this time it was the mid-noughties. The New Labour dream hadn't yet crashed. The banking crisis was no more than a distant cloud on the horizon. The property boom was in full swing. No longer were drug operations set up in disused warehouses and backstreet two-up, two-downs. Terence's vans unloaded their multimillion-pound contraband at some of Liverpool's plushest loft developments, including Beetham Tower, Cornwallis Court and City Tower. The raw cocaine was diluted with industrial-sized quantities of a cheap and semi-legal dental anaesthetic called benzocaine, which was especially imported from China in massive barrels by specially set-up Cartel subcontractors. Enforcers protected the safe house with sub-machine guns. During the first year of the operation, Terence acted as tenant at one of the drug-factory properties at Royal Quay. He'd been sucked in deep. He'd gone from being a fairly ordinary teenager to a powerful manager in one of the UK's biggest crime groups. His family were adamant. They blamed it on the trauma brought on by finding James Bulger's body.

CHAPTER 1

TEN YEARS LATER

2003

By 2003, underworld financier Yael Feeney was embroiled in gang wars on several fronts. Yael's main dispute was with a gang of young upstarts led by an up-and-coming drug dealer called Kallas. The conflict was vicious, involving shoot-outs, torture, murders and bomb attacks, and it took place on an unprecedented scale. Kallas's criminal record was so long you'd have thought the police's printer had gone haywire, spewing out endless lists of violent incidents, drugs crimes and weapons offences. The 24-year-old *pistolero* eschewed the traditional trappings of underworld wealth. There were no golfing jumpers, suntans or forty-grand Rolexes bought from the lobby of a six-star hotel in Dubai. Kallas looked the part. He was King Rat in an environment where urban warfare thrived, surviving like vermin in the smoking rubble left after a nuclear holocaust. Pasty-faced and skinny, he looked like he'd been raised on a diet of Haribo sweets, cheap Chinese takeaways and bottles of Coke until he was old enough to snort cheap cocaine off his WAG's false breasts. He embraced the technological age that had revolutionised the underworld, routinely using his mobile phone to film his molls performing sex acts. Some were humiliated; others were blackmailed. He had the pasty trademark complexion of the hundreds of street urchins who rarely climbed out their North Face jackets to see daylight. To blend in, Kallas sported state-of-the-art all-weather wear in just one colour: black. He looked like a cross between a black-bloc anarchist, a hiker and an urban terrorist-cum-superhoodie, and for many years there were no photographs of his face. Only a small, close-knit group of gang members knew what he looked like – and he looked just like them, looking down at the floor wearing an expression of boredom and disdain. Kallas was the new face of Britain's underworld: and if you didn't like it, you were going to have to kill him.

According to the old underworld code, the war should have never happened. Yael Feeney was a big fish and Kallas a mere minnow in the established order. But instead of making them feel intimidated, Yael's status had the opposite effect on the new kids on the block such as Kallas. The fact that Yael had a house worth one million pounds, a business with assets, new offices in London and Liverpool, a fleet of nice cars and a family with children made him weak. He was, in their words, a 'victim'. They laughed at him. They were gang members known as 'creatures' and 'rats', and with no assets and no fixed abodes, they were almost impossible to exterminate. They only met their basic needs: a chippy meal every evening, a new set of Lowe Alpine all-weather shells every month and an armoury of state-of-the-art weapons, including SA80 army-issue assault rifles, Spider machine pistols and Tokarev hand guns. Similar kinds of weapons were being used in the wars unfolding in the outside world. In Iraq and Afghanistan, guerrilla fighters were rising up against the big powers, underworld-style, just as it was in Liverpool. The conflict between the old guard and the younger generation was asymmetrical.

An arms race between Yael's gang and his enemies ensued. Each side rushed to enlist back-up and hired guns. Kallas joined forces with a gang from a notorious area called the Grizedale estate in Everton, led by a drug dealer called Daniel Gee. Accordingly, and to counter the threat, Yael ripped a page out of Sun Tzu's *The Art of War*. He agreed to sponsor the sworn enemies of Daniel Gee: a rival gang led by drug dealer Michael Wright. Yael knew the Wrights through the Cartel; he had underwritten big drug deals to which Michael Wright had been connected. The bond was strengthened because Wright also did business with a Toxteth dealer known as Bubbley Shalson, who was also at war with Kallas and

Sidious. Kallas and Sidious had fallen out with Shalson, who they considered a rival up-and-coming drug dealer from the Liverpool 8 area of the city. Shalson was a mixed-race crack dealer with a string of drug dens in Liverpool and Manchester. Shalson had teamed up with a Somali gang to try to sell drugs in the North End of the city. Yael Feeney decided to back Shalson in his war with Kallas and Sidious by providing him with money and arms. Another nightclub-owning gang also declared war on Sidious and Kallas.

The Wright family began to act as 'agents' for Yael's outfit. Wright wasted no time in shooting at Kallas and flanking his gang members with machine-gun fire, in the hope of keeping them pinned down. The hope was that Yael could get on with his day job of running a money-laundering empire.

But it was bigger business of a different nature that was causing concern: Cartel business. The problem was clear. Both the Wright gang and Gee gang were fully signed-up members of the Cartel, whose distribution networks were key to offloading huge amounts of Cartel drugs quickly. Their economies of scale and their closeness meant that the Cartel could quickly claw back money from freshly imported cocaine and use the cash to reimburse suppliers in Amsterdam and South America. The cash flow was then used to fund longer-term returns in Scotland and other parts of the UK. The internal squabble put the Cartel's senior members into a quandary. They had previously learned that internal wars were bad for business. They wanted it stopped. But a strange thing happened, something previously unheard of: their pleas for peace were ignored. Neither the Wrights nor the Gees cared what the old guard thought. And although Yael worked for the old godfathers, he no longer cared either – the fighting had gone on too long. The godfathers were told to go back to their golf clubs and their villas in Marbella or they would be the next victims.

As 2003 rolled on, the dispute between two rival factions of the Cartel deepened. The Gee family were now in all-out war with the Wright family. In days gone by, this dispute wouldn't have had much significance: turf wars down the food chain came with the territory. But both the Wright family and the Gee clan signified an important change: they now represented the new face of Cartel power, and they knew it. No longer was the status and wealth of the Cartel concentrated in the hands of the old-guard drug lords at the top of the pyramid. The Wrights and the Gees were very much at the bottom of the hierarchy. But a new politics had emerged: street politics. Essentially they were street-level distributors. But that's where the real money was being made now: power was trickling down from the importers at the apex to the salesmen who collected the cash at the bottom. Suddenly, the street dealers realised that they were in a strong bargaining position, because the whole business rested on their interface with consumers.

The new crime groups essentially organised themselves like massive street gangs, employing hundreds of sellers and couriers who peddled drugs for fixed wages. The distribution cells were marshalled into cells or 'rounds'. Each discrete patch was rather like a window cleaner's round, and the local bosses were sometimes known as 'roundsmen'. Each roundsman had a circle of punters who called him on a mobile phone to place orders for crack, powdered cocaine or heroin in the same way that they might buy pizza. The rocks, stones and wraps were then delivered by kids on bikes or served up at prearranged 'points of sale', such as a local park, or sometimes in an alleyway close to a local doctors' surgery, a favourite pitch with 'brown' addicts who frequented clinics at specific times to pick up methadone 'scripts'. A highly efficient dial-a-dealer service evolved. Consequently, the most important asset in the set-up was soon identified as the mobile phone number on which the orders were placed and the SIM card, for this was the number that the punters knew, often off by heart. Enterprising dealers could build up a 'round' that served up scores of drug users and generated a fixed income every day. The phone 'operator' and his runners were arranged so that there were two or sometimes three shift changeovers per day. When the dealer had made enough money, or was being watched by the police, or wanted to step up to the next level in the Cartel, then he could sell on the SIM card as a going concern to other up-and-coming dealers. SIM cards were soon changing hands for prices ranging from £10,000 to more than £100,000. An ex-dealer called Colin Borrows was offered a

SIM card in Liverpool for £200,000. When he got out of prison following a 14-year sentence, a former Cartel heroin supplier called Suleyman Ergun was offered a London-based SIM card 'round' for £1 million. He revealed how a mobile 'call centre' had been established around this lucrative round. The call centre could be moved at a moment's notice between different safe houses and was closely guarded by armed men. The call centre was based in and around Brixton in south London, but the sales were made to hundreds of punters each day in the Euston and King's Cross areas in north London.

Back in Kirkdale and Grizedale, SIM cards were bought and sold frequently. As long as the new managers continued to buy the drugs from the local wholesalers, either the Wright family or the Gee family, depending on the area of business, no one minded much who controlled the SIM card.

As the two families expanded their respective territories, it was only a matter of time before they fought. But with each side being stoked by third parties – Kallas and his gang backing the Gee family, and Yael Feeney and Bubbley Shalson backing the Wright family – the disturbance became increasingly vicious. There were also wider consequences. As power shifted down the Cartel and young gangsters were turned into multimillionaires overnight, street-level gangsters decided that they wanted to be the new bosses of the Cartel. Like Kallas, they didn't wait to be asked. David Hibbs-Turner was a next-generation street dealer and protection racketeer who wanted to start importing drugs as well as distributing them. In many ways, Hibbs-Turner was like Kallas, but he was a few years older and had already established a multimillion pound network. In order to progress, Hibbs-Turner knew that he'd have to align himself with the new generation in a struggle for power with the old guard. Hibbs-Turner threw in his hat with Daniel Gee and Kallas in their war against Yael Feeney and Bubbley Shalson. It was a headache that Yael didn't need, but he'd have to sort it.

But the process wasn't all plain sailing. With the help of intelligence-led policing and an increasingly sensitive network of sources, Merseyside Police picked up on Hibbs-Turner almost immediately. For the first time in a fight against the Cartel stretching back 30 years, the police were getting ahead of the curve and identifying future bosses on the way up the ladder. More accurately, they now had the capability to exploit their advantage to the max. The Analyst was Britain's number-one anti-drugs cop: he dedicated his life to fighting the Cartel.

The Analyst: 'Within their respective areas, this gang war had a big impact. Kids started picking sides in the playground. But it wasn't cowboys and Indians. It was who wanted to be the Wrights and the Gees. They were pretending to be criminals.

'Amid this, then the police started picking up intelligence about a drug dealer. His name was Hibbs-Turner. He was not unusual in any sense: he had perceived criminality. But he was already considered to be Level 3 because his distribution network was wider than just Merseyside. For instance, he was selling drugs into Scotland.' 'Level 3' was police jargon that referred to criminals involved in serious and organised crime who operated on a national or international scale. The classification was derived from a Home Office policy known as the National Intelligence Model. The hunt was on.

The investigation wasn't helped by all of the noise going on around the central targets. The gang war between Yael Feeney and Kallas was by now the number-one concern of Merseyside police. Senior members of Yael Feeney's gang began picking off any of Kallas's foot soldiers who had strayed too far from their bosses' sphere of protection. Members of Yael's gang were getting frustrated by the lack of action and, without his knowledge, began targeting a 24-year-old deputy within Kallas's gang known as Sidious. Yael Feeney was also paying Bubbley Shalson and his gang to take potshots at the Gees and Hibbs-Turner in a bid to disrupt their drug empire. It was part of a strategy by the rogue members of Yael Feeney's gang to keep the pressure up on their enemies. They had rightly guessed that Sidious was the weak link in the gang. Kallas was a well-camouflaged moving target and was hard to hit. By normal standards, there was little to prove that he even existed. He kept a very low profile. He had no fixed abode: he refused to live in a normal home, preferring to crash in one of several safe houses dotted around Liverpool council estates. He didn't own a car and spent his time lying down on the back seats of high-powered vehicles, being driven at high speed from one meeting to another. He didn't have credit cards. Yael's ally Bubbley Shalson had a shrewd plan. He knew that if he could draw the Gees and Kallas out into the open, in an all-out war, then the police would move in on them. Effectively, the bait would be the Wright family, whom they would use to fight their battles. The trap would involve Sidious.

CHAPTER 2

INSIDE THE BELLY OF THE BEAST

2003

As the Cartel matured and the police started catching more kingpins, prison became a fact of life for the narcotics millionaires who'd once enjoyed a life of little work but lots of luxury.

A drug dealer known as Dylan Porter was two years into a twenty-one-year stretch for managing one of the most successful heroin-importation cells the Cartel had ever known. Porter was the opposite of what many would believe a drug lord to look like. He was skinny and bespectacled, and he was quiet by nature. Humility and humour were more apparent than ruthlessness or aggression. Dylan claimed that he was sorry for all the misery he had heaped on his community by flooding the country with drugs, but he said that he'd known no better. He'd turned to selling drugs on a street corner when he was an unemployed youth during the recession in the 1980s and carried on because that was the only way he knew how to make a living. It may not have been much of a defence, but he was determined to do his time without complaint and, once he was out, turn his back on crime for ever.

In the 'jug', as prison was known, Dylan missed out on seeing his kids grow up – and they never knew what his life was like. To make up for it, Dylan wrote a diary so that one day they might understand what their father went through. The account reveals that, alongside violence, drug dealing and homosexuality, prison life was an extraordinary and extreme

32

mixture of camaraderie between senior villains and a hatred of the system and its screws.

Dylan landed in Whitemoor Prison in 2001. In his diary, which he has titled *The Belly of the Beast*, he recalls, 'The first thing that hit me was the noise. The wings in Whitemoor are open plan and consist of three landings. I was located on the second one. At the end of the landing there was a kitchen. In dispersal, you can cook your own food.' A dispersal prison is a high-security jail equipped to accommodate the most dangerous inmates. Dispersal prisons are separate from local prisons, which tend to house general criminals close to their families. Hardened villains are 'dispersed' from the mainstream jails into separate facilities outside their geographical region of origin.

Self-catering was an important part of life. Groups picked their fellow diners carefully based on both their friendliness and their status in the criminal hierarchy. Whether they were eating Jamaican rice 'n' peas made by a Yardie or Irish stew made by an IRA terrorist, the process was as much about bonding as cooking.

Dylan describes the surreal induction process into a new prison, during which he was asked how he thought jail was preparing him for release: 'I'd just started a 21-year sentence, for fuck's sake.' The meeting was a 'strange' mixture of formality and threat. After inquiring about his prospects of rehabilitation, Dylan claims he was threatened by a notorious prison officer known as A-to-Z that if he stepped out of line he would be arrested and more years would be added to his sentence. But Dylan was still sore: 'The soft cunt – I'd just got 21, I didn't care about daft nickings.'

Dylan was soon introduced to all the big gangsters, from cartels in Liverpool, London and elsewhere. He met the leader of the Dome diamond gang; a con who'd tried to blow his way out of jail using Semtex; the gang that tried to escape from Gartree in a helicopter; and a couple of IRA active service units. The elite cons had a word with a prison officer so that Dylan was moved over to their wing.

Dylan's cell was searched regularly, as he was suspected of flooding Whitemoor with drugs. He claimed that the authorities targeted anyone linked to the Cartel: 'People told me that the screws were offering money to other inmates to set me up. They said me and my mate were the biggest drug dealers that had ever been in Whitemoor. Here we were surrounded by the IRA, Palestinian terrorists, major London villains, Turkish mafia, Russian mafia, Colombians and Americans, yet a feller from Bootle and one from Netherley were public enemies number one and two.'

Shortly after he arrived on B wing, Dylan became friends with Jason Fitzgibbon, a Cartel drug dealer from a notorious south Liverpool crime family who was serving eight years for drugs. Dylan complained that Fitzgibbon was 'given hell' by the authorities. He'd been moved from Frankland Prison for attacking an IRA guy. The *News of the World* had described Fitzgibbon as Britain's dumbest convict, but he boasted he'd become a multimillionaire without having ever done a day's work in his life. Dylan described his fellow Cartel boss as 'staunch' and 'far from a bully', saying he was one of the most generous lads he had ever met. Outside, Dylan Porter had earned £30,000 a month from one single heroin-smuggling route. Inside, he earned £30 a week making coat hangers. Outside, too, his family suffered. Dylan had been one of the few Cartel bosses not to engage in money laundering. Ironically, he hadn't trusted the methods to keep his money safe. Now he was paying the price. His fortune had disappeared: some was seized by the police, but much more was paid off in debts to the Cartel, which held him responsible for the heroin that had gone down in his bust. One day, Jason Fitzgibbon sent £200 to Dylan's young daughter as a birthday present. But the prison guards were watching over the Cartel bosses' every move. They misinterpreted the good deed as Fitzgibbon trying to extort money from Dylan. Fitzgibbon's cell was raided by riot cops. Later, Fitzgibbon was shipped out of Whitemoor for knocking out a 'dickhead' football player for refusing to pass the ball. His mistake was to attack the man in front of the horrified governor during a VIP's visit.

Fights over football were common. In an unrelated incident, toilet brushes were sharpened to a point in a planned hit on a spectator who'd got in a fight over a goal. Another game led to two stabbings, a man being 'swilled' with boiling water and two prison transfers.

Even violent drug dealers with big reputations found themselves cut down to size in the presence of the Cartel and their allies. One drug dealer called Brock tried to collect a drug debt from one of Dylan's jail neighbours. Dylan said, 'Brock was about 6 ft tall and about 17 st. He was dripping in gold and had a Rolex watch on his wrist. To complete the set, he even had gold teeth. He looked every inch the rap star.

'Brock had a reputation for selling drugs in the system and the lad apparently owed him money from a previous jail. The lad was only small, but he didn't seem intimidated. As Brock approached, the lad stabbed him in the face and then just walked off laughing. Brock stood there with a handkerchief trying to stem the blood flowing from his face.'

Brock had become the latest victim in Britain's increasingly violent jails. He stayed in his cell for three weeks. He'd gone from predator to victim, and was soon relieved of his Rolex, his Cartier chain and everything else – except his gold teeth. 'Brock came to Whitemoor like Puff Daddy and left like Trevor Macdonald,' recalled Dylan.

Drugs were freely available in jail and one day Dylan was caught walking along with 'a piece of cannabis between the cheeks of me arse wrapped in tissue'. When two guards asked him to strip and squat in his cell, the drugs fell to the floor. But instead of giving up the pot, Dylan brazenly snatched it and ran out of the cell. The officers were trapped in the cell by Dylan's pals while he made his getaway. He threw it to a fellow inmate, knowing that if the prison officers didn't have the evidence they couldn't convict. Dylan was thrown into solitary confinement, known as the block, for three months. Dylan was cooped up for 23 hours a day. His cell was equipped with cardboard furniture. Meals were served only when the prisoner sat on his bed with his legs on top, hands on his knees. Later, for good behaviour, prisoners would be allowed to put their legs on the floor. The only way Dylan could get tobacco was when the other prisoners showed solidarity and made noise all night until the authorities relented.

Back 'on the wings' in the main prison, Dylan claimed that one of the perks was 'guards willing to bring cannabis in for a price'. Contraband was brought in and traded by prison officers. This trade was carried out using coded letters. So if a cannabis-using inmate ran up a £2,500 bill and the debt needed to be paid off, Dylan or another inmate would write a letter saying that someone wouldn't buy his daughter a cartoon video on the outside even though the price was £2.50: this would be clear to a seasoned hand on the outside that a £2,500 debt needed payment. The fact that the letter had come from Dylan would put the receiver of the letter immediately on message.

Prisoners united in their hatred of paedophiles. One day when Dylan was making a phone call to his three-year-old daughter, he saw a cleaner brushing the landings (a privileged job) and recognised him: he was Sidney Cooke, a child molester who had killed a fourteen-year-old boy and was serving two life sentences. Astonishingly, none of the other prisoners had realised who their new cleaner was. So Dylan made it his business to out him to his inmates so that 'every night from then on this creature got a torrent of abuse'.

But not all Cartel godfathers could cut it as easy as Dylan in jail. Doing time was a life skill that required tolerance, patience and the ability to accept one's fate. Many spent their time trying to overturn their convictions: a bureaucratic and frustrating business. One was Dylan's mate Tony Sleevey: gang boss Carli Sleevey's nephew. Tony Sleevey was serving time for a gangland hit he claimed he hadn't committed: he would later appeal against the conviction, and in 2007 it was overturned. Another was Sam Cole, a young foot soldier jailed for killing a drug dealer in Preston. Many witnesses in the case later changed their evidence, casting doubt on whether Cole had been at the scene of the crime, and Cole spent most of his time fighting the system. However, he later lost his appeal and is still in prison.

Other godfathers found prison overwhelming. Outside, they had been big cheeses. Inside, they crumbled under the pressure. Such was the fate of Cartel drug lord 'Fast Eddie' Gray, who was slowly being ground down by prison. Gray went into solitary confinement for his own protection after being convinced that inmates were going to 'serve him up' (stab him with a knife). The 6 ft 4 in. ex-gangster, who claimed he was being targeted for his money in a blackmail scam, was known on the outside as the Bear, but inside he was terrified of a rival called Warren Slaney.

Meanwhile, the tedium of prison life was occasionally broken by the odd surprise. One day a female prison officer who'd taken a shine to Dylan tipped him off about a fellow prisoner who was an informer and was feeding information about Dylan and his pals to the prison authorities. This was an extraordinary situation and showed that guards often cooperated with their charges in order to build up a relationship. On another occasion, another prison officer discovered a Palestinian terrorist serving a 40-year sentence having sex with a younger man in his cell. The prison officer was disgusted and spread the gossip around so that Dylan and his gang would punish the terrorist for preying on more vulnerable people. Dylan said, 'The sight that greeted him turned his stomach: the young man was bent over the sink and the terrorist was behind him, balls deep. It looked like rape but no one could ever find out if it was consensual or not. Either way, this behaviour was heavily frowned upon on my wing.' After being confronted by the gang, both the terrorist and the other inmate were shipped out of prison the next day.

Dylan said, 'This terrorist was a horrible man. When the planes hit the Twin Towers, he was celebrating like he'd scored a goal. He came to borrow a frying pan off my pal one day and I told him to fuck off and that he was a nonce. He tried to tell me that he was a soldier, but I told him that soldiers don't use pregnant women in battle.'

Inmates like Dylan could avoid homosexual attacks because they were tough. Homosexuality wasn't rife, but there was a strong subculture in some parts of the prison. One wing of the prison was dubbed the 'pink spur' because it contained three well-known gangsters who were gay. One of the villains used to coerce some inmates into performing sexual acts in the prison chapel, one of the few places where inmates could mix freely with a high degree of privacy.

Dylan said, 'These three used to compete for any young lads that come on the spur. Monday night there used to be a church group and one of them turned it into his own little massage parlour. The church group would scurry back into the pink spur, heads down, apart from this one gangster who would stroll on last, head held high, with a smile on his face like the cat who'd got the cream.'

Violence between inmates and prison officers was common. On Christmas Day, a low-level Cartel street dealer, a heroin addict with a pathological hatred of 'screws', was paid to throw a bucket of excrement over a female prison officer in revenge for her harassing some high-up inmates. He'd been filling up a container for three days and was paid with a few bags of heroin.

CHAPTER 3

FAME

2003

For Yael Feeney, Kallas was a hard target to hit because of his low profile and the way he kept moving. But underboss Sidious was the exact opposite. His profile couldn't have been any higher. He had started dating a 21-year-old soap star turned reality-TV celebrity whose every move was tracked by the tabloids. Sidious moved into her new-build mini-mansion in Liverpool, making him easy to find. He was forever being photographed with his famous girlfriend falling out of showbiz parties and C-list film premieres, thus making his movements relatively easy to follow. Sidious did himself no favours; he enjoyed the attention and was a regular at Liverpool's new raft of nightspots, such as the Newz Bar and Baby Blue. As soon as Sidious turned up in a restaurant or an office for an underworld meeting, informants who were on Yael's payroll would call him up and say: 'He's in.' Yael had a particular dislike for Sidious. As a teenager, Sidious had approached him to underwrite a drug deal with an underworld loan. Yael had thrown him out of his office on several occasions. Sidious had always threatened to come back with a gun.

In order to encourage more random attacks against Sidious, Bubbley Shalson put a contract on Sidious's head. However, the contract was put out without Yael Feeney's knowledge. The prospect of a payday and a shot at the big time encouraged many up-and-coming hoodlums to think about having a go at Sidious, even though many of them didn't even know what the dispute was about. For Sidious himself, the simple fact that a bounty was out there played on his mind. Threats to kill were as much about psychological warfare as carrying them out.

Repeated attacks were made on Sidious and the £300,000 home he shared with his starlet moll in the city's Croxteth Park area. It didn't help that the new estate that the couple lived in was close to Croxteth and Norris Green, where pools of unemployed young men hung around, many of whom were armed and desperate to prove themselves. The areas would soon become blighted by American-style gang warfare.

On one occasion, Sidious was involved in a high-speed car chase in his partner's £50,000 Range Rover. When Sidious's girlfriend landed a lucrative record contract and launched a pop career, his enemies were determined to scupper it. They 'sprayed up' her house with an AK-47 assault weapon. Attempts to burgle the property were made by professional 'creepers', who were looking for any dirt that would compromise her. The gang were convinced, wrongly, that there were videos containing homemade porn movies, which they planned to spread around the Internet to discredit her. None were found.

Yael's alliance with Michael Wright was soon tested to its limits as the war with Kallas and the Gees span out of control. An arms race ensued. Instead of backing down, Kallas and Daniel Gee went right off the scale and ordered a series of bomb attacks against Yael and his business partners. Gee and Kallas also struck back at an unconnected firm that owned a string of nightclubs. This strand of the war became the most visible, as it was carried out against nightclubs and pubs, and members of the public were caught in the crossfire. To carry out their guerrilla war, Kallas and Gee recruited the perfect patsy: Richard Caswell, a disaffected doorman who used to work for Yael but had been sacked for misconduct.

Gee and Kallas arranged for 21-year-old Caswell to be given a war chest to plant car bombs filled with industrial fireworks, petrol and nails. Days after the AK-47 attack on Sidious's home, his boss, Kallas, ordered revenge on Yael and Bubbley. They were shot at and attacked with machetes. Gee and Kallas decided to use the cover of the underworld war to attack their other enemy, a legitimate nightclub-owning family who had refused to let them sell E tablets and coke in their venues. On 20 September 2003, a massive car bomb blew up outside Club 0151 in Liverpool's city centre, shattering windows in nearby hotels, shops and offices. Miraculously, no one was hurt. The detonation struck at the heart of the owner's business. Six days later, Kallas and Gee ordered another attack. A nail bomb was thrown into the middle of the packed Dickie Lewis pub in Kirkdale. The device skidded across the pub's dance floor and lit up but failed to detonate. Police later discovered that the bomb was filled with razor-sharp shards of metal. Had it exploded, it would certainly have cost lives.

On 18 October 2003, a car bomb was parked at the home of a family member of the owner of the nightclub. The devices were crude: Chinese fireworks, each costing £5 and containing up to 70g of flash powder, were placed under the petrol tanks of the cars. It might sound amateurish, but the bomb squad said they caused the biggest explosions on mainland Britain between the fall of the IRA and the 7/7 terrorist attacks on London's tube. The next day, a third explosion caused devastation outside another house connected to the same family. Detectives began an investigation code-named Thornapple, and then chief constable Norman Bettison launched a national campaign to control the sale and import of fireworks.

Buoyed by the success of their attacks on the nightclub owners, Gee and Kallas turned their attention back to their underworld rivals Yael Feeney and Bubbley Shalson. Some of Yael's other rivals sensed weakness and homed in for attack. Yael was at the centre of a hugely lucrative money-laundering company, which included legitimate businesses and a property portfolio. However, the intangible assets of his company were as valuable as the businesses he ran. Yael's influence and status as an advisor also gave him power within and without the Cartel, despite the fact he had never personally dealt drugs. Other money launderers and loan sharks were jealous and wanted to dismantle his empire piece by piece, so that they could become the preferred bankers to the Cartel.

Bubbley Shalson was also feeling the heat. A rival drug dealer from the South End area of the city decided to move against Bubbley, knowing that he was bogged down in a war with Kallas. They demanded that Bubbley sell them a string of his crack houses and heroin rounds, ones he had built up on their manor, for a knock-down price of £10,000 each. The area was controlled by a drug-dealing family whose leader was in prison. One of their other leaders was a professional identity thief known as the Fraudster. The Fraudster was an extremely powerful organised criminal who was juiced in right at the top of the Cartel, because of his expertise in high-tech financial matters. The Fraudster wasn't a white-collar criminal. He ran a multimillion-pound crime firm that was involved in drugs, protection and contract violence. The Fraudster worked for the Cartel's boss, Colin Smith. He could also supply false companies with false IDs and had access to an international market of contract assassins.

Bubbley had managed to fend off their approaches so far and was looking to catch the Fraudster alone so he could beat him up. But the Fraudster, who was a master of disguise, proved elusive. Bubbley didn't even know what he looked like, never having seen him in person. When he asked his underworld contacts for a photograph, they told him that there were none in existence except his police mug shots. The Fraudster always refused to be photographed.

One day, out of the blue, the Fraudster turned up at an expensive clothes shop in Liverpool's city centre. Luckily, Bubbley knew the owners.

Bubbley said, 'The lads who worked in this boutique knew I was looking for the Fraudster. One day they phoned me and said, "The Fraudster has just walked in." This was very unusual, as he rarely went out, never mind shopping for jeans and jumpers and so on. Few people knew what he looked like. He was a proper fraudster who wore disguises – wigs, glasses, false beards, the works – like he was right out of a film. No one even had a photo of him. All I wanted to do was attack him on sight, because I knew he was behind the people who were trying to take my crack houses off me. My first reaction was to say to the lads who worked in the shop, "Keep him there, don't let him leave." But it was quite a posh shop and they were just normal lads, so how were they going to restrain a very violent man?

'Immediately, I sent down one of my best enforcers to get him. He was equipped with special apparatus to carry the job out. But then, as he was on the way, I got a call from my insider. He told me, "The Fraudster has bought some stuff and he's leaving the shop, and there's no trouble."

'I had to be careful. Obviously, I didn't want to bring it on top for the shop or the lads who worked there. If I did the Fraudster in the shop, this would have backfired on my insiders and led to a big murder investigation in broad daylight. So I said, "OK then, let him out of the shop, but make sure you get me a smudge of him on the CCTV." If I couldn't bash him up then the next best thing I could do was get a picture of him so that next time I could find him.'

Meanwhile, as far as the bigger picture was concerned, Merseyside Police were continuing to strike blows against the Cartel. The successes were based on the rigorous implementation of a new crime-fighting system called intelligence-led policing. The force also had the ability, unique outside London, to track villains across international borders, known as 'Level 3 capability'.

In the summer of 2003, Merseyside police officers were celebrating yet another conviction against a Cartel cell. Liverpool-based gangster Francis Smith was a mid-ranking Cartel manager who worked for an old Cartel stalwart known as Stan 'the Big Fella' Carnall. Carnall was serving ten years in Kilmarnock Prison after being caught with six kilos of heroin in a previous sting. Nevertheless, even in prison Carnall managed to work with and for Curtis Warren, the richest Cartel boss, who'd been jailed in Holland in 1996. The case proved that even when the Cartel leaders were imprisoned, they still managed to operate from behind bars. Meanwhile, Francis Smith and an associate called Anthony O'Toole tried to smuggle £6 million of drugs in a consignment of bananas. The gang's runners included Anthony Healy, Harold Camello and Alan Gerrard, who all later admitted conspiracy to smuggle the drugs. The heroin, cocaine and Ecstasy were concealed in a lorry owned by Scottish haulage firm boss Alexander Thom, who'd fallen into debt after a previous drug run had gone wrong. After noticing that Francis Smith was spending more and more time with known Cartel bosses,

Merseyside police spent months observing the gang's movements as part of an operation code-named McArthur. Smith himself was also one of Britain's most wanted men at the time, but instead of picking him up, Merseyside police took a big risk. They decided to let him roll in the hope of catching a wider conspiracy. It was a tough call but one that was consistent with the new intelligence-led doctrine and one that eventually paid off.

The legitimate load had consisted of 19 tonnes of bananas imported from Belgium. But hidden underneath a false floor in the lorry were 21 kilos of heroin, 19 kilos of cocaine, 65 kilos of Ecstasy and 100 kilos of speed. The groupage loads were becoming increasingly common.

CHAPTER 4

LONG LARTIN

2003

In March 2003, Dylan Porter was transferred to Long Lartin high-security prison in Worcestershire. Built in the 1970s, the jail was electronically controlled but had no in-cell toilets or washbasins, except in the 'block': the notoriously strict punishment cells, whose officers were despised by the prisoners.

Immediately, Dylan settled into a life of relative luxury. He was greeted by Robbie McCarthy, who was doing a life sentence for the murder of Stephen Cole. Cole had been the main bouncer at Cream nightclub, and his allies included Scarface, Kaiser, and Poncho, who had helped smuggle the Cartel's first 1,000-kilo load of cocaine in 1989. The consignment enabled them to set up a permanent Cartel hub in Amsterdam, and they went on to become very rich. Kaiser and Scarface had started out as petty drug dealers in post-riots Toxteth. They got their big break by travelling to South America personally and making contact with a cocaine trafficker who agreed to supply them on credit. Poncho was Scarface's nephew, who acted as a middle manager for the gang in Liverpool and Amsterdam. Stephen Cole was a former Liverpool football player who'd got involved with the nightclub scene.

For Britain's criminal elite, Long Lartin was a place of extremes. On the one hand, Category A cons were allowed to brew alcohol, drink and throw parties on a Friday night. They enjoyed privileges and customs that had grown up over the years. A food 'boats' was a system of allowing prisoners to choose what they ate and who with. Each 'boat' was made up of a small group of like-minded prisoners who cooked fine foods together. Access to a boat was by invite only. Dylan claimed that a female employee even put on illicit sex shows: 'There was one female worker in particular who used to put on a show for the lads. She was a big, fat, ugly thing, but sometimes you have to make the best of a bad situation.' But if the prisoners abused the limited freedoms, then punishment was far worse than in normal jails.

When he first arrived, Dylan was told by a prison officer that the prisoners on the Category A landing were allowed a drink and that he didn't mind as long as the prisoners behaved themselves. Dylan said, 'I know a lot of people reading this will be shocked by what the PO said. But you have got to understand that we were all doing massive prison sentences and that by allowing us our little bit of freedom of a Friday night, he knew there would never be a problem on his wing.'

For the first party, the gang of hitmen, drug dealers and gangsters had 50 litres of ice-cold hooch – a crude homebrew made with fruit, sugar and Marmite – and 12 jars of distilled pure alcohol. After that party and the ones that followed, the gang staggered back to their cells blind drunk and sometimes naked. One Sunday morning, Dylan and Jason Fitzgibbon, who had also ended up in Long Lartin, enjoyed four Ecstasy tablets washed down with pure alcohol. For the birthday party of Ray Betson, one of the Dome diamond robbers who'd been transferred to Long Lartin too, the cons baked a cake with a diamond shape in the middle and put a sticker of diamond merchant Graff of London on the side. The soundtrack was Motown classics.

Dylan's neighbours included John 'Goldfinger' Palmer, a quietly spoken criminal mastermind who was doing eight years for masterminding a £30 million timeshare swindle on Tenerife. Another neighbour was snooker player Ronnie O'Sullivan's dad, who had been sentenced to life when his son was just 16. O'Sullivan senior, who acted as a mentor to the snooker champion even while behind bars, was jailed in 1992 for the brutal stabbing of Bruce Bryan, a driver to Charlie Kray, in a nightclub in Chelsea.

Screws who refused to be lenient were squirted with bottles

full of urine, scalded with hot cooking oil and stabbed. At other times they were assaulted by 30-strong gangs armed with DIY knives and long pieces of sharpened metal that were used like swords. On one occasion when a prison officer interrupted a party and tried to confiscate the booze, a Mexican stand-off occurred, with a prison riot team at one end of the landing and the boozed-up cons at the other. The revellers were thrown into solitary confinement. Another time, there was a riot in the block after the gangsters were refused their Christmas dinner.

Dylan said, 'I got back on the bed frame and started rocking back and forth like a lunatic. And then I heard this crack as the bed frame snapped. I quickly ripped the bed up and set about smashing my toilet and sink. The hardest bit to smash was the spy hole in the door, but I managed it, and as soon as I got the glass out I shouted, "Honey, I'm home!" A big cheer went up on the landing.'

The disturbances ended when several inmates went on a protest called a 'shit up', which involved smearing faeces over the cell walls. 'The smell was absolutely disgraceful,' said Dylan. They were eventually extracted by MUFTI (minimum use of force tactical intervention) squads, dressed in crash helmets and wielding riot shields. Dylan was shipped out to Strangeways, in Manchester, before being relocated to Full Sutton, in Yorkshire.

Meanwhile, on the outside, business was booming for the Cartel. The effective boss of the Cartel was a career drug dealer called Colin Smith. Smith had taken over from Curtis Warren following his incarceration in Holland in 1996. A cautious man who enjoyed continuity and disliked violence, Smith was more business-minded than Warren and grew the Cartel's operations. Without exception, the Cartel was the most surveillance-aware criminal organisation Britain had ever known. From the lowest street rat to the cocaine kings at the top, like Colin Smith, they all knew that talking on the phone would get them nicked. They had seen it on their favourite films, like *Goodfellas*, and had taken heed. They had read the phone transcripts that had got Curtis Warren nicked in 1992 and in 1996. Colin Smith was doubly aware of the dangers. He'd been roped in as part of a 1,000-kilo bust in the early

'90s with Warren. Both of them had walked on a technicality, but it was a close shave, and Smith had seen his name in black and white all over the various phone-tap transcripts, contact sheets and surveillance logs. Never again.

Smith went to extremes. It wasn't just about arranging face-to-face meetings in unusual places, not even out of town. The whole world was now his oyster. He and his associates would arrange meetings in foreign countries at the drop of a hat, exploiting the boom in budget flights to move lower-level gang members from A to B. And no matter how far the delegates had to travel, as soon as the meeting was over – even if it had lasted only a couple of hours – everyone was instructed to disperse and go back to the safe houses in the countries in which they lived.

The Analyst said, 'Someone like Smith would not use his phone. His view would be: his phone is just about general talk. When he was communicating with his contacts, it would be a case of, "Are we meeting at the other place tonight?" And of course it would be case of the "other place" would mean something, a specific location, to them. And tonight would be an eight o'clock meeting, as the time would have been sorted out before. But then you'd have them meeting, for example, in Spain. So they're thinking, "Are we meeting at the other place?" And the other place meant Puerto Banús. For them, there were no borders and boundaries. So that means they literally went straight down to the EasyJet desk at John Lennon Airport and on the plane to Spain.

'Within two or three hours they're standing in the sea with their Speedos on and having a conversation with somebody. The person they're talking to in the sea doesn't have to worry that they've got a surveillance device on them. It's a one-to-one, face-on situation.

'And then afterwards you're back on the plane to the UK.'

By crossing borders like most people cross the road, the Cartel thought they were safe. But by 2003, 30 years after Britain's biggest drug dealing gang was founded, Merseyside Police had also grown, in size and scale. Merseyside Police were now the most sophisticated police force in the UK as far as drug enforcement was concerned. The force was the only one outside the Met to have Level 3 capability, giving it the back-up in terms of officer support, resources, training and legal permissions, and the authorisation to travel outside the UK almost instantaneously to track drug dealers. If Smith or one of his gang jumped on a plane to watch Everton playing in Europe, it was no big deal to have a couple of officers on the plane. If business was being discussed in a five-star hotel afterwards, Merseyside Police simply asked the local force to help out. By now they had protocols in place with nearly every major police force in Europe. Merseyside Police had become a beacon; their best practice became textbook tactics for other forces around the country. Their officers flew around the world studying how policemen in South America and the USA tackled gangs and drugs. They saw what worked then came back to Liverpool and road-tested different tactics during investigations. If they were successful, they codified them in manuals. These operations won awards and the Association of Chief Police Officers (ACPO) and the Home Office spread them around the country.

The Analyst said, 'The view of the main players like Smith was that law enforcement didn't have the authority to travel out of the UK after them. On some occasions that was correct – but not always. That's the thing: it all rests on how organised the investigation is. And by then we were well on top of our game. That's where the drug traffickers fall foul sometimes: they assume too much.'

In a bid to stay low-key, Smith made further anti-surveillance changes. Unknown faces became key personnel, in addition to men with reputations. He broke with tradition and began to recruit drug dealers from outside the Cartel, and from outside Liverpool, into key positions. The further removed from Liverpool the better; the fewer links with the established players the better. In Holland, Smith recruited a 35-year-old low-level trafficker from the wild backwaters of the Forest of Dean, in Gloucestershire. Simon 'Slapper' Cowmeadow was a plumber turned drug dealer. Like many young men in the Forest of Dean in the 1990s, he found himself getting mixed up with the rave scene. The Forest of Dean had a reputation for mystery and hard partying. Slapper was mates with dance band EMF and he found himself serving up tablets at illegal raves in the countryside. The story of what happened to

Slapper would become a warning to relatively ordinary criminals who got mixed up with the Cartel.

Cowmeadow had started out as a regular guy. He lived with his then partner in a cottage in Flaxley, a picturesque English village. He was a family man with a 12-year-old son. He was a regular at a nearby country pub and had a reputation for playing practical jokes. Though he was a self-employed plumber by trade, he also dabbled in second-hand car dealing. Slapper was the lad about town who lived by his wits because he was intelligent and good-humoured.

He was also good at laying his hands on E's. Slapper's weakness was that he loved to live a double life. In November 2001, the National Crime Squad busted Slapper with 100,000 Ecstasy tablets with a street value of £1.5 million. Slapper tried to bluff his way out, acting as if he was just a roguish country bumpkin who got drawn into a caper and got in above his head. The drugs were discovered concealed among 26 pallets of frozen chips in the back of an articulated lorry at an industrial estate in Thurrock, Essex. It turned out that on the side Slapper had turned himself into an expert in arranging transport for drugs gangs. Six months later, Slapper and his two accomplices appeared at Southend Crown Court, but on the day he was meant to take the stand, Cowmeadow did a runner. He was sentenced to 18 years in jail in his absence.

With nowhere to go, like most drug dealers on the lam, Cowmeadow turned up in Holland looking for work. He was soon introduced to Colin Smith. Smith immediately recognised Cowmeadow's potential. He was desperate and therefore cheap, despite having lots of good contacts in the transport sector. He had experience. He was alone and for that reason would probably remain loyal if he was treated right. He had little knowledge of the Cartel and would not be dragged into their internecine feuds. Here was someone who could be one of Colin Smith's men in Amsterdam. Cowmeadow was soon recruited into the firm.

CHAPTER 5

DIAL-A-DEALER

2003

At the top of the Cartel, everything seemed fine. Hundreds of millions a year in drug revenues were rolling in and the vast majority was flowing into the hands of the established godfathers. The Cartel's hierarchy was stable and clearly defined. At the top, there were rich and well-protected gangsters who kept everyone in line using a combination of reputation and custom. At the bottom, there were the street soldiers, the criminal equivalent of urban peasants, who did most of the hard work and took many of the risks.

In 2003, a small revolution began in isolated pockets of the city. In essence, several street soldiers began to question the old order. If most of the money was made at the distribution level, why should they have to hand over their profits to those higher up the chain? When the dealers argued with the middle management, they were told that that was the way things were: it took a lot of brainpower and money and contacts to smuggle shipments between continents; therefore, it was only fair that most of the rewards went to the traffickers at the top of the tree.

However, resentments still simmered. The soldiers couldn't form themselves into a trade union through which they could organise themselves into a powerful force of dissent. However, what they did have was ultimately more powerful. They became united by several social and cultural beliefs that they shared. For the first time in the UK, the phenomenon of US-style street gangs began to emerge. Street gangs had been around in Britain for hundreds of years, but the difference now was that the gangs were well armed with state-of-the-art automatic weapons and an array of older weapons, such as shotguns and First World War pistols. The gangs differed from previous generations in that they were bigger, they were able to extend over large neighbourhoods and they were gelled together by better communication. In short, they were better organised.

Many of the gangs were a natural extension of Britain's burgeoning underclass, a huge body comprising the unemployed and low-paid workers that had been clogging up the sink estates since the days of Mrs Thatcher. Now the third generation had emerged, some of whom were the sons of heroin and crack addicts. They were poorly socialised and quick to anger.

The gangs unified their look by wearing the same clothes. Black weatherproof outdoor wear became the trademark look of the urban street gang. Black North Face jackets, Lowe Alpine microporous bottoms and Berghaus trapper hats became de rigueur for gang members, who used their large number of pockets to hide numerous bags of green skunk cannabis. The loose-fit shells were ideal for concealing machetes, pistols and disassembled shotguns. Outdoor wear was good for standing around on street corners in harsh weather. It was the evolution of the hoodie to the maximum. It was anti-CCTV, in as much as one black-clad figure looked like any other on film, making it difficult for police and witnesses to identify criminals.

The most noticeable street gangs emerged in the Croxteth and Norris Green areas of the city, and what started out as a dispute between children from local estates would ultimately lead to the downfall of the Cartel. The feud started in 2003. At that point, both gangs cooperated in the sale of drugs and firearms. Joe Thompson, then twenty-two, was one of the leaders of Norris Green's most prominent group, the Strand gang. His friend Wes Brown, then 18, was a prominent member of the Croxteth crew. The flashpoint occurred in 2003, when there was a fatal shooting in a local pub. The dispute then spiralled out of control and both formed larger, better-armed gangs, starting a war that has now left four dead, scores injured and shot, and a catalogue of firearms incidents numbering in the hundreds.

The new generations of gangs were far from cohesive. There was rivalry between the younger leaders to see who was going to become top dog. One of the contenders was a drug dealer called Nicky Ayers. Ayers was ruthlessly cruel, but he'd managed to create a network smuggling E's and cannabis into Jersey. If only Ayers could stay alive and stay out of prison, he was one of the few gang leaders who could challenge Kallas for supremacy. But Kallas had luck on his side. In 2003, Ayers got nicked in connection with a parcel of drugs in Jersey and was jailed for six years, effectively taking him out of the game at a time of crucial change for the Cartel. This left the field open and Kallas free to make a run for the big prize. Ayers simmered bitterly in jail. One day he would get revenge on Kallas.

However, at the top of the Cartel, Colin 'King Cocaine' Smith was too busy consolidating his power to notice the threat emerging at street level. Smith had close links with a gang of former IRA hitmen known as the Cleaners. The Cleaners often visited a pub owned by the Smith family. One bonfire night, a party had got out of control and one of the Cleaners had pulled out his gun and started firing it into the air like a cowboy. It was a rare indiscretion and the police were called. Several gangsters were arrested; however, nothing much came of the case.

Smith was also forging close links with an Irish criminal gang from a tough area of Dublin. The outfit was led by an Irish godfather called Freddie Thompson. Thompson was the leader of a Drimnagh-based drugs gang that has been involved in a bloody feud with a rival gang from Crumlin. Since 2001, at least 11 people have lost their lives as a result of the feud.

But it was the younger generation who caught the eye of Smith. Paddy Doyle had been a hitman for Thompson. Doyle was a career criminal who had been the chief suspect in two murders carried out in Dublin in 2002 and 2005. He went on the run via Liverpool and Manchester, eventually ending up on Spain's Costa del Sol. From there, with the help of Colin Smith, he helped run a drugs empire, smuggling vast amounts of cocaine from Spain into Ireland. In return, Doyle agreed to work as a hitman for Smith. He was also an enforcer to secure the Cartel's drugs route once cocaine had been landed on the Spanish coast from Colombia.

Doyle was ideally suited to the work. Though he was typical of the third generation of gangland 'soldier' in that he was young and extremely violent, he was more loyal: unlike the hotheads from Norris Green and Toxteth, he was easy to control. Doyle was aggressive, showy and started fights on a whim, but he followed orders and he had respect for his elders. The downside was that, unlike Smith, Doyle loved to show out. Other Irish criminals on the Costa enjoyed the quiet life and just got on with their business. Doyle loved fast cars, high-class hookers and burning money. The other big problem was that Doyle was ambitious. Smith hadn't set a limit on Doyle's independent activities, so he was free to do business with the Turks and the Russians. He was getting out of his depth.

CHAPTER 6

NEW BLOOD

2004

Happy New Year! On 1 January 2004, a 19-year-old gang member called Danny McDonald was shot dead in the Royal Oak pub in the West Derby area of Liverpool. McDonald was a prominent member of the Croxteth Crew. The shooting was proof that the dispute between the Croxteth Crew and the Norris Green gang was escalating.

The dispute was widening. The younger generation was learning how to form alliances and build networks across the city, a development that would prove crucial when they later launched the coup on the leadership of the Cartel. The Croxteth Crew had formed an alliance with Kallas's gang. Kallas was paying the Croxteth Crew to attack his enemy Yael Feeney with guns, grenades and firebombs.

Yael's gang had blamed McDonald for a recent machine-gun attack. They made a coalition with the Norris Green gang and lured McDonald to his death. The bullet hole can still be seen in the pub's radiator. In retaliation, the Croxteth Crew, Kallas and the Gee family hit back with more explosions and 'spray and pray' drive-by shootings.

But revenge begot more revenge. Daniel Gee's 21-year-old brother Ian was shot in the back and his friend Craig Barker was killed when their car was hit by a hail of bullets. Speculation was rife that the shooting was a case of mistaken identity and that Sidious was the actual target of the hit. Retaliation was swift. A few days later, on 11 April, 19-year-old Michael Singleton was shot down in Kirkdale, the manor run by Michael Wright, after several men burst through the back door of his house and fed bullets into his head and chest. He died on the floor next to the kitchen sink. A month later, car-wash boss David Regan was murdered on the forecourt of his business in the Old Swan district. Once again, the MO was the same: masked gunmen came out of nowhere and shot the father of three in the back.

The young gangs were getting out of control. The police launched various operations to contain the violence. However, unlike the older generation, whose response to police activity was to either lie low or go on the run, the younger generation decided to stand and fight. Why should the police be allowed to stand in the way of the growth of the gangs? Most of the gang leaders were too young to understand the consequences of their actions. None of them had yet served long prison sentences. Death in combat was glorified instead of mourned. Kallas's scornful response to the police was a huge car explosion outside West Derby Road police station in Tuebrook.

That bomb, on 13 May 2004, created by packing industrial fireworks into a petrol container, was the biggest blast on the British mainland since the IRA ceasefire. Bomb-disposal experts said more than 20 shock rockets were used, enough to kill. As the gangland feud continued, Merseyside Police urged all residents living near police stations to be on guard. The blowing up of the car outside Tuebrook police station came at a time when officers had a breakthrough in the inquiry.

Merseyside Police decided to fight fire with fire. What happened next was unprecedented in British policing – but the tactics would mark a turning point in how gang crime was dealt with. Police responded with a massive show of force. More than two hundred and fifty people were arrested on the Grizedale estate – astonishingly, this accounted for one in ten of its population – more or less at once. The operation looked more like a counter-insurgency manoeuvre than a criminal investigation, as hundreds of officers swept through the streets at dawn, flanked by armed cars as the force chopper hovered above. But it worked. Hundreds of weapons were seized, including a powerful sniper rifle complete with telescopic sight and ammunition. Like an enemy force trying to keep hold of the ground they had gained, the police moved quickly to set up strongholds. A mobile police station was set in the centre of the estate to coordinate more raids. A tactic known as 'disruption' was introduced, which involved deliberate and continuous hassle of 18 'high-impact players'. Gangsters who were known to be involved in Level 3 crimes, such as transnational drug dealing, were stopped and arrested for Level 1 infringements, such as possession of a stolen phone or having no road tax. Zero tolerance was enforced. If a drug dealer parked in a disabled car space at the local Mothercare, he was swooped upon and then searched, arrested or moved on. The police's thinking was: 'The criminal mind does not see any difference between running a red light and selling a kilo of cocaine. We might not be able to catch you red-handed selling drugs, but we can disrupt your activities by pulling you for speeding and a broken brake light.' Graffiti was removed from the estates and personal attack alarms were handed out to residents, in a bid to make them feel secure, in the hope that they would start shopping their criminal neighbours. The five brothers who made up the Gee family were arrested. By the end of July, police had stopped the vast majority of low-level incidents. Only the high-level gang attacks continued.

Merseyside Police went back to the drawing board. They sent Detective Chief Superintendent Steve Moore, one of their cleverest and most senior officers, around the world to research best practice on how to deal with gang activity. Moore had come up through the ranks. He'd been brought up on a tough council estate in the Netherley district of Liverpool, a place that later became synonymous with crime. He'd won a place to study a degree in philosophy, politics and economics at Oxford and was one of a new breed of officers, like the Analyst, who was not afraid to use rational processes against the Cartel. Moore proposed setting up a semi-independent elite unite known as the Matrix: Britain's first anti-gang unit. The Matrix would have hand-picked officers, a fleet of transport and command vehicles, and an autonomous covert surveillance unit. Moore adeptly pushed his ideas through the police's bureaucracy.

However, the bloodlust of the Grizedale Crew wasn't

satisfied. They hated the police for invading their estate, and they hated the chief constable, who was trying to block their access to explosives. Their reaction was to turn their guns on the police. On 12 August, a second massive car bomb exploded outside the police station in Walton Lane, strewing wreckage more than 100 metres away.

While their enemies fought with the police – as had been planned all along – another gang then decided to target Sidious's celebrity girlfriend by trying to ruin her career. It was all-out asymmetric warfare. Shortly before she took up a leading part on the latest hit reality TV show, her reputation was blighted by an Internet hate campaign. Chilling threats to kill both her and Sidious were posted on her official website. The message warned: 'I'll kill her! Watch your back, you cow. Your boyfriend is mincemeat and so are you!'

The gang followed up by launching a propaganda campaign against Sidious by calling him a grass. The allegation, a serious one in the underworld, dated back to four years earlier, when Sidious had told police the names of six attackers who had macheted his pal to near-death.

Fearing that the vendetta would eventually cost him his life, Sidious and his girlfriend moved to London. But the attacks didn't stop. Two weeks later, a fire-bomb was thrown into their uninhabited Liverpool house. Army bomb-disposal experts were called in after the device smashed glass in the front door. A second bomb hit a neighbour's car.

On a visit back to Liverpool, Sidious and his girlfriend visited a restaurant, which happened to be owned by the Cartel's boss of bosses, Colin Smith. The night ended when a gang of lads beat up Sidious. Following a celebrity fashion show, a gang of masked men armed with baseball bats and a machete surrounded their Range Rover. Smashing a window, they attacked Sidious with the machete and left him with a stomach wound.

CHAPTER 7

GENERATION X

2004

The constant chaos horrified the Cartel's bosses who, despite the nature of their business, wanted nothing more than a quiet life, at least in relative terms. The incessant violence was held up as evidence that the new generation was out of control and could not be entrusted with the future of Britain's biggest drug gang. The kids were irrational and impulsive. How could they be relied upon to sit down with representatives of the various South American cocaine cartels and get respect? They were street hoodlums, not businessmen. But what could the bosses do? When they complained, the new generation hit back, throwing hand grenades at them and shooting up their multimillion-pound mansions in blatant shows of disrespect. In normal circumstances, they would employ onside drug dealers like Bubbley Shalson to fight fire with fire, bringing in his private army of loyal gang members to maintain order. But even this was out of bounds: Shalson himself was under attack and his lieutenants were engaged in an unauthorised gang war against the upstarts already. The only rest Cartel bosses got was when the young gangbangers were sent to jail. The senior bosses started to complain that the police weren't doing their job and locking up the yobs. Like *Daily Mail* readers, they began to call for tougher sentences, deriding teenagers for being lawless and irresponsible. In June 2004, they breathed a collective sigh of relief when the inspiration of the new subculture, Kallas, was sent to prison for a 30-month stretch after being caught with an imitation firearm.

It gave the bosses time to think. It gave Yael Feeney an opportunity to reload and recuperate.

The hiatus gave the Cartel's leadership time to focus on more serious issues further away from home. Things weren't going so well for the Cartel's South American contacts. In 2004, Colombia's Cali cartel suffered a number of arrests, with its founders, Gilberto and Miguel Rodríguez Orejuela, extradited to the US.

One of the big problems faced by senior members of the Cartel was what they called an 'imbalance of policing'. By 2004, Merseyside Police had become really good at catching the big bosses. By following the drugs and money, and by forging links with strategic resources such as the National Crime Squad, they were taking down the traditional bosses at a rate of knots. The police had not yet gained the same expertise at dealing with the new gangs, as they were only a relatively recent phenomenon. The Cartel bosses complained that they were getting all the heat from the police while street rats were left free to run amok. They complained that they were being unfairly 'squeezed' out of crime because they were being attacked on two flanks by the gangs and the police.

One example was long-standing Cartel godfather Edward Jarvis. Jarvis had a pedigree underworld heritage that could be traced back to the start of the Cartel in 1973, when he was just eight years old. Jarvis had been a protégé and close contact of the Banker, who'd taken over the Cartel from founder Fred the Rat. The Banker passed on the title to Curtis Warren when he retired. Jarvis had been heavily in the mix ever since he'd been old enough to hold a five-pound deal. He served his apprenticeship during the boom years of the 1980s. By the 1990s, he was a multimillionaire drugs baron who was so high up that he was shipping contraband himself by the boatload in private yachts.

In the 1990s, he'd run rings round the police. In 1998, Dutch police raided a house and found cannabis and amphetamines with an estimated street value of £600,000. The job had Jarvis's hallmarks all over it, such as the type of drugs found and the transport used to smuggle them. Three of his workers were arrested at the house. A false passport in the name of Peter Jones but with Jarvis's photograph in it was found at the scene. But he'd gone. When the Dutch authorities contacted Merseyside Police to pick him up for drugs, they said there was not enough evidence to make a conviction stick. The National Crime Squad said it would put it on file until they plucked him again. The only thing they could get him on was a second-hand income-tax-evasion charge that had come through the Banker after he'd been nicked for money laundering.

But six years later, in 2004, it was all change. Merseyside Police were the number-one drug hunters in the UK and now they had the Level 3 capability enabling them to track down the likes of Jarvis on sea, land and air. Along with the National Crime Squad, they built a file on Jarvis linking him to a £48 million haul of cocaine that had been intercepted in a yacht called *The Pulse*. Jarvis had supervised the plot from his Liverpool home and then from a second temporary HQ in Margarita, a tropical island in the Caribbean, off the coast of Venezuela. Getting his lackeys to buy the boat for £30,000, paid for in cash on the Greek island of Rhodes, before sailing it to the Caribbean in preparation to pick up the cocaine from Venezuelan contacts, Jarvis hid his involvement using a string of aliases and false passports, but was finally caught after he wired money from a Spanish bank account to the yacht's crew members under the falsified name of Andrew Rainford. Two weeks later, the crew were arrested unloading large packages of white powder onto the yacht. Jarvis was sentenced to 28 years in jail.

But Jarvis was just one of many of the millionaire gangsters to fall foul of the police's more intrusive approach. A few years earlier, dealers from a major Cartel cell had got their fingers burned after setting up Britain's biggest-ever amphetamine factories. The enterprise became the victim of the police's newfound effectiveness at dealing with the Cartel. In an early coup for intelligence-led operations, Merseyside Police 'turned' one of the Cartel's leading chemists into a witness and the National Crime Squad attacked the speed ring with a number of secret infiltrators and informers. The model was now up and running, and there was no way they would ever again allow amphetamine factories to be set up and run for any length of time.

In 2004, four men began plotting to set up a string of similar factories across Liverpool and Southport. The police were ready for them. Just like the previous operation that had been busted, the men tried to disguise the illegal factories by pretending they were part of a legitimate chemicals company. Shortly afterwards, they established two facilities with the potential to turn over £1 million of speed per week. But this time the factories weren't even allowed to get going. The National Crime Squad shut them down and the four men were each sentenced to twenty years in prison.

Meanwhile, there was a madman on the loose. According to a contemporary report in the *Liverpool Echo*, one officer said the car-bomb attacks against the police had 'freaked them out'. A massive manhunt got underway before the next one went off. At the end of August, Richard Caswell's home was raided. Ironically, he lived in the heart of his enemy's territory, in the middle of Kirkdale, close to the Wright family. Caswell was arrested after DNA linked him to the attacks, and a haul of firearms was also discovered at the house he was living in at Newman Street, Sandhills. He always claimed that he lacked the knowledge to build a car bomb, but he admitted driving the cheap cars filled with fireworks to the scenes of the crimes before the cars were ignited by someone else.

Anyone and everyone seemed to be carrying a gun, even those villains who didn't sell drugs or who had little to do with the Cartel. It wasn't hard to get dragged into a lethal dispute. Carli Sleevey was a tough, no-nonsense director of a major north-west waste-disposal firm. He didn't sell cocaine. His nephew Tony was serving time with Dylan Porter, though the former eventually had his conviction overturned after an appeal. Like Yael Feeney, Carli Sleevey wasn't a drug dealer but was a gangster turned legitimate businessman. He and Yael Feeney had a lot in common and often did each other favours. Sleevey had been dragged into a long-running tit-for-tat dispute between members of his family and a former Cartel underboss who worked directly for the Cartel's main godfather Colin Smith. In 2002, Carli Sleevey's nephew Tony was wrongly jailed for murdering the underboss, who was stabbed several times. A month later, a member of Sleevey's family was gunned down in revenge. One month after that, a member of the underboss's family was killed in a revenge attack. To protect himself from further attacks, and from the increasingly unpredictable new generation, Sleevey began carrying a gun. One day, he was caught carrying a handgun.

In 2004, the Matrix team got up and running. Immediately they identified David Hibbs-Turner as the new-generation gang leader who was behind much of the upsurge in teenage violence. Matrix covert operations launched an investigation into Hibbs-Turner from 2004 that would last 20 months. At first, police intelligence discovered that his gang was running drugs including coke, Ecstasy and amphetamines into the UK from Spain. A police officer said it was a 'determined' gang that was drug trafficking on an 'industrial scale'.

In Britain, a struggle for power between the generations was about to embroil the Cartel in a long-running conflict. But in Holland, the Cartel was achieving supremacy over other international gangs because its image was exactly the opposite of the reality. In Amsterdam, the Cartel had a reputation for being stable and easy to do business with. Its representatives were seen as resilient and not quick to anger. The local Dutch godfathers were getting bored of the Yugoslavian gangs that had flooded in after the civil war and then started shooting at them. Three of the Dutch crime lords had been killed in quick succession. Their Middle Eastern connections were forever getting gunned down too. In July 2004, Egyptian drug dealer Mounir Barsoum became the latest victim in a series of gangland hits when he was shot dead at the wheel of his car. His brother Magdi, who had run a coffee shop and café called Bar Red Light, had also been involved in illegal drug dealing, but had been shot dead in 2002. The Cartel now presented the acceptable face of international drug dealing; it was an organisation whose older members were very experienced and could be trusted not to turn. This was the Cartel's competitive advantage, and they soon began displacing other foreign gangs from the Dutch capital.

CHAPTER 8

MEXICO

2005

Modern cocaine production began in Peru in the 1960s and '70s, not Colombia, as is widely believed. It was only in the 1980s that the influence of Peru's crime gangs began to drift across the border into Colombia.

At this time, few people outside Mexico had heard of the Mexican drug cartels. The North American republic was not a cocaine producer. The Mexican mafias did not grow coca plants; neither did they process the crop into paste. The Mexican mafias were simply traffickers and smugglers who took the cocaine from South America and shipped it up north to the world's biggest market for cocaine: the USA.

In 2005, Eduardo Tomás Medina-Mora Icaza was a 48-year-old Mexican lawyer. For the previous five years, he'd served as head of the Center for Research and National Security (CISEN). While researching Mexico's national-security problems, Medina-Mora had noticed several changes in the way the country's cartels were doing business. First, they were growing fast. Second, since 2003 the Mexican cartels had become increasingly violent. Third, the Mexican cartels were looking to expand vertically down the supply chain: put simply, they wanted to control the coca growers, processors and traffickers in South America. Fleeing police activity in their home country, a number of Mexican drug lords headed for Central America, from where they could exert more influence on the growers. Medina-Mora was rapidly becoming one of the world's authorities on the cocaine trade, so much so that in 2005 President Vicente Fox invited him into his cabinet to become the Secretary for Public Safety, with a brief to find a solution to the problem of organised crime.

Speaking to this author, Medina-Mora said, 'To go back to the beginning, Colombia used to produce marijuana and poppies for heroin. Then they started to trade with "contrabandits", exchanging the drugs they produced for merchandise such as clothing and TV sets. Once they had consumer goods, the Colombians then started to trade these with the neighbouring Peruvians, who would in turn pay them with illegal products in kind. That established a Peruvian play – the cocaine came from Peru. That totally changed the play in South America.'

After coca plants became common in Peru, the influence migrated back over the border to Colombia and largely replaced pot and heroin. Before the 1990s, harvesting coca leaves had been a relatively small-scale business in Colombia, but when the harvest began to grow Colombia's ascendancy coincided with the decline of coca harvests in Peru and Bolivia, countries that had dominated coca-leaf production in the 1980s and early '90s. But several factors began to impact on cocaine production in Peru and Bolivia. First, the US and the local governments encouraged manual-eradication campaigns. With US help, the government were also successful in rupturing the air bridge that had previously facilitated the illegal transport of Bolivian and Peruvian coca leaf to Colombia to pay for their contrabandit trade. Then a fungus wiped out a large percentage of Peru's coca crops and made it more difficult for the cartels to obtain coca from these countries.

In response, Colombia's drug cartels purchased land in their home country to expand local production, pushing coca cultivation into areas of southern Colombia controlled by the FARC terrorists, also known as the Revolutionary Armed Forces of Colombia. Colombia replaced Bolivia and Peru as the primary producer of coca leaf between 1996 and 1997. Colombia's supremacy coincided with the growth of the Cartel, who went on to purchase much of the European-targeted output.

By 2004, Colombia was responsible for 80 per cent of the

world's cocaine production. One estimate has Colombia's coca cultivation hectarage growing from 13,000 in the mid-1980s to 80,000 hectares in 1998 to 99,000 in 2007.

By 2005, there were three dominant producers: Bolivia, Peru and Colombia. However, all of these producers were now under pressure from the numerous and extremely violent drug cartels from Mexico to hand over their wares at a price set by them. Mexico controlled trafficking to the west.

At first, the Mexican cartels had started off as middlemen who distributed cocaine produced in south Colombia and Venezuela and shipped it on to the US. Within the hierarchy, they were lower down the chain than the producers, such as the Cali cartel in Colombia. During the 1980s and early 1990s, Colombia's Pablo Escobar was the main exporter of cocaine and dealt with organised criminal networks all over the world. When enforcement efforts intensified in south Florida and the Caribbean, the Colombian organisations formed partnerships with the Mexico-based traffickers to transport cocaine through Mexico into the United States.

This was easily accomplished, because Mexico had long been a major source of heroin and cannabis, and drug traffickers from Mexico had already established an infrastructure that stood ready to serve the Colombia-based traffickers. At first, the Mexican gangs were paid in cash for their transportation services, but in the late 1980s, the Mexican transport organisations and the Colombian drug traffickers settled on a payment-in-product arrangement. Transporters from Mexico usually were given 35 to 50 per cent of each cocaine shipment. This arrangement meant that organisations from Mexico became involved in the distribution as well as the transportation of cocaine, and became formidable traffickers in their own right. Currently, the Sinaloa and the Gulf cartels have taken over trafficking cocaine from Colombia to the worldwide markets.

However, the Mexicans soon outgrew the suppliers and started asking the question that the new generation of gang members had asked in Liverpool: 'Why should we be of lower status and get less money when distribution is as important as production?' Like the proverbial scorpion on the frog's back, the Mexicans turned on the Colombians and Venezuelans and gave them an almighty sting. Mexican gangs were sent down to South and Central America to take over and oversee production of cocaine.

Eduardo Medina-Mora not only became one of the world's number-one authorities on cocaine crime, he also began to work closely with his own security services and those of other countries in a bid to curtail the power of the Mexican cartels. Medina-Mora said, 'The Mexican partners evolved into being dominant. At first, shippers from South America started paying the Mexican transport people in kind and gave them product – cocaine. So that gave the Mexican-based cartels a relevant role in the value-added chain. The South Americans allowed the Mexicans to have cocaine because they thought that they could distance themselves from the final leg of the smuggling route, that of passing over the border to the US. In this way, they thought that they could avoid extradition to the US, thinking that the one before the last mule could not be tried in the US. That was a very powerful trigger for the Colombians to get involved with the Mexicans. The Mexicans then got a degree of access and control to wholesale distribution in the US. Then the Colombians and Mexicans started partnering themselves in cargo, from production to the North American route. Instead of buying cocaine for $12,000 as it came into Mexico, they started buying it very cheap direct in Colombia. Then there were joint operations and cross-ambassadorships from each other crime groups.'

Eventually the Mexicans became the dominant partners because they had a monopoly on distribution in the US, and also because they were much feared. This in turn led to great rivalry between various Mexican cartels, which fought for control of the lucrative trade. By 2006, the problem was no longer simply a socio-economic problem: the power of the Mexican cartels was also a threat to national security. In 2006, Medina-Mora was appointed Attorney General in the cabinet of President Felipe Calderón. Within months the new President had declared war on the Mexican cartels, sending in the army to take on the well-armed bandits.

Medina-Mora said, 'The drugs trade cannot be stopped when demand is inelastic. The objective then is to remove groups that have accumulated throughout the years. The idea is to remove the drug lord – remove their ability to kidnap tranquillity from the Mexican people.

'The violence started in 2003. In Mexico it became a national-security problem because they have accumulated so much economic power, so much firepower to intimidate local people and local government.'

The military offensive against the cartels was designed to stop war breaking out in Medina-Mora's country. Over the next five years, more than thirty-five thousand people were killed. By 2011, the Mexican government was using US drones to collect intelligence on the drug cartels threatening Mexico.

The events several thousand miles away in Mexico would have several important developments for the business of the Cartel. First, within a few years, such was their power in the global market, the Mexican crime groups would have a big influence on the price and quantity of much of the cocaine shipped to Europe, even if it was smuggled from other countries, such as Colombia. Second, the Mexican drug barons took a strategic decision to actively target Europe as a secondary market following the saturation of the US market. Third, within a few years the Cartel would also find itself in the position of needing a new cocaine supplier. The big question was: would the two groups do business with each other?

CHAPTER 9

JOHN SMITH

2005

For over a decade John Smith had enjoyed special status within the Cartel. His brother Colin was the de facto boss of bosses of the organisation. Colin had once been Curtis Warren's deputy but since Warren's incarceration in 1996 had taken over the number-one spot. For many gangsters, having such a high-profile criminal for a brother would have been a problem, but John Smith was no Fredo, the character in *The Godfather* haunted by an inferiority complex. John Smith wore his status well, profiting from the big deals that came his way through Colin and doing his own stuff on the side. He had become somewhat of an expert on trafficking Class A drugs out of Amsterdam. In the late '80s and early '90s, Colin and John Smith and Curtis Warren acted independently. But they were so busy that they often met up by accident in the lobbies of hotels in Amsterdam, where they would laugh and joke about their graft. They would be in and out of each other's rooms, asking about what drugs they were buying, swapping contacts and catching up on the latest underworld gossip. A short while later, Colin Smith and Warren formalised their relationship and became partners.

By 2005, John Smith was running several drug running operations, both big and small. He was basically an overseer, cruising around Liverpool in his £35,000 Toyota Land Cruiser, stopping for cups of tea in anonymous suburban houses where he would give instructions to his underlings. Every couple of weeks, he would stop off at the home of his mate Francis

Gallagher to discuss the distribution of drugs. They would often be joined by their associates John Traynor and Gary McEvatt.

Smith would leave with three cases of Stella Artois. But instead of lager, they contained 15 kilos of Class A drugs, worth an estimated £1.5 m. While Smith took the cocaine and pushed it via street-level dealers into Merseyside, the heroin headed for St Helens and a dealer known as 'Eddie'. The police are still trying to track him down. By Cartel standards, the amounts were small. But the method was beautifully simple, and each load netted John Smith a cool 60 grand.

Gary McEvatt was Smith's man in Amsterdam. He was trusted because he was only 22 and from Smith's manor in Speke. In those days, Smith preferred to stay away from the Dam, as the dealers nicknamed the city – the father of four liked the comfort of his mini-mansion in the exclusive Calderstones area of Liverpool and his villa in Marbella. McEvatt did the legwork in the 'flat place', collecting 30 half-kilo blocks of cocaine and heroin from a Cartel supplier in Rotterdam. The suitcases were then passed on to a courier called John Traynor, who walked them onto the P&O ferry at Rotterdam disguised as a daytripper on a booze cruise.

During the 11-hour voyage back to the UK, Traynor stocked-up on duty-free booze to shore up his cover story. But the props had another use. The bottles of Stella were removed from the boxes and drugs were stuffed inside in their place before the lid was carefully resealed. When no one was looking, the boxes were passed to an insider who'd been corrupted and recruited onto John Smith's firm: a P&O worker called Francis Gallagher, who used his trusted position to stroll past customs officers without being stopped.

Everything went smoothly until a weak link in the set-up appeared on the police's radar. Hundreds of miles away in Warrington, Cheshire, a low-level dealer called Lee Mortimor was caught on camera passing half a kilo of cocaine to a buyer. In times gone by, the handover might have been regarded as insignificant, but with the wonder of intelligence-led policing and some very switched-on officers, this small window was seen as a gateway into opening up the hierarchy.

The police simply followed Mortimor until he led them to Cartel members higher up the chain. Operation Copybook was launched by Merseyside Police in September 2005 and was to become an award-winning model of how to carry out a complicated drug-following, asset-recovery-chasing operation. Officers estimated that, taking into account all the trips they saw booze cruiser John Traynor make, the gang had smuggled around £10 m of drugs. For seven months, the officers followed their every move.

Later the gang was hit and jailed for a total of 68 years. Bang! The race was on. The police were catching up, getting closer and closer. For Colin Smith, Operation Copybook was too close for comfort. After all, it was his brother John's outfit that had been under the microscope.

Between 2002 and 2005, Colin Smith's hitman Paddy 'Wack' Doyle had been slipping back into Ireland to do jobs. Officially, Doyle was on the run following the murder of Timothy Rattigan in the Crumlin area of the city in 2002. Like Liverpool, Dublin was experiencing the new phenomenon of well-armed street gangs revolting against their bosses and killing each other. Doyle had been drafted in by his Irish boss Freddie Thompson because he was a controllable upstart. Eighteen-year-old Rattigan was a member of a rival Crumlin gang and was shot outside his home.

Doyle was already well known to the Garda, having amassed 42 convictions for drug dealing, serious assault, theft and road-traffic offences. A police report described him as 'psychopathic' and someone who enjoyed inflicting pain on others. In one fight, he beat a man to within inches of his life in a pub. Doyle was useful to the Cartel for the same reasons that he was useful to Freddie Thompson. Although he was a young gang member who shared the new generation's belief in shooting first, Doyle was considered old school at heart. He was curiously conservative when it came to the criminal hierarchy and he liked things staying the way they had always been. Unlike Kallas, Sidious and the army of teenage 'creatures' that were running amok and disrupting Cartel business in Liverpool, Doyle didn't want to upset the old order. He saw the well-trodden path of the elders as his route to wealth and power. For the Cartel, this was a godsend.

He would be Colin Smith's secret weapon in controlling attacks from the young bucks in Liverpool. In addition, he would stop the young gangs from encroaching on his key battleground in Spain.

International flight was fast becoming accessible for the 'rats' who'd never been further than the Strand and bought their clobber from the Broadway, the Rodeo Drive of Norris Green. It was easy for young gang members from Norris Green or Kirkdale to jump on an EasyJet flight from John Lennon Airport in Liverpool and start wreaking havoc in Malaga two hours later. This could not be allowed to happen. Freddie Thompson began hiring out Doyle to the Cartel to do more and more of their dirty work.

One of the great things about Doyle, in the eyes of the Cartel, was that he was loyal. Unlike the new generation, he wouldn't try to turn someone over for a few kilos of coke. In fact he'd go the extra mile, especially if it meant turning the streets into the set of a Quentin Tarantino movie. In autumn 2005, Doyle slipped back into Dublin to see his old pal Thompson. Doyle often wore a wig as a disguise. He had no need to get dragged back into the turf wars of his boss, Freddie Thompson, but Doyle couldn't help sticking his neck out. When Freddie told him that he had a problem, Doyle was off like a rocket trying to solve it.

On 13 November 2005, Doyle went for a meeting with two of Thompson's drug dealers. He got into the back seat of a car at a housing estate in Firhouse. Darren Geoghegan and Gavin Byrne believed they were there to discuss an impending drugs delivery, but Doyle produced a 9 mm pistol and shot both men in the back of the head. They died before they realised that anything was amiss. The pair were murdered as a result of internal gang tensions over the control of drugs money. Doyle was taking up the mantle of the Cleaners, the gang of ex-IRA members who cleaned up internal disputes for the Cartel and the Irish mafia. For one so young, Doyle was good. Bloody good. In some respects, he was better than the ex-IRA guys. What he lacked in discipline, he made up for in ferocity.

But his holiday in Dublin wasn't over yet. Two days later, on 15 November 2005, Doyle received a call on his mobile phone informing him that a member of a rival Crumlin gang was attending a Phil Collins concert at the Point Theatre. He picked up a Glock pistol and went out to confront the man, who turned out to be 27-year-old Noel Roche. Along with another member of the Thompson gang, Doyle followed his prey to Clontarf. With the sounds of 'Sussudio' still racing around his head, Roche was shot dead outside the Yacht pub. Doyle then drove the getaway car to a nearby estate and set it alight to destroy his fingerprints. All in a day's work. Standard Procedure. As a hitman, he had done it countless times before.

However, Doyle had got sloppy. He fled before making sure that the car exploded. The fire fizzled out and traces of Doyle's DNA were recovered. Following procedure, after carrying out three murders in two days, he boarded a flight to Alicante days later and then moved to Marbella a few days after that. He linked up with Gary Hutch, a nephew of the Irish boss of bosses known as 'the Monk'. The Monk had rock solid links with the Cartel at the highest level. Colin Smith was happy. Doyle could no longer go home to Dublin. The Cartel had him all to itself.

Back in Liverpool, life was good for Colin Smith. Like most Cartel godfathers, he was able to afford a mansion in Liverpool's most exclusive neighbourhood. He'd also built up a property empire, buying pubs and an amusement arcade, while a restaurant he owned was frequented by Liverpool and Everton footballers. On one occasion they'd had to duck after a gunman burst in and let off several rounds.

He also had a property in Puerto Banús on the Costa del Sol but kept a close eye on his empire, jetting in and out of Liverpool on cheap EasyJet flights. Smith was a fanatical Evertonian with a VIP box at the Goodison Park ground. He was friends with many of the players and had flown back and forth for European games. When ex-Everton player Mark Ward fell on hard times, Smith paid him to play for a semi-professional team. But Ward later got mixed up with drugs and in 2005 was jailed for eight years for possessing cocaine worth £650,000.

To keep his position secure, Smith made sure that his middle management was well paid. He made a lot of crime families and gangs rich by making them high-level distributors on generous terms. As a result, he was well loved. By 2005, many of the middle management who had been loyal to their first boss, Curtis Warren, were now becoming increasingly loyal to Colin Smith. Warren was losing his grip on the Cartel. If only he could get out of prison and reclaim his position . . . But this was never going to happen. In February 2005, while Warren was still inside a Dutch prison, he was charged by Dutch authorities with running an international drug-smuggling cartel from his cell. During the trial, he was moved around six jails for his own safety. Eventually he was found guilty and he would have to spend many more years inside. Colin Smith's position as the number one was secure.

CHAPTER 10

OPERATION COPYBOOK

2005

The success of Operation Copybook, which focused on Colin Smith's brother John, gave intelligence-led policing a big credibility boost. Soon the policy was on the statute books as the core principle underpinning a big overhaul of organised-crime policing.

It had been an uphill struggle. For the past decade, Tony Blair had been pouring money into community policing and tackling antisocial behaviour. The policies reflected the New Labour refrain 'tough on crime, tough on the causes of crime'. Organised-crime intelligence had been taken away from some police forces and made part of MI5's remit. But in 2001, after 9/11, everything changed. MI5 was instructed to focus on anti-terrorism measures. The focus on asset recovery moved back to the police; in fact, MI5 no longer even mentions organised crime on its website.

Organised crime was once again high up on the police's to-do list. In a bid to find a home for intelligence-led policing, the Serious Organised Crime and Police Act 2005 created the Serious Organised Crime Agency (SOCA). The crime squads of all police forces were coagulated into a national agency, headed by Sir Stephen Lander. The Financial Intelligence Unit section of the National Criminal Intelligence Service, which had operated alongside but independently of investigation agencies, was subsumed into SOCA.

The Cartel's number-one enemy, the Analyst, was recruited into SOCA as a VIP asset. The Analyst told them that fighting the Cartel wasn't just about kicking in doors and James Bond-style hi-tech surveillance. It was about studying law books in great detail to find out how they could trip up drug dealers while simultaneously making sure that the police themselves were not going to get tripped up by the defence if a case got to court. The days when drug dealers could wriggle out of court through a loophole found by a highly paid lawyer were numbered. The Analyst was determined to stamp it out. And it wasn't just about drug legislation: the Analyst urged his officers to become experts in the laws on murder, money laundering, you name it.

The Analyst said, 'You've got to have part of the team who are aware of the law. As the senior investigating officer you've got to know it all, so that you don't take a line of inquiry that scuppers what you've done already. Of course, we use the CPS as our lawyer. But the bottom line is that you've got to get your books out yourself, because you can't keep knocking on the CPS's door and asking about the legislation.

'So, for example, if I was dealing with a murder which had been carried out by a gang and not just one person, then instead of going after the main targets, I would go for the lot on joint enterprise. I dug out stated cases on joint enterprise such as R. versus Rahman and others and used them to convince the CPS that we could do this. I built my case and then sat down with the lawyers and said, "I believe I've got a case."

'When they came back at me and said, "You're vulnerable because of this point," I said, "I've done the research: here's the case law. We can get around it." It's fascinating. Oh God, it's fascinating.'

Effectively, the Analyst not only had to be a police investigator but a frontline lawyer. Many officers found this boring, but the Analyst convinced them that by continuously going over legal points over and over again, it actually improved investigative powers and led to safer convictions.

The Analyst said, 'It's not just about building a case around a suspect because you fancy that they are the ones responsible. If you go back to miscarriages of justice in the past, that's the way things have happened. For instance, I had one job – a murder – in which there were thirty-six named suspects. We put each person under a microscope just to prove it wasn't them. It was a process of elimination rather than the other way around, that is looking at the one we thought it was most likely to be. I applied the same logic to the main suspect and everyone passed the test except him. The others had alibis, or forensics proved it wasn't them. So it's not just building a case, it's proving and disproving.

'The reason why was simple: when I got to court, the main suspect's barrister would probably have said it wasn't my client, it was someone else. I could respond immediately with the facts.

'As regards the miscarriages of justice in the '70s, the critics would say that they chose the suspect and built the case. It's a different issue today. We are thorough and we're right for the right reasons.'

In 2005, a different cell within the Cartel discovered a near fail-safe mechanism of smuggling huge amounts of cocaine into Britain. They were using scaffolding bars stuffed with cocaine.

Three men – John Mullally, David Baker and Keith Burke – masterminded the operation. Burke set up a front company called KBE Engineering. He tendered for fake construction jobs in Spain, Holland and the Balkans. The scaffolding bars were sent out of the UK to the phoney sites and filled with drugs. Then they were driven back to Liverpool, where the drugs were distributed. A gang of 17 workers were employed on the continent and in the UK to manage the operation. Each load bore £2.5 million of drugs.

Unluckily for them, the police had been tipped off about the scheme. In 2005, Merseyside Police launched Operation Lima and began secretly watching the gang at work. It was a testament to the newfound expertise of Merseyside Police that all of the various pieces were slotted together like clockwork. Using their Level 3 capability, officers immediately alerted Customs and Excise and set up a link. Then they set up partner operations with units in Holland, Spain and Eastern Europe.

CHAPTER 11

DAVID HIBBS-TURNER

2005

The Cartel's new kid on the block began to put together the team he hoped would help him make his final ascent to the top of the tree. He was only 27, but already he had considerable leadership skills. Police later said he was convinced he was untouchable. Hibbs-Turner spent a lot of time in Amsterdam organising deals and fake passports. One of the key requirements of a gang in Amsterdam is possessing property, which was required to accommodate large numbers of gang members as well as acting as safe houses in which to store drugs, weapons and money. It sounds like a simple requirement, but it requires care and local know-how if you don't want to draw attention. The properties were supplied by specialist underworld estate agents who drew up false lettings contracts and supplied fake details to housing authorities and local councils.

Joint second-in-command were brothers Stephen and James Kelly, aged 30 and 24 respectively. The Kelly brothers were in charge of distribution in Liverpool and spent their days going from one luxury pad to another in a fleet of top-end cars, organising the cutting and packaging of the drugs.

Next in line was Terence Riley, the boy who had discovered James Bulger's body on railway lines 12 years earlier. Now he was 25, and his grandmother Ann Nesbitt blamed his criminality on the trauma of finding the body. Riley never spoke again of what he saw – he only ever spoke about graft. How many kilos, how much and how to get them from A to

B. If anyone could become a poster boy for the new generation, it was Riley, a child who'd been warped into a drug dealer by the vices of society. When the family tried to get him to talk about James Bulger, Riley became hysterical and started screaming. Riley shut himself off. His personality changed completely and he rarely visited his family. He turned into a drug-dealing machine whose professionalism impressed Hibbs-Turner.

Kaim was the next member of Hibbs-Turner's inner sanctum. Kaim was related to Sidious. He even lived next door to Hibbs-Turner so he could be on hand to arrange drug deals or carry out contract killings.

Lee Cole was a seasoned importer with convictions for heroin and cannabis. He carried a gun and spent much of his time flitting between Liverpool and Amsterdam. He and Michael Kinsella were involved in sending money and delivering large quantities of cocaine. Wesley Barton was just 23 when he was put in charge of a drugs factory at a yuppie docklands development called Royal Quay.

Lower down the chain, there were a number of smugglers and distributors who had specific jobs, such as David Surridge, a 'bashman' and a runner. He bought hydraulic presses to compact cocaine once it had been mixed with a bulking agent called benzocaine. Benzocaine was an ideal adulterant for cocaine because they had very similar properties. Once the white-coloured benzocaine had been mixed with the moist, yellowing, freshly imported cocaine, the mixture was blended in a food processor and had a white, fluffy appearance, which to buyers was a giveaway that it had been 'danced on'. In order to give the appearance of purer, higher-quality drugs, the powdery mixture had to be compressed into blocks using hydraulic presses. One gang in the Halewood district of Liverpool had six Magimix food processors in operation round the clock and used to place the blocks of cocaine underneath a car chassis, which was lowered by a jack for compression.

The Cartel began using so much benzocaine that several drug dealers stopped dealing illegal drugs altogether and switched to trading purely in benzocaine, importing containers of 'beno' directly from China to meet demand. One of the gang said, 'The lads who are bringing in beno are making more money than cocaine smugglers. It started off around 2005. Lads were buying 25-kilo barrels from pharmaceutical wholesalers in Nottingham for £3,000 each. Then they started importing it for £2,000 each and selling it on to the underworld for £10,000 a barrel.

'One man from Halewood made so much money from beno and spent so much time in the polluted and druggy air of a beno factory that he literally went mad and was sectioned.'

Teenagers Nicholas Miller and Stephen Phillips were ex-gang members who'd been given a chance to work in a more organised network: a common career path for Cartel foot soldiers. They spent their days moving between safe houses. One group of men concentrated on moving money around. Anthony Wignall made regular journeys to Amsterdam and was responsible for sending money from the UK to Holland. Michael Riley was a bag-man, or courier, who travelled to Holland carrying bags of cash, which was used by Hibbs-Turner to pay for the next importation of drugs. Adam Joynson and Jamie Quirk sent out substantial amounts of cash to Holland.

Hibbs-Turner had bought his own nightclub to hang around in and turned it into a gangster's paradise. Hibbs-Turner's gang's HQ was called the Velvet Lounge, which was in Bold Street in Liverpool city centre. The venue had been set up with dirty money and its tills overflowed with it. In days gone by, Merseyside Police might have let it go. But now every time anyone set a foot wrong inside or outside, they raided the place with riot cops and dog handlers. If the club overshot its licensing hours by one minute, then officers mounted on horseback were sent in to break up the crowds that spilled onto the streets while Matrix officers searched the punters in the queue for drugs and weapons.

The frontman appointed to run the club was a smooth-looking licensee called Harish Aggarwal, who later wished that he'd never got involved. He took over the licence on 10 May 2005 after buying the lease at a knockdown price of £35,000. He was strictly hands-off and stayed away, so he didn't know that the bar was turned into a rug joint straight out of *Goodfellas*. Heads were smashed against the porcelain sinks in the toilets, blood was spattered up the walls and there was so much cocaine on the surfaces that one punter thought the cleaners had forgotten to wipe away their Ajax cleaning products. As the mayhem got out of control, Aggarwal rarely turned up for fear he might be hit by a flying champagne bottle – or worse.

A month later, Aggarwal was asked by officers to visit the police station to explain how he was financing the deal. On two occasions, he failed to appear. In mid-September, a man was injured in a shooting outside the club. When the club was hit by a temporary 24-hour closure, members of Hibbs-Turner's gang responded by storming a pub in Bootle and intimidating staff and customers. A fortnight later, a senior police officer shut the club again after spotting a man with a serious head injury outside following a large-scale disturbance inside. Mounted officers and a special dog team were called in to drive revellers away. In desperation, the owner of the building changed the locks. The police were determined to shut down the venue, and kept up the pressure.

About 40 of Hibbs-Turner's gang converged on the Velvet Lounge from all over Europe on a Friday and Saturday to snort cocaine off the tables and bar and have sex in the dark corners. Violence was common, but witnesses were too scared to come forward. Instead of trying to get a traditional conviction, the police used a new method born of the tactic of 'disruption'. Instead of concentrating on the individual, they concentrated on the 'consequences' of Hibbs-Turner's behaviour. They catalogued fights, took videos of after-hours parties and looked for evidence of drug-taking at Hibbs-Turner's private parties. They were gathering hearsay evidence. The club was eventually closed down.

In 2005 the police began to hit Hibbs-Turner's bash-houses. A raid was carried out on the docklands safe house at Royal Quay, where Terence Riley had been seen loading bags full of drugs into cars. Forensics revealed drugs worth £500,000 had been produced there. Riley's fingerprints were also found. But luckily for Riley, he wasn't there on the day. For the past couple of years he had been spending more and more time in Amsterdam. Ironically he'd been trying to dodge a low-level warrant for dangerous driving from 2003, which again the police had pursued to disrupt him. In Holland, his job was to collect money transfers and to provide a safe house for his fellow conspirators.

During the police's surveillance of Hibbs-Turner, they noticed that there were now as many people involved in money laundering as drug distribution. Or at least it looked as if the gangsters were taking both tasks equally seriously. Cartel dealers had learned to take money laundering seriously, boring though it was, and managing money transfers was seen as being as important to survival as knowing how to hide skunk cannabis in the hollow plastic roof of an old Land Rover. Colin Smith began using the hawala banking system to transfer money around the world instantly. Hawala banking is an ancient Arabic money-moving network based on trust, not accounting. The traditions were set up thousands of years ago to help Arab traders do business around the world without them carrying large amounts of gold from one city to another.

The Analyst explained, 'Money laundering became sophisticated. When you've got rooms full of cash coming in, literally huge amounts of cash, you have got to think, what's your distribution network for this cash? Colin Smith chose to go over towards Bradford with a hawala bank. Hawala banking is defined as an "informal value transfer system". It's untraceable, and records, if any, are often destroyed. Emails are written in dialects that are a de facto encryption.'

The hawala system consists of thousands of agents, usually Muslim, dotted around nearly every city in the world. If a rag-trade immigrant worker in London, for example, wants to send £1,000 back to his wife in Pakistan, he will begin by going to a local agent, usually a small shopkeeper in his neighbourhood. He gives the hawala agent the £1,000 in cash. The agent then phones his colleague in Pakistan and asks him to instantly pay out the £1,000 in local currency rupees to the customer's wife. She has to produce ID of some form, or maybe a code word, to make sure that she is the right person to give it to. Both agents, the one in London and the one in Pakistan, take a small fee for the transaction. But the beauty of the system is that it is simple, instantaneous and few records are kept. It's based on trust, and the hawala agents get to know their regular clients. In modern times, the hawala system has been very useful in helping millions of migrant workers legally and cheaply remit their wages back home. But at the same time, because there is none of the red tape and delays associated with Western bank transfers, hawala can easily be exploited by organised crime gangs and is a great way for drug dealers to move cash around.

The Analyst continued: 'On one occasion, Colin Smith was seen to take a quarter of a million pounds in cash into a shop in Bradford. He walked out, drove away and was watched by a surveillance team. Later, when he was picked up by the officers, of course, Smith had nothing on him. The officers then went back into the hawala shop and found that the bag with the £250,000 was still there. But when they confronted Smith with the evidence, of course he said, "The money has nothing to do with me." In other words, he made a complete denial.

'During the interview, we said to Smith, "We saw you take a bag in."

'He said, "Well, there was nothing in it."

'We said, "Well, there's quarter of a million pounds in it."

'He said, "Well, that feller in the shop must have put it in there."

'We said, "Well, the shopkeeper says he didn't."

Smith said, "I don't know what you're talking about; it's nothing to do with me."

'And that's that – he walked away. But what was also significant was that, by denying the cash was his, he also chose to walk away from the quarter of a million pounds itself, because by now it had been seized under the Proceeds of Crime Act. And if you want to get it back, the onus is on you to prove where you got it from. Can't prove it? Gone. That's what the act says. However, by saying it wasn't his, he was forgoing that opportunity. But Smith didn't complain. He just saw the whole episode as an occupational hazard. To him, it was just another business risk which hadn't paid off. He looked at the drugs industry like a business. Sometimes your shares rise and sometimes they fall: such is the fickle nature of drug dealing and organised crime. They take hits along the way and that's the nature of it.'

At the time, the Analyst and his colleagues at Merseyside Police were one of the few forces who took asset recovery seriously. By studying the law books incessantly, the Analyst was confident that he could use the Proceeds of Crime Act 2002 as part of his arsenal in his battle to destroy the Cartel. The Analyst liked the fact that the law had created the concept of 'criminal lifestyle': if the police could prove that a person had been convicted of a crime then a court was entitled to look at all of that person's assets. He liked the fact that the Assets Recovery Agency (ARA) had been set up. He liked that there had been changes in the definitions of the crimes to which the Act applies.

Unfortunately, most officers in other forces weren't as forward thinking as those in Merseyside Police and they couldn't be bothered. To them, it looked like a load of hassle. Booting in doors and feeling collars was a copper's job, not running through spreadsheets and consulting Swiss experts on the technicalities of Liechenstein's ancient fractional reserve legislation. For this reason, the Proceeds of Crime Act was getting a bad rep. In reality, the law had made sweeping changes to the offences of money laundering and was trumpeted as being aimed at the 'Mr Bigs' of the criminal world. However, because so few people knew how to enforce it, insofar as the bulk of the law was concerned it made no difference to them at all. Even when the act worked and Merseyside Police could confiscate £250,000, it allowed enough loopholes for the Mr Big to go through.

CHAPTER 12

SMIGGER

2006

The gang war between Croxteth and Norris Green rolled on. A Norris Green Strand 'soldier' called Liam 'Smigger' Smith was one of the main names to emerge from the dispute. Smigger was a textbook 'solja'. His mum and dad were jobless alcoholics and struggled to control their son, who started off selling small quantities of green skunk cannabis and powdered cocaine. He only ever ate out of chip shops and Chinese takeaways, and if he got bored in the queue he'd drop people at random with a roundhouse kick. The conflict spread into the jail system, fuelled by the proliferation of mobile phones, which inmates could use to stay in contact with their gangs on the outside and to pass messages to fellow cons, even if they were held in other prisons. Rival gang members called each other in prison and made taunts and threats. The nexus between mobile phones, gang members and inmates was as useful as it was deadly. Gang members' enemies found it hard to pin them down, but when one booked a visit to see an inmate, this gave their enemies crucial information on where a gang member would be and when. This information could then be communicated to their rivals on the outside by mobile phone so that an ambush could be put in place. When a gang turned up to visit one of their incarcerated members, their enemies could identify them and shoot them. Such was the fate of Liam 'Smigger' Smith. In 2006, Smith was blasted to death with a shotgun by the Croxteth Crew as he left Liverpool's Altcourse Prison after visiting one of his soljas.

According to eyewitnesses, the force of the blast was such that his body fell backwards and went into shock, and reportedly jumped up from the ground after being shot. He later died in hospital.

Smigger's funeral was typical of a young gang member's, featuring floral tributes in gangster lingo. The police fought to close it down. Smigger's body was put under guard at a secret location after threats that the Croxteth Crew were going to steal it from the funeral parlour. At the wake, cocaine was snorted and a mini-riot erupted, which was broken up by the police.

The Cartel godfathers continued to ignore these disturbing events that were threatening to destabilise their multimillion-pound business. They preferred to concentrate on more sophisticated matters such as money laundering and internal procedures. Inside the Cartel, the smugglers were developing rules to regulate the deals that were taking place within the organisation itself. For example, to cut down on blood letting, if a dealer could prove that his stash had genuinely been seized by the police then he wouldn't have to pay for it.

The Analyst said, 'When police operations take out a lot of drugs, somebody in the organisation has to take a hit. When we seize 100 kilos, ultimately somebody is going to have to put their hands in their pocket and pay for it. We don't know who that is, but it's a fact. If the dealer responsible for the drugs can prove that the police have seized it, for instance by showing the higher-ups a police charge sheet, then it's beneficial to them. They call it "the greens": if they can show the carbonised copy of the sheet, which is green in colour, to the people they got the drugs off, then that would be their insurance policy. They could say, "It wasn't me. It was the police. I did not rip anyone off." Of course, there would be a steward's inquiry into how law enforcement had got onto them and what was the weakness in their system, and they would learn from it.'

The Analyst continued, 'So you've got different levels of financial distribution. Your money is coming into the organisation: how do you legitimise it and bank it?

'One method is gambling. They will go into a casino or into a bookie's and bet £50,000 on an evens favourite.

Betting-shop winnings are now legitimate income. I know one individual who laundered £1 million through online betting. He put down £1 million in bets and got £800,000 back over the year. He's £200,000 down, but now that £800,000 is legitimate winnings. As far as we the police are concerned, that doesn't mean we can't get the money off him eventually. It just means that we will have to use a more complex investigation and a different approach in court. In the end, we will have to "proceeds of crime" that £800,000 through another form of asset-recovery operation, one that is more complex than usual and one that is capable of proving that the winnings from gambling are in fact the proceeds of a criminal lifestyle. The cover story of gambling makes it harder for us, but it can be done. In reality, he can say that he won it, and unless there's a complex investigation, that's fine. It's not perfect, but it goes somewhere.

'Once they start moving the money around to offshore banks, they can always point to the betting win as a starting point. Some of them have binders full of betting slips to back that up. But the difficulties come when they start bouncing the £800,000 around the international banking system.

'The same thing happens when the drug dealers buy property. They keep moving the fraudulent mortgages around, so that it means that you have got to chase the money. As police, we've got people who are trained to deal with that. When a case like that comes up, I give it to the specialist unit who deal with it. They will asset-trace the criminals. They are trained by the banking industry. They are experts in what they do; some of them are qualified to the level of financial accountants. Every opportunity to move money around illegitimately, even if it's deep in the murky world of criminality, they know about it. They will take a person's life and start looking at it under a microscope.

'For example, we recently had a suspect. The suspect had a child seven years of age. During the asset-trace, we found that the child had just banked £16,000 into a kids' account. That's a pretty good paper round if you can get that sort of money. The suspect had put the money in the child's name hoping that if we looked at them, we wouldn't be looking at the children. Eventually, it turned out that the kids, who had not yet reached their teens, were worth hundreds of thousands of pounds in their own right. They've had offshore bank accounts.

'To the credit of the police, we are good adversaries to the criminals. We've done asset recovery for years. But the Proceeds of Crime Act was a piece of legislation that gave us more opportunity to do that, because it puts the onus on the criminal to prove that their earnings are legitimate. And that's not an easy job really, if you're a drug dealer.

'As far as Curtis Warren and Colin Smith were concerned, it did become incredibly difficult, because criminals don't put things in their own names. So their aim was to realise the benefits of their own money, in terms of raising their own quality of life, but it had to be done in such a way that it didn't show, which became very hard to do if you had to do it over and over again with a lot of money. So it makes sense if other people become the beneficiaries of their money. Companies are set up in other people's names. Investments are made, and property is bought using other people's names. Some people will have a role within the organisation, which is specifically to be the guardian of their assets. They will sit on a property portfolio or, lower down the chain, own a sunbed shop. They will front any business that can turn money round more readily as a service. Service providers are better for money-laundering purposes than businesses that sell products. For example, a taxi could be doing the airport run twenty-four hours a day, seven days a week. The reality is that the taxi might not actually exist. It's just a set of plates that never go anywhere. If you've got 30 or 40 of them on your books then that's a good way of attributing income. According to the books of the sunbed shop, they have 200 customers a day all going in for a spray tan. But how many times do you drive past the place and there's no one in there? That's 200 people at 50 quid a go. We do have to put these businesses under surveillance and that's when your investigation starts to unfold.'

CHAPTER 13

SUPERHOODIE

2006

In 2006 Merseyside Police became the first force to ASBO a major gangster. From a crime-fighting perspective, it was a suave operational move that took disruption tactics to the maximum. It showed that the policy of disruption – making the lives of 'high-impact targets' a misery, while the police waited to get enough dirt to put them away in jail – was finally paying dividends. ASBOs for grown-ups stopped gangsters doing some of their favourite things, such as going out to party on a Saturday night, or showing off and snorting lines of cocaine in nightclubs. Suddenly the social behaviour of the kingpins, as well as their criminal behaviour, could be used against them. No longer were they free to wander around the city centre knocking people out right, left and centre during long and violent drinking sessions. If they talked loudly and aggressively while holding court in Chinese restaurants in the early hours of the morning, police officers could have them turfed out. For David Hibbs-Turner, the ASBO was not only irritating; deep down it was also a bit humiliating. He was being treated more like a hoodie than a major-league hoodlum.

Witnesses had been too scared to go to court to testify against the well-known drug baron, protection racketeer and hitman. The police had come to the conclusion that securing a fully-fledged conviction was tricky. But the ASBO application allowed the authorities a lower burden of proof. Anonymous hearsay evidence could be used in a magistrates' court. In the case of Hibbs-Turner, much of that evidence was based on how the 27-year-old terrorised pubs and clubs in the city centre. The magistrates lapped it up and were only too happy to help. Astonishingly, they slapped a ten-year ban on the underworld playboy, preventing him visiting central Liverpool at night.

But the Cartel had other concerns: namely, structural worries. In 2006, the legitimate economy in Liverpool was booming for the first time in a quarter of a century. This should have spelled doom for the Cartel. Since its inception in 1973, the Cartel had only ever prospered during periods of economic gloom. The city of Liverpool had served the Cartel well, because the downturns had come one after the other, each one seemingly deeper and longer than the last. Essentially, the Cartel preyed on human misery. They had benefited from the oil crisis in the 1970s, when the authorities had been doubly distracted by decimalisation and entry into the Common Market. In the Thatcher-led deindustrialisation of the 1980s, their ranks had been swelled by a small army of unemployed foot soldiers who would rather sell drugs than stand in the dole queue. In the 1990s, the Cartel had put on a growth spurt fuelled by dance drugs, a windfall that had coincided with the property slump: a fortuitous mix that led to the growth of mainstream money laundering. Now everything was under threat. Stubbornly, Liverpool was defying its recent history and becoming economically stable.

In 2006, according to Liverpool City Council's Liverpool Economic Briefing 2009, the city's total income in the legitimate economy was £7,626 million, providing a per capita figure of £17,489, which was above the north-west average. There had been a staggering increase of 71.8 per cent in the value of legal goods and services being made and traded in the city, between 1995 and 2006. During the same period, employment rose by 12 per cent. The A-plus stats presented a two-fold problem to the Cartel. First, where was the next generation of Cartel workers going to come from? If a potential recruit could get a proper job or open a small business, which would involve less risk and more money, why would he or she enter the drugs trade? Going up the ladder, why would anyone want to be a godfather when legitimate businessmen were making more money from investing in property than smuggling coke? Why go to the Cartel to underwrite drug deals when the banks were falling over themselves to lend to people with little or no track record, giving out money for investment in everything from art galleries to construction firms, from lifestyle ventures to Internet businesses.

The second big problem for the Cartel was demand for product. On paper, a boom should have sounded the death knell of the underclass, or at least caused it to shrink. The underclass had become a main market for the Cartel, consuming huge amounts of green skunk cannabis (aka 'homegrown'). Heroin and crack cocaine were still big sellers.

On paper, it looked like the new millennium, New Labour boom was going to finish off the Cartel. Finally, the good money was going to push out the bad. Even the stats began to back up the theory, proving that the police and the government were actually winning the war on drugs. The UK government said that this was no surprise. They boasted that since 1998 there had been a record level of investment in tackling drugs. As a result, they boasted drugs misuse had fallen by 21 per cent. A refocusing on treatment and education, as well as law enforcement, meant that the numbers entering drug treatment increased by 113 per cent. It looked like the boom was depriving the Cartel of its lifeblood – desperate punters. Even drug-related burglary and shoplifting was down by 16 per cent between 2004 and 2006.

But all was not as it seemed. Critics began to complain that the numbers behind the war on drugs were deeply flawed and no more than an exercise in New Labour target-setting and spin that had simply displaced crime elsewhere in society. Not everyone was happy with the new anti-drug techniques, particularly the raft of laws that New Labour had brought in to tackle drugs. The *World Money Laundering Report 2007*, published by Vortex Centrum, claimed there was a 'lack of comprehension' of the effect of the law in practice. The author of the report, Nigel Morris-Cotterill, an expert on financial drug crime, said that 'short-sightedness' meant that the laws were extremely difficult and expensive to implement. Some parts of the law were so difficult to understand that they were described in the report as 'tortuous' and 'incomprehensible'.

The complexity led to uncertainty as to how the law was interpreted in court.

In reality, both scenarios contained an element of truth, but the picture on the street was more complicated. It was true that demand for heroin and crack was falling amongst traditional users: addicts and other vulnerable groups. Working-class people were also turning away from both cannabis resin, because it was low quality, and a synthetically made substance called formula. But behind these factors, there was a secret lifesaver for the Cartel. Demand for powdered cocaine amongst middle- and working-class people was rocketing. The Cartel had been clever in helping to reposition the drug in the mass market by branding it a 'recreational' drug, then lowering the price and spreading it far and wide on an industrial scale. This was the core market that was sustaining demand and keeping the Cartel's tills ringing. The Cartel was adapting to the booming conditions.

The fact that there was so much money sloshing around the economy not only boosted profits; it also helped to launder money. The Cartel found it much easier to move money around the world. After all there was so much dirty money in circulation, it didn't seem to make much difference. In 2006, the IMF said $600 billion was laundered – and between 11 and 12 per cent of that was drugs money.

Another strange phenomenon was happening. The underclass, including millions of the poor, had been cut off from mainstream society during the Blair-era boom. They didn't have jobs, but their fixed living costs were being paid for by the benefits system. Bucking the expected trend, the underclass didn't shrink. Despite Blair's war on child poverty, the underclass entrenched itself and grew. Two consequences were important for the Cartel. First, the growing underclass provided the recruits for the Cartel's diminishing human resources. The teenagers formed street gangs. At the top, the boom was making the super-rich godfathers lazy. Second, the new underclass began growing and smoking homegrown herbal skunk cannabis on a grand scale in spaces known as lofts, using DIY hydroponics technology. Herbal skunk cannabis was much stronger, and the new generation smoked it faster and harder than traditional potheads, making it similar to heroin and cocaine in the nature of its use. A young gang member might smoke £20 of 'green' in an hour and go out robbing to fund the next £20 bag. The effects of smoking green skunk cannabis suited the teenagers' lifestyle. It was strong and the buzz fitted well with Tupac and Biggie Smalls and playing *Scarface* on the Wii and the Playstation. Mood swings, aggression and forgetfulness were side effects, but that was all part of the scene. The Cartel recognised a bandwagon when it saw one. It was quick to get involved in investing in lofts or buying dealers' harvests.

CHAPTER 14

COLIN SMITH

2006

By the mid-noughties, Colin Smith was the single most powerful drug dealer within the Cartel. He wasn't officially the Cartel's leader, but in terms of revenue generated and weight of drugs imported, he was by far the most successful. Merseyside Police estimated that Smith directly employed more than 100 senior managers outside of the UK. The Analyst described his cell as a 'global enterprise'.

The Analyst said, 'The people abroad had several roles. There were people involved in the negotiations for the purchase of drugs. Then, you've got people involved in the preparation for transport stage. Then you've got the transport to a safe location from the source. That would involve people who move it from point of entry, say, Spain, to a safe place in Europe. Finally, you've got the redistribution into the UK, whether it comes across in a lorry or whatever.'

Within the basic structure, Smith employed a myriad of specialists lower down the chain to carry out specific technical roles. The Analyst said, 'When the cocaine comes over from South America to Europe, you've got people whose job it is to fly out from Britain to South America. Their job is to escort the ship over. They have a satellite phone, and when they are getting within a short distance of Spain, they put a call to the people onshore. They give them GPS location of where they are in the sea. At that point, the parcel will be thrown over the side of the ship into the water. The parcel is designed so that it part-floats, so that it will sink under the water to a certain depth and remain there, hidden but gettable. The people on shore will be told to get everything ready to go. They have a yacht that is moored in Spain, but the purpose of that yacht will be disguised: for instance, it could be owned by a dive crew who are pretending to dive on holiday. They would then sail out to the coordinates and recover the parcel from under the sea and take it back in.'

Nothing was left to chance. Further subdivision of roles took place, so that one person's job was solely to arrange the satellite phone and other forms of communication. His responsibility also included arranging the timing and structure of messages between parties. The priority was the man on the ship with the satellite phone.

The Analyst explained, 'The man with the satellite phone will remain on the boat. He's a British man and that's his job. He's also been responsible for security, so that no one interferes with the product en route. You've got the crew on the ship, who might see an opportunity to steal the product, if they know that it's there. But the crew probably do not know, so that becomes less of an issue. But somebody on the ship has to know, in order to get the drugs on there in the first place. Somebody on the ship has to know the real reason as to why there is a Brit national travelling with them, and that person must know the cover story that hides that fact. For instance, the Brit might be linked to some other legitimate cargo on the ship. That may be the "front" that is used. If they are linked to a cargo, the key question for the police is not only what the cargo is, but also who else it is linked to. Is the legitimate cargo linked to the smugglers or have the smugglers hidden the consignment without the owners knowing? Who on the ship is the British man directly linked to? Who is the British man linked to on land? The British man would essentially be a paying passenger on a commercial ship.

'We had one man involved with a cargo of Italian marble fireplaces. The drugs were hidden inside parts of the fireplaces. We have seen cargoes of lead ingots. There was another man caught with a cargo of pineapples. So in that case, the satellite-phone operator may purport to be a pineapple seller. But the pineapples have been hollowed out, and each one contains a kilo or half a kilo of cocaine.'

Forward planning was also key. It was essential to the operation that the cargo ship on which the drugs had been smuggled was free to go once the contraband had been jettisoned. The ship would be beyond suspicion and left to sail to its legitimate port of call, carrying on as normal. Even if it was not economically viable to unload the proper cargo, the plan was stuck to so that the ships' records appeared on the up and up.

The Analyst explained, 'Everything is OK on the ship at that point because there is no contraband onboard. Meanwhile, the drugs have landed on mainland Europe. So then who is responsible for recruiting the lorry drivers who bring it back to the UK? That's another specialist role. Once it hits the UK, then you've got to think about logistics. Do you use a legitimate distribution warehouse? If so, what's the front business for all of that?'

When 1,000-kilo loads of cocaine and heroin reached the UK, Smith was forced to think about the wider aspects of his business. He was in possession of a very expensive commodity that rivals wanted to steal. The key question was: what did the security set-up look like? When opposing criminals made threats, Smith needed effective security to deal with them. His most efficient member of staff was the Fraudster – the very same professional assassin that Bubbley Shalson was after.

The Analyst said, 'If you listen to the rumours, then you could say the likes of the Fraudster could be Colin Smith's security manager. He would go out and do his bidding, go out and be the enforcer on his behalf, obviously with other people who would work with him. When there are threats to the organisation, such as people who are trying to take the commodity away or destabilise their business, or not paying as they should do, then the security side of the business will go and deal with that.'

The Cartel godfathers were experts at covering up their dirty work. The most common method of distraction involved disguising the real motives behind gangland assassinations. For instance, targeted killings were often blamed on family disputes, but underneath there was more often than not a drugs link. The real reasons were easy to hide because nearly everyone within the Cartel was interlinked. The various factions were interwoven to an incestuous degree. For instance, one assassination victim was the relative of Carli Sleevey. Carli Sleevey was Yael Feeney's ally. Both Carli and his relative had been involved in a long-running dispute with a family that was linked to Colin Smith's deputy.

The Analyst said, 'A man was murdered because of the fallout from the Stephen Lawlor murder. There's a personal element to all of that. But what underpins that dispute? Is it drug related? What we can say is that the enforcement side of that business does what they do, and they go to kill somebody.'

Stephen Lawlor was an enforcer and security boss who had worked directly for the Cartel's main godfather, Colin Smith. Lawlor was also involved in running nightclub doors, but this was separate from his duties as an underworld debt collector for Smith. His job was also to protect Smith from enemy attack and lean on rival drug dealers when required. In 2001, Lawlor became involved in an unrelated dispute, which arose as a result of his nightclub-door business. He was shot five times. A man was found guilty but later freed on appeal. Lawlor had been shot at an unfortunate time. Under Colin Smith's guidance, he'd been organising a huge shipment of cocaine from Amsterdam. Just before his death, the cocaine had landed in Amsterdam and was 'lined up on the docks like a row of new cars', according to a Cartel insider. When the Colombian suppliers tried to get hold of Lawlor to collect their £70 million fee, there was no answer. According to the Cartel insider, eventually they were told by Smith that Lawlor was dead and that the coke had gone missing. The Colombians weren't happy. They weren't happy with Smith. They didn't trust him. There were rumours flying around that the Fraudster had been involved.

CHAPTER 15

ARREST

2006

The war between Yael Feeney and Kallas was hotting up. Both sides had dragged in reinforcements. Feeney and Bubbley Shalson had asked Michael Wright, who was allied to several street gangs such as the Norris Green gang, to join forces with them. To counter the threat, Kallas had lined himself up with the Gee family, who lined themselves up with the Croxteth Crew to fight wars by proxy all over the city. As part of the up-and-coming generation, Kallas was prepared to go to extremes. To give him the edge in an increasingly out-of-control arms race, Kallas was banking on a secret weapon: David Hibbs-Turner, the new godfather he had been courting.

An assailant armed with a shotgun tried to break into Yael Feeney's penthouse flat to shoot him. However, the state-of-the-art security was too much and the man ended up shooting at Feeney from a distance. Yael began wearing a bulletproof vest during the day. In his offices in Manchester, there was always a gun close to hand and a group of bullet-headed bodyguards sitting around waiting for a 'call-out'.

In May 2006, the police visited Yael to tell him that they had received intelligence that his life was under threat. 'As if I don't know,' he told them. The police officers were patient: 'We're just following procedure,' they told him.

Just in case, Yael bought another gun, an assault rifle. In September, Yael was arrested in the city centre after a car crash that later led to a fight. A routine search of his home unearthed computer disks that exposed his money laundering activities. Yael was charged and remanded to prison.

Yael Feeney explained, 'The busies came into the jail. I was sent to jail down south, just outside London. They wanted me to do a deal. First, they asked me to give up all my bank accounts in which I laundered money. They told me that they knew I had lots of businesses through which I laundered money for the Cartel. I was looking at ten years for money laundering and they said if I cooperated that they would have a word with the judge.

'But that wasn't all. They then asked whether I would grass up all of my enemies, whether I'd make a statement and name Kallas, the Gee family, Hibbs-Turner and all the rest of them. I could have grassed them up but, as much as I hated them, I couldn't do it. I told the busies that they couldn't have my computer hard drives and that I wasn't gonna put pen to paper for no one.'

One of the computer disks revealed financial links to an active drug dealer called Bubbley Shalson. Shalson was picked up and charged with a drugs conspiracy. For his own safety, he was remanded to a jail in Scotland. Shalson remained in jail while his enemy David Hibbs-Turner remained out on the street.

However, the police were determined to change that, and fast. In many ways, David Hibbs-Turner was too good at being a gangster. He was an expert drug trafficker and a no-nonsense hardman with the ability to organise large, complex operations. Moreover, his skill at being able to deal with street criminals and big gangsters alike had won him loyalty. The police stepped up the pressure. A two-pronged attack was launched. The plan was to squeeze Hibbs-Turner between the two arms of both an overt and a covert operation. In addition to the publicly acknowledged ASBO, Hibbs-Turner was put under constant surveillance by the Matrix unit covert investigations team. But he was good at tap dancing through the raindrops. In the hope of pushing him into making a mistake, the ordinary police kept up the disruption pressure.

However, in the end it was his own vanity that led to his downfall. In autumn 2006, Hibbs-Turner's ex-girlfriend began an affair with a rival gangster. She began dating Michael

Wright, the drug dealer who was at the centre of an ongoing gang war with the Gee family and Kallas. The underworld politics were murky. But, put simply, Michael Wright was allied to Cartel financier Yael Feeney. However, neither Wright's reputation nor his connections would help him in the end. Hibbs-Turner had become good friends with Kallas. For months, Kallas had been urging him to throw in his lot with his gang and the Gees and wipe out Wright. Kallas had argued that once Wright was out the way, they could join forces and gang up on Yael Feeney. Once he'd been killed, the path was clear to take over the whole Cartel. It was time for the new generation to take over. But Hibbs-Turner refused. Getting dragged into a battle followed by all-out war was bad for business – and, after all, though Hibbs-Turner might dislike Wright, he bought gear from him. No, Hibbs-Turner said. Kallas would have to fight his own battles. But in autumn things changed. Now it was personal. Hibbs-Turner found out that Wright was 'shagging his bird'. This fact coloured his view of the Wright situation.

Hibbs-Turner was seething. He called together his closest lieutenants and gave the order that he wanted Wright killed. Kaim was Hibbs-Turner's right-hand man. His brother, Sidious, was Kallas's right-hand man. The brothers were the key link between Hibbs-Turner and Kallas. Kaim even lived next door to the drug lord, playing an 'integral role' in the higher levels of Hibbs-Turner's drug-running gang, as police told the courts later. Hibbs-Turner instructed Kaim to manage the contract that would lead to Wright being blown off the face of the earth.

Meanwhile, as Hibbs-Turner's anger boiled, Merseyside Police kept up the disruption pressure in the hope that he'd go too far and make a mistake. They wanted to trip him up and shake him down, make him take his eye off the ball. Then they would close in.

Hibbs-Turner and his boys planned how they were going to kill Michael Wright. Kaim subcontracted the hit to two gang members lower down the food chain: Paul Hollands and Philip Woolley. Hibbs-Turner approved and began speaking to Woolley. One day he called Woolley to give the final go-ahead.

In the meantime, Merseyside Police had intensified their investigation into Hibbs-Turner. By then, the police actually had a covert video camera on Hibbs-Turner's property, so they could observe him walking up and down making mobile phone calls. In addition, they had a listening probe that could pick up the audio, and they also had wiretaps on various phones. Astonishingly, the police recorded the actual conversation in which Hibbs-Turner gave the order for Wright to be killed.

The Analyst said, 'We had a covert camera on Hibbs-Turner's house while the murder of Michael Wright was being organised. So we recorded Hibbs-Turner making a call to Philip Woolley.'

It was a great coup for the investigation into Hibbs-Turner. Finally, a lot of the police's hard work was being rewarded. But success came with a bitter aftertaste. As always, things were complicated. The investigators were now faced with a moral and an operational dilemma: should they stop the operation now, arrest Hibbs-Turner and charge him with conspiracy to murder, thus saving Wright's life? Or should they carry on to ensure that they gather more evidence on his drugs offences: the primary purpose of the probe in the first place? The dilemma was this: carrying on risked Wright being killed with the police's knowledge.

The Analyst said, 'That was the big question: do we show out on this, when it's got a value, or do we carry on to make sure we can get more evidence and more members of his gang? In the end, we decided to continue the operation.'

David Hibbs-Turner and Kallas were the main criminals who treated the low-lit rooms of the Velvet Lounge like the venue for a private orgy. Their gangster underlings fixed their drinks behind the bar. Police repeatedly burst in. They found drug-taking, fights and people sneaking in after hours. Shootings were common. Several closure orders from the police were ignored. On the day after one such order was received, the gangsters threw a party to celebrate. An astonished policeman who came to enforce the ban found the club 'in full swing', in complete contravention of the authorities' orders.

When officers tried to investigate beatings and stabbings,

there were no witnesses to be found, of course, and the doormen who had been on duty would be replaced by a new set of Hibbs-Turner's henchmen and never seen again. On one occasion, officers investigating a reported assault in the club requested a CCTV tape. But when it turned up, they found the reel had been burned and was impossible to play. When patrolling officers asked to see the door security register, a standard book for a city centre bar, it could not be produced.

Instead of complaining, the police simply took it as an opportunity to monitor a honey-pot for villains. They mounted a stakeout and took photos of criminals leaving the club at 5 a.m. Police officers, both covert and uniformed bobbies, were sent inside on several occasions. They found customers, including known villains, in the manager's office or making their own drinks behind the bar. By October 2006, they had enough evidence to present a damning dossier to the magistrates' licensing committee. Within minutes, the club was closed down for good, one of the first ever to be shut on the basis of attracting bad lads. The licensee was out of the country on holiday, still refusing to answer questions about where he got the money to open the club.

CHAPTER 16

MICHAEL WRIGHT

2006

Liverpool in December was cold, dark and wet. The clouds sweeping in off the Irish Sea were fat and black. The population was punished with freezing rain and a few hours of weak light per day. Liverpool's new class of rich people had turned the city centre into a cross between a game show and the last days of the Roman Empire. Designer products were everywhere. Boutiques were springing up specifically to sell overpriced clothes to WAGs and molls. The air was filled with the stench of burger vans and the sweet odour of roasted nuts from the fake German markets in the run-up to Christmas. Acres of the shopping areas looked like a bombsite as the city raced to build the Liverpool One shopping centre in time for the city becoming the European Capital of Culture 2008, two years in the future. The roads were gridlocked.

Michael Wright didn't like Christmas shopping. But he did like Kentucky Fried Chicken. He'd been bombing around town seeing his boys and sorting things out, and on a visit to see one of his allies in Norris Green, Wright was spotted by an enemy foot soldier. He made the mistake of pulling into a KFC in the Stonedale retail park, which was on rival territory controlled by the Croxteth Crew. An assassination squad that had been put together by David Hibbs-Turner quickly swung into action. They scoped Wright's car before moving in. They felt confident enough to strike. Michael Wright was shot at close range as he sat eating his takeaway in his car.

When Hibbs-Turner received the news, he was buzzing: it was the best Christmas present he could have wished for. But the celebrations would soon turn sour. The big problem for David Hibbs-Turner and his gang was that they were already under surveillance for their drug-running activities. The secret police surveillance squads that were tracking their every heroin and coke deal were able to rapidly tweak their investigation to monitor any communications that had taken place before, during and after the murder. Every single mobile phone connected to the gang's core was tapped. It was standard procedure for Cartel members to dispose of their pay-as-you-go phones every few weeks, but Merseyside Police had developed secret techniques to detect the new phones and pick up where they left off.

The Analyst said, 'We have people who look at phones in detail – contact and cell site analysis. It's used an awful lot in the courts. A good example is the Michael Wright murder. Telephone evidence was incredibly valuable to the investigation. We had used it a lot on murders before, so we were well prepared when it happened. The suspects kept "dropping" the phones, but we just tried to stay one step ahead. There are ways around that. Foolishly, the suspect's attitude was: "Well, I'll ditch my phone every week and I'll be all right." But that just means that we expect you to ditch your phone every week and we have contingency plans. There are ways of finding out what the new phone's number is and where that phone is going. And it doesn't just have to be a phone: it can be Skype, or conversations over the Internet. We can do it all, and we did.'

Luckily for the police, Hibbs-Turner carried on as though nothing had happened. He continued to talk about his criminal activities on the phone as if he was talking about football or *Coronation Street*, convinced that he was covered because he was 'all day' – a scallywag phrase derived from 'I can do this all day long', meaning that the risk of being caught was low. So blasé was his attitude that the murder was soon forgotten by him, as though it was just one of many mini-crises that had to be handled during the working day of a top-five UK supercriminal. New crimes were more important. He began leaning on a rival security company for protection money. He made a string of threats to the boss of a company called Step Up, complaining that one of their sites was on 'his patch'.

When Step Up refused to pay up, Hibbs-Turner warned the firm's area manager that he would find out where he lived and 'bomb his house with him in it'. He also threatened to 'spray the site with bullets'. Weeks later, a fire was started at the company's site and an £18,000 digger was destroyed. Now that he'd got their attention, the firm agreed to pay Hibbs-Turner £900 a month. Everything was routine.

Meanwhile, another completely separate cell within the Cartel, run by a different villain, was about to get a shock. The gang had been smuggling cocaine in scaffolding bars from Europe and had made millions of pounds by staying low-key and not going down the Hibbs-Turner 'I couldn't give a fuck' route. But the police's Operation Lima was about to catch up with them. The Force Crime Operations Unit raided the houses of the Mr Bigs – and not only in Liverpool. As part of a new level of cross-border cooperation, doors across Europe were going in. Merseyside Police worked together with Her Majesty's Customs and Excise, the Dutch police, the Spanish authorities, NCIS and other UK forces, and the case resulted in heroin and cocaine worth £2.5 m being seized. Just over 11 kilos of cocaine were found by Customs officers at Dover in a shipment of scaffolding heading for Liverpool, and a second seizure of 16 kilos of cocaine, imported by Eastern European lorry drivers, was found at an address in Halewood in Liverpool.

In all, 21 people were busted and jailed for a total of 200 years. No stone was left unturned. Every member of the gang was jailed: even the money launderer got six years. The wife of one Mr Big got twenty years just for helping out. Shadowy figures from Croatia and Serbia were roped in. At Liverpool Crown Court, Judge Mark Brown, who presided over the trial, said he was sure that the seizures represented 'the tip of a very large iceberg'. He then went on to commend the detectives involved in the extensive investigation and said, 'The investigation highlights the dedication and skill of Merseyside Police in combating international drugs trafficking.' Focussing on particular skills that the force were getting better at, the judge went further, complimenting the team for the management of the investigation, disclosure and surveillance skills, file composition, gathering of exhibits and professionalism displayed, and said it was a 'major success for the major crime unit' and that the 'population of Merseyside should be justly proud'. They weren't empty words. What they were was a coded message to the Cartel, a message telling them that their sworn enemy, the police, were now up to speed on the War on Drugs. There were going to be more upsets in store for the drug dealers. David Hibbs-Turner should have realised that the writing was on the wall. Instead of reading court reports, which some of the old godfathers did religiously in order to pick up on the police's latest tricks, Turner was busy, partying and leaning on doormen for £1,000 a month protection money.

CHAPTER 17

POTTED OFF

2007

In 2007, Yael Feeney was jailed for ten years for money laundering. Yael's defence team pleaded with the judge, arguing that their client was a legitimate businessman who had had no idea he was funding drug dealers. But the judge was not interested. He told Yael that he was a criminal. Yael was potted off to jail like one of the gang members he'd spent years trying to eradicate.

Yael was sent to an open prison in the south of England to begin his sentence. Even though it was a relatively relaxed prison, almost at once Yael witnessed just how cruel jail could be. One inmate was a drug-addicted dwarf known as Half-Pint. The dwarf was raped by one inmate. Then he was ritually humiliated in exchange for 'jaily', a small wrap of heroin. At first, Yael, the old-school gangster, was shocked.

Yael said, 'Half-Pint had worked as a dwarf in show business all of his life. He had been abused in showbiz all his life, too. He'd got into trouble for some reason and ended up in jail. But he wasn't your normal dwarf. He'd give out wanks to other inmates, and some of them would go "suck that" for a jaily. But one day a well-known deviant tricked him. He said to Half-Pint, "I'll bet you a chicken eye you can't climb through that chair." The chair that he was pointing at had like a gap in the back of it. A chicken eye is the same thing as a jaily, by the way: just prison slang referring to a small bead-sized bit of gear, hence it looks like a chicken eye.

'Half-Pint was so desperate for gear that he started to try

to get through this little hole in the chair, as though it was a circus trick he used to do. Then, when he was getting through the back of the chair, the feller locked him in place, getting down on him with his body weight, restraining both the dwarf's arms before pulling down his trousers and bumming him from behind. This deviant then threatened Half-Pint: "If you tell anyone, I will kill you."

'That was the kind of place prison was. That was the kind of place I was going to have to live in for ten years. It was dog-eat-dog, and I was going to have to wise up fast.'

For the first few months, it was fun and games. Dwarf-throwing was a regular spectacle. Yael didn't approve of Half-Pint getting bullied and raped, but he didn't mind having a laugh at his expense. Political correctness, inclusion and equality weren't part of prison culture.

Yael said, 'Half-Pint would still do anything for a jaily. We used to see who could throw him furthest along the billet, which was the little hut where we lived. It had a corridor down the middle of it, and we measured how far he travelled by seeing how many cell doors we could throw him past. I got seven doors – that meant I could bowl him past seven cell doors.

'Then we did this other thing with him, to see who could throw him off the roof. It wasn't a good thing to do, but it was better than him having to get shagged for his gear. We kind of took care of him. I know it doesn't sound like it, but we did. Prison is harsh, and what looks like cruelty can be kindness in disguise.

'But one day another bunch of lads started to take it too far. One feller put him in a big tumble dryer in the laundry along with five hundred pairs of jeans. The dwarf was promised a jaily if he could stand ten spins. But once the door was locked and it went round, getting red-hot, Half-Pint just started panicking.

'I got told about it and I wasn't very happy. In the next football game, I said to the feller who'd put him in the dryer, "That's bang out of order," and I knocked him out.'

The message was clear. There might have been double standards, but what mattered was who laid down the law. There was a new daddy in town, and his name was Yael Feeney.

Later, Yael was transferred to a normal jail in London. The new place was a tough nick, and Yael decided that he had no option but to make his mark by force immediately. Soon he ruled the wings. One day he was tipped off by a prison officer about a remand inmate being a paedophile. The prison officer was, in effect, encouraging Yael to beat him up. It was an opportunity for Yael to stamp his authority on the wing and win the support of the general cons, who all hated nonces. In prison, the accusation was a serious one and could have got the inmate killed. To cover his back, Yael asked for proof, just in case the prison officer was leading him on to settle an old score. To make sure, the guard showed Yael the paperwork: a computer print-off of the inmate's prison record, including a detailed list of his crimes. The dossier revealed that the inmate had committed several penetration offences against a minor and thirty-five other sexual offences over a period of four years.

Yael said, 'I couldn't believe it: the inmate in question had been on the wing for six weeks, telling jokes and playing pool with us – and he wasn't a bad-looking feller either. He didn't look like a monster. What I mean is that he didn't look like a nonce; he didn't look weird. You wouldn't know he was capable of it. I decided to do him in. I just couldn't have a paedophile on a wing that I ran.

'I was working in the kitchens at the time. Me and another porter, who were let out in the morning before the others, knew when the nonce was at his most vulnerable: in the showers, where he couldn't run anywhere.

'One morning we took off the overalls that we wore and both put on full blue tracksuits, so that we wouldn't be picked out by our clothes later. We cut the sleeves off an old jumper, cut eye holes in them, put them over our heads and used them as balaclavas.

'Then I pounced on him in the shower using a table leg as a weapon. I stabbed him with it. It's only thick wood, so it was only gonna gouge him, his eyes and that. All the other lads in the shower started singing to drown out his screams. I was on him for a minute and a half, which is a long time when you're knocking the fuck out of someone. Both of us booting the fuck out him with our steelies on.

'Then afterwards we ran back to our cell. On the way, I deliberately hit the button to set the alarm off, knowing that would cause chaos, to cover our getaway and so that we were covered while we got changed. That happened on five occasions, when I battered paedophiles.

'I only got ten years – so I'm not going to fuck my job up, waiting to go to Cat. D, for nonces. Normally if you want to get access to nonces so you can bash them up, you have to wait until you are assigned a lower category, such as Cat. D. Then you'll be put in an open prison where there are nonces who aren't segregated from the rest of the prisoners, so you can do them in. But I wanted to do them in now, while I was in the London nick. But I had to balance that with not getting caught. I was only doing ten years and I had a cushy job in the kitchens, so I didn't want to risk my job or getting time added to my sentence by getting caught attacking a paedophile. So that's why I was careful to do some personally but farm others out to my lads: to lessen the risk of me getting caught. I did two personally, and I paid smackheads to do the other three. I got a £100 worth of jailies and paid all the lads to do the nonces in: money well spent, in my humble opinion.'

Yael was learning that in jail drugs gave you power. Drugs were the currency of life and death. Drugs got things done.

On the outside, the Cartel, which Yael had once worked for as a money launderer, was going through ups and downs. Liverpool's booming legitimate economy was helping to curb organised crime. In the early days, the Cartel had been started because most people worked on the docks and were experienced at smuggling contraband. However, those blue-collar jobs were long gone and the local economy had matured. In 2007, over 60 per cent of all employment in the city was in the public administration, education, health, banking, finance and insurance sectors. Historically, the economy of Liverpool had been centred on the port and a related manufacturing base. Now in the post-Blair age, that accounted for less than 10 per cent of employment in the city. This was good for demand. Well-paid jobs meant punters bought more gear. The Cartel sold cocaine to the growing middle class. But now there were fewer workers seemingly prepared to go and work for organised crime direct.

CHAPTER 18

DOWNFALL

FEBRUARY 2007

On 15 February 2007, drug-dealing killer David Hibbs-Turner was arrested and charged with the murder of Michael Wright. Another 13 people were arrested and charged, including Hibbs-Turner's button-man Phil Woolley. None of the 14 had known they'd been under police investigation. But one of Hibbs-Turner's underlings managed to stay clear. Terence Riley, infamous for finding James Bulger's body, was away in another city when the doors went in. It was a lucky escape: Riley had been in contact with Hibbs-Turner the day before he was arrested alongside the rest of his gang. The question was: how long could he 'stay on his toes'?

Like most modern criminals, Hibbs-Turner wasn't fazed by murder charges or prison. In fact, he sat on his bed in his cell and simply continued to run his empire from behind bars. Like most incarcerated gangsters, he had access to a bank of mobile phones. For instance, he continued to extort the owner of Step Up security for protection money. Hibbs-Turner made it plain that the fact he was in jail and no longer available for facetime made no difference: he was still in charge and he was still directing operations. And he was still getting paid.

Terence Riley didn't stay on the run for long. He was brought back to the UK by Dutch police on 13 March 2007 and charged with conspiracy to supply Class A and B drugs and with a previous bail offence.

Merseyside Police were on top of their game. Their expertise was recognised within the trade and they won a host of awards. In a bid to boost the status of complex drug investigations, the Home Office had launched a police awards ceremony. Officers were going to get recognition for running complex cross-border operations. The aim was to spread good practice and new ideas. One of the new big ideas was that police work wasn't all about just feeling collars. Follow-through was also emphasised and the importance of tracking down drugs cash was also seen as vital. As part of a big restructuring to emphasise this, in 2007 the government announced that ARA would be closed and most of its functions transferred to SOCA in the hope that more dirty money could be seized.

In 2007 at the police 'Oscars', known as the Tackling Drug Supply Awards, officers from Merseyside Police won the Best Practice in Asset Recovery award for Operation Lima and Operation Copybook. There were big smiles all round at force HQ and lots of pats on the back.

But come Monday morning, it was back to business. Accolades aside, the flow of drugs onto the streets and into the prisons hadn't stopped just yet. Outside prison, Yael Feeney had refused to deal drugs. He had acted as a money launderer for the Cartel, but he had never sold their products. Now that he was in jail, he was faced with a dilemma.

Yael Feeney said, 'I'm not into selling drugs and never have been. But in jail drugs are a way of life: if you've got drugs, you've got power. End of story. I know that sounds hypocritical, but in the underworld it's a very important point of difference. I came into jail on my own: I wasn't part of a big crew who'd all been locked up together and could look out for each other. I couldn't expect to go in there and survive on my reputation alone. It wasn't enough that everyone knew I had been running all these big businesses around the country.

'Of course, I knew loads of drug dealers and hard-case lads in the jail. But, again, that's not enough – you can't just call on them for favours all the time. You've got to do it yourself. You've got to have your own army around you. And that means you've got to build it, pay for it and command it yourself, without anyone else.'

In jail, the foot soldiers who made up the private 'armies' were the long-term drug addicts. The heroin users were the only people desperate enough to carry out contract violence on behalf of the daddies, like Yael, who ran the wings. Drug addicts were the cannon fodder used to wage war and keep order. Without drug addicts, a godfather was powerless.

Yael Feeney said, 'You've got to have your rats around you, no two ways. You've got to have your common-and-fucking-scumbag rats at your beck and call 24 hours a day. You've got to have the addicts who will be prepared to die for you in return for a wrap of gear. You've got to have wave after wave of junkies you can send against your enemies. That's just something you've got to have if you are going to survive. Feed them with a few jailies and they will do anything for you. They will die for you. Outside, you wouldn't mix with them if your life depended on it. You wouldn't walk on the same side of the street as them: they are truly vile life forms. But in jail, you've got to have them.'

Drugs had changed the whole of society. The working-class recruits might have disappeared from the Cartel's ranks, but it now had the underclass to do its bidding on the street. The new hierarchies had penetrated into the jail system as well, and to an even greater extent, because their social structures were distilled into a concentrated form. The atmosphere was more intense. In jail, the underclass was exploited by bosses like Yael. On the outside, the teenage street gangs were now challenging the old order, taking on the old godfathers; in jail, it was the same.

Yael Feeney said, 'You can be the hardest feller in jail, you can be the richest, the King Kong, the Big Daddy. But these lads, these smackheads, will just come past and stripe [slash] you in the yard with a razor four or five times – and they will do it if someone gives them a "henry" of gear [an eighth of an ounce of heroin] to do it. If you get them that fucking bad, when they are turkeying for gear, when they need heroin desperately, they'll give people a wank. They are the lowest of the low who will go to any extreme. Of course, we never used them for sexual favours; we were straight-up people. But we used to play with the creatures like gladiators. We'd make a DIY boxing ring in a cell. We used to tip the beds up to one side and put the mattresses against the wall to make the ropes. Then we used to make the bag-heads fight each other

– no gloves non-stop – for a jaily. Purely for our amusement. They would be paid to fight each other to near-death for a little bit of heroin while we sat back and laughed. 'But because there's no calcium in their body, because their bones have been ravaged by years of drug abuse, their teeth would be falling out of their heads and their bones would be cracking.

'They're in and out of jail all their lives. They're like slaves. We had them running around like servants. Every Thursday, one would hoover our pad. Then he would do all my washing and ironing, make sure all my bedding and underwear wasn't creased. He'd go right through my pad for three hours for a jaily. I lived like a lord.

'It's survival. People think jail is easy. It's not.'

Yael feared that the gang war that he'd been fighting outside would spill over into the prison. Other gang bosses had armies of teenage addicts as well. He said, 'I made a lot of enemies on the outside. I was thrown in jail without my mates behind me. There's me and 1,500 cons. I was still running my property business that generated millions of pounds a year from my cell, but that kind of power meant nothing in jail.'

Luckily for Yael, Bubbley Shalson had also been sent to prison and this took some of the heat off him. Shalson was jailed for seven years for drug dealing. He continued his war with Kallas and Hibbs-Turner as though nothing had happened.

Bubbley said, 'My enemy Kallas had lads inside the prison. Don't forget: Hibbs-Turner had been nicked as well, and 15 of his crew were now in the system and they had all threatened to kill me.

'I was sent to a far away prison in Scotland, but their reach was tremendous. Their weapon of choice was a toothbrush with a melted handle into which two razor blades had been inserted. They were going around saying, "See you on the yard on Saturday: ching, ching." That meant I was getting two slashes from a toothbrush knife. "You're getting it ching, ching." That's what was being said. That was the mantra.

'So I thought, "It's me or them." I made a decision. I had to strike unilaterally before it got out of hand. It was a case of "do it to them before they do it to me". I began with a scattergun approach. I just started running into cells of anyone I suspected of being with Kallas and knocking fuck out of everyone. Afterwards, I would say to them, "There's your little kicking, but in future, if you come for me, I will kill you."

'But it would be foolish to think you can rely on violence alone. Like everyone else, I started dealing drugs in jail. It's about getting them onside a bit as well: a bit of carrot and stick. A bit of psychological warfare, if you like. So after I'd booted the fuck out them, I'd say, "In the future, come to me for your bits." Meaning come to me for your heroin and weed. Meaning that there's some business there, if you want to stop fucking about. There's not only gear but money to be made. And that's how I started selling tackle in jail as well as outside jail. I started selling drugs purely and simply to keep my enemies close, to keep them pacified, and to fund my war chest. I did it purely to survive. I had zero option.'

Bubbley believed that drugs were being used to control the jail population from an official position. Though he had no direct evidence, to him it was clear that there was a tacit agreement between drug pushers and senior prison officers. The amount of drugs in prison was evidence in itself. Bubbley was determined to use the situation to his advantage by becoming part of the power structure, a key player in the conspiracy.

He said, 'Contrary to popular belief, people don't get shagged in jail every five minutes. On the whole, people don't get raped in the showers every time they bend over for the soap. Anyway, cons use shower gel. Bottles of shower gel are the official, non-drug currency that has taken over from tobacco, because a lot of people don't smoke any more.

'But there are certain people who'll rob their own ma and grandma. They are drug addicts who will give other inmates a wank. What they think when they are doing it is that "it's just a piece of skin". That's how they rationalise it. They'll just turn their heads and give other cons a wank. All for a jaily.

'So if they will go that low for drugs, you can get them to do serious violence against your enemies. They will go around swilling screws: that's throwing boiling water or buckets full of piss over them. I've seen it done, and I've had it done on my behalf, to people whom I have fallen out with. The smackheads are known as creatures. Creatures are the underclass of the prison system.'

CHAPTER 19

RHYS JONES

AUGUST 2007

In August 2007, an event occurred that would shock the world and come to symbolise the grip that US-style gangs were having on Britain's streets. An 11-year-old schoolboy called Rhys Jones was shot and killed, caught in the crossfire between Croxteth and Norris Green gangs. The Everton-mad youngster had been walking home from football practice when a stray bullet fired by Croxteth Crew gang member Sean Mercer pierced his back. Once again, the 21-year-old pistolero had form. Mercer was solid third-generation underclass from a first-rate Cartel pedigree. His dad had been a doorman at one of Fred the Rat's nightclubs and had strong underworld connections to Curtis Warren and the Banker. His mother was a prostitute.

In contrast, Rhys Jones's parents were model citizens, hard-grafting strivers who lived on a respectable housing estate especially built for Liverpool's burgeoning strata of self-employed and service-industry-worker families. Unlike the older Cartel members, the young bloods did not care whether they killed criminals or civilians. Mercer had been firing at a group of lads from Norris Green who had wandered into a nearby chip shop. The gunman was later jailed for life, but the postcode hatred between the neighbouring estates remained rife. Lads quickly armed themselves with weapons from gun runners in their area and recklessly opened fire on busy streets. In examples of the terrifying violence, a mum fled her home with her baby and toddler after a gunman shot

117

at her house in Fazakerley. Three seventeen-year-olds and a fifteen-year-old were shot in another attack in Bootle, just a week after children had fled when a gun battle broke out in Toxteth. Another gunman opened fire in a place called Stockbridge Village.

The shooting had a big impact on the Cartel. Several high-up drug gangsters condemned the shooting not only because it was plain wrong but also because the increased police activity it brought with it was bad for business. For the gangs, it was even worse. The police clamped down even harder on street violence. Anti-terror legislation and public-order laws were used on a mass scale to stop and search thousands of teenagers. Newspaper reporters and TV crews flew in from around the world and shone a light on Liverpool's gang culture for the first time.

CHAPTER 20

THE OPERATOR

2007

By the end of summer 2007, Colin 'King Cocaine' Smith was at the zenith of his power. But, like any king, his position had come at a price. He'd made several enemies on the way up and there were always subplots bubbling under the surface, mainly hatched by up-and-coming criminals who wanted to take Smith down. The police knew the big picture, but they couldn't answer the key questions yet. Who was going to overthrow him? When was the coup going to happen? What would the Cartel look like after he'd gone?

The treachery that cost Smith his life came as a surprise to many Cartel gangsters, for Colin Smith had always been careful to tread more carefully than most. He wasn't a bully who'd made his name by killing and injuring rivals. He was simply a businessman who'd risen through the Cartel's ranks because of his ability to make and retain contacts. His negotiation skills and his high levels of organisation had carried him far.

However, over the years he'd made a number of small slights against his partners. He didn't mean anything by them, but they had built up ever so slowly. An unpaid bill here. An argument there. The gossip gave way to jealousy. Several of these injured parties began to coalesce into a quiet conspiracy. As in most underworld disputes, if Smith was to be killed, it wouldn't be because of one clear-cut issue. The killers would be a group of people with shared interests and mixed motives, going back over a number of years.

The primary motive to kill Colin Smith was his sheer wealth.

119

His estimated £200 million fortune made people envious in a business where wealth equalled status. Suddenly his partners were covetous of his money. They wanted it to be theirs – at all costs.

The Analyst said, 'He was a wealthy man. If you ask me honestly, he could well have had that [£200 million], plus more. The difficulty arises when you start looking at his assets. You can find one company that is a property business, the company in which he was a co-director. And you can find those assets, and the value of the money, that he's got with his wife in their joint business ventures.

'For instance, they had a couple of restaurants. He owned them. In short, it's not difficult to find some of the properties that they owned, in either his or her name. Then you go a little bit under the surface and start looking at more complex financial arrangements, investigating some of the other companies in which he's got an interest: an "interest" being something like a bearer bond.'

This was more complicated. A bearer bond is a certificate that proves that an individual has an investment in a business entity, such as a corporation. The beauty of these mysterious debt securities is that they are totally anonymous. As certificates, they differ from the more common types of investment, such as stocks and shares, in that they are completely unregistered: no records are kept on the owner or the transactions that took place to acquire the bonds themselves. No names appear on paperwork in any shape or form. Bearer bonds were becoming increasingly popular with Cartel bosses simply because whoever physically held the paper on which the bond was issued owned the investment. It was like having a super-denomination bank note under the bed that only you knew existed: money issued by the Bank of You. A bond with '£50 million' written on it, or '50 per cent' of such and such a business, can be presented to the directors of that company, and they have to pay up what it's worth. The downside was that if the bearer owner lost the piece of paper, that was the end: it was like money going up in flames. Recovery of the value of a bearer bond, in the event of its loss, theft, or destruction, was usually impossible. Colin Smith had one bearer bond worth £75 million. The bond represented a massive share in a big, well-known company.

The Analyst said, 'So you find that someone is holding a bearer certificate for a company that is worth £150 million in total. Now, if you believe what you're being told, Smith owned bearer certificates of over 50 per cent of that company. It was a certificate that says he owned half of that company. The piece of paper doesn't give it a physical value, but it's a legally binding certificate, which means you can go along and cash it in. It's quite accepted as a financial instrument. The company in question was a waste-management and recycling company.'

Bearer bonds have historically been the financial instrument of choice for money laundering, tax evasion and concealed business transactions in general. The American government was the first to spot that bonds were a drug dealer's dream. In a bid to crack down on illegal use, the United States Treasury began to reduce the issue of bonds in 1982, as Colombian cocaine and the Cuban crimewave swept the Gulf states. However, the practice remained widespread in Europe. In one single swoop, the Italian financial police seized bearer-bond documentation totalling $134.5 billion, split up into $500 million and $1 billion denominations. The waste-management company that Colin Smith was part of was not his only investment: he had secret chunks of several profitable businesses in the UK. Some of the links were tenuous, but Merseyside Police were confident that they were his.

The Analyst said, 'Some assets were directly linked to Colin and others indirectly. With some businesses, some of the family say, "That was our Colin's, because he invested his money to buy it, and we know he owned 50 per cent." But how do you prove that? If you go there, to one of these companies, and look at the books, the actual registered shareholders aren't named. For example, if you look at the building company that he allegedly invested in, you look at the people there, and all of the properties they've built over the years: it's a big, well-known company. The only trace of the link left is that you will see Colin's name in the annals of history in an old record at Companies House. You will see the owners, who, funnily enough, are associates of Colin's, who run this building and management company. The business is a completely separate company involved in property development. They've built some quite big properties and businesses, so do you link Colin to something like that? You might find that in the early days he was registered, and you might find that he's simply associated with the owners.'

Colin Smith's big investments in legitimate companies were long-term assets that gave him security and provided a proper-looking income over the long-term. But big drug dealers also need smaller, more mobile chattels in which to store wealth for a short period or which they can use to transfer value on a deal at short notice without exchanging cash or cheques. In essence, dealers need to be able to use benefits in kind to pay bills and receive income.

The Analyst went on, 'So, then you look at the cars. One of his mates came and collected a Bentley. It wasn't registered in Colin's name, but they took it away, because it was Colin's at the time. He wasn't using it to drive in, but it was also a tangible asset. When you talk about assets, about money laundering, it's not just about cash, because companies use vehicles as assets. So if I have a £100,000 Bentley, we can use that as an asset. If I'm going to pay you for something, instead of giving you cash, I will give you the car instead. No money changes hands, but £100,000 has been transferred between me and you.

'First, we will put a value on it – but to do it properly, there might actually be companies out there, specialists, who actually do all that for you independently. So when you get a group of people turning up in really nice cars, and then they just disappear, that's just about moving assets around.'

The specialist companies are car-finance experts who will value a high-performance car independently and even raise a loan on the back of it, if necessary, thus giving the money launderers even more options. The process is known as asset finance. If Colin Smith paid for a couple of kilos of cocaine with a Bentley, the new owner could access the cash by getting a loan from an asset-finance company using the Bentley as surety. The cash has been paid out by a legitimate company, with a receipt to prove it. In effect, Colin Smith's money has been washed. Alternatively, the new owner could simply sell on the Bentley to get the cash.

THE OPERATOR

The Analyst explained, 'Criminals don't see it like us – we would think that we're gonna lose £500 in depreciation. They can take that loss if, at the end of it, the money looks legitimate. So a £100,000 Bentley might have a nominal value of £80,000, because we can always realise that. Then we can move that car to somewhere, give it someone else so that they can sell it and realise the money from it. It's like an Internet betting scam.'

In the US, the authorities have spent a lot of time and effort clamping down on money laundering through the auto trade. The FBI has brought forward many cases in which drug dealers buy expensive cars with cash so they don't have to put money in the bank. In London, there are whole networks of professional fraudsters who work closely with drug dealers to wash money from asset finance.

CHAPTER 21

RIPA

2007

Colin Smith and several members of his inner sanctum were under surveillance. The Regulation of Investigatory Powers Act 2000 (RIPA), which had been in place for seven years, had been put on the statute books to bring down people just like Smith. But few forces apart from those in London and Liverpool were using it effectively. Colin Smith was jumpy, so a light touch was required. In a bid to avoid ruffling feathers, the police began to concentrate on those around Smith instead of the main target himself.

The Analyst said, 'Again, a lot of it comes down to the art of how well you run your investigation. If you don't put all your eggs in one basket, if you run a number of lines of inquiry, then that pays dividends. We learned not to concentrate surveillance around your main target but the associates of that target too. The main target is completely aware of surveillance, but the other person that's with him, such as the driver, isn't, and they might be speaking to somebody. They will take you to the main target, and the main target will take you to where you want to go. There's other ways around it as well.'

The Analyst had learned a lot by targeting people like Colin Smith. Members of Smith's gang insisted on flying to Spain at the last minute to meet associates while swimming in the sea. They could not be overheard, nor could they be taped by someone waist-deep in seawater; they didn't even need to be frisked for a undercover recorder. Ironically, however, taking over-cautious anti-surveillance measures had lulled the Cartel bosses into a false sense of security. The police simply put a policeman on the beach to watch the scene, and they were gathering crucial evidence.

The Analyst said, 'There might be someone in the water, but you don't have to know what they are saying; you just have to prove that they are together. They didn't realise that.

'We've had officers in other places, such as Amsterdam. There are ways for officers to work with forces right across Europe. You will set up an operation. If you know that you've got to work in Amsterdam and Spain, you just go out and set up a protocol for working there. You get it approved by the Home Office. Then the protocol is in place, so we don't have to mess about on a case-by-case basis. And it works both ways. If the Dutch criminal comes over here, then the surveillance is authorised over here. We'll just run the surveillance and then give it to the Dutch.

'Section 27.3 of RIPA says I can authorise surveillance anywhere outside the UK. By setting up protocols beforehand, the relationships are already established, so when we need to do something, it's as quick as making a phone call. If the bureaucracy is in place on an operation, it doesn't matter if the target hops on a plane tomorrow morning: we will be ready when they get there.'

The operations started rolling and were executed like a military campaign. Officers learned to think on the move and react to events quickly. The police squads began to mirror the Cartel cells they were tracking. The bureaucracy still had to be dealt with, but a new generation of officers were prepared not to let it get the better of them. In Amsterdam, members of the Cartel were becoming suspicious that Merseyside Police were staking out a Marks & Spencer store in the city centre. The shop was popular with Cartel drug dealers and their molls who missed home comforts such as tea bags, Chinese chicken wings and croissants.

The Analyst said, 'You can have all the meetings with your foreign counterparts as you prepare your operation. But the point is that you've broken the barriers. The criminals make it difficult. They will literally hop on a plane for a meeting and then come back again. But the meeting won't go unnoticed. That was the crucial thing. We might not have been able to listen to what was said, but we can now prove that two suspects were together.

'That's why cases take time to build. If you're going to follow someone's lifestyle, you're going to know what their patterns of behaviour are. You've got to check out the opportunities, but you've got to know enough about them to know where those opportunities are. There might be a trigger for surveillance which presents itself. If they go to Marks every morning to get the croissants, that's where we will pick them up. They are creatures of habit. Police officers do go abroad fairly regularly. The boundaries no longer exist.'

The big question was: Who would get to Colin Smith first? Merseyside Police or the enemies he was making inside the Cartel?

CHAPTER 22

THE CORPORATION

2007

Merseyside Police became experts at tracking the flow of drugs from suppliers through the Cartel and onto the streets. Officers estimated that Smith's wholesale operation alone employed 500 criminals – and that encompassed only the sellers, not all the people involved with peripheral activities, such as money laundering and security.

The Analyst said, 'If you've got a tonne of cocaine coming into the UK, that's a realistic amount. The 1,000 kilos is then broken down into 200-kilo batches. So you've then got five people who are going to take that 1,000 kilo load and distribute inside the UK. For each one of those 200-kilo units, it will be batched into 20-kilo parcels. For each of the five people who initially got 200 kilos each, they have got ten distributors sitting below them, each with 20 kilos. So now you've got a total of 50 people taking 20-kilo batches to redistribute. And below each of one of those 50 people, there are ten people, who each will take two kilos. That's 500 people. The network is even huge before it hits the streets. Then you've got all the other business interests that are related to that, so it's huge.'

The Analyst said that Colin Smith was 'running around with all this in his head'. In addition to the core chain of 500 drug handlers, the police were beginning to map out the superstructure that surrounded and supported them. Colin Smith's part of the Cartel became the subject of close scrutiny, and the police were surprised by how big and complex it was.

The new additions were mainly to do with money management. Smith was being forced to bolt ever more circuitous networks onto the central wholesale operation to mask its true purpose in an increasingly hostile world. It was becoming clear that the police, SOCA and the asset-recovery agencies were making life difficult for him. Smith was feeling the heat, particularly from the raft of new money-laundering laws that were hitting the statute books. New agencies seemed to be popping up all over the legislative landscape, not only within the UK but overseas, too. Government grants were being dished out to NGOs and academics that could help with the big push.

The Analyst said, 'I could point to a police organisational chart on the wall, showing a complicated hierarchy of police units, personnel, ranks and reporting lines. That would look like a child's version compared to that of the crime group we were looking at. We watch films, the traditional gangster films: *The Godfather*, for instance. If people are involved in a high level of criminality, then that level of sophistication goes on.

'If you were involved in a legitimate international company that dealt with hundreds of millions of pounds worth of assets every year, then you would need a similar level of sophistication. You'd need an incredibly sophisticated company of people to manage the money, the security, the distribution: you would need all of that in place. Then, on top of that, you need someone to manage the money that is coming in, to distribute the profits that you make, and all of that has got to sit in an underworld environment that's not legitimate.

'Then you've got to expose it to the legitimate world. You've got to create a whole sequence of legitimate companies and business interests across the world, so people then become involved in legitimising the money. They would effectively put a legitimate front on an illegitimate business. So now you're starting to network.'

The ballooning structure of Smith's firm brought with it political difficulties. If anyone was trying to kill him, the first motive would obviously be money. The second motive involved a dispute with the Ex-Sportsman, whose family owned a successful Cartel franchise on Smith's patch. They expanded from drug sales to protection rackets and nightclub security. Using the Fraudster as muscle, they had forced Bubbley Shalson to sell his crack houses and drugs rounds at the knockdown price of £10,000 each. He had been too busy fighting Kallas and the Gee family to take much of an interest. The Ex-Sportsman was becoming increasingly cocky. One day he challenged Colin Smith over a deal and they fell out.

The Analyst said, 'If Colin was in dispute with this man, and he had decided that the Ex-Sportsman's time was up, then what next? There was a situation where things had to happen and the Ex-Sportsman had to disappear by choice. If he stayed in Liverpool, he might be killed. This put pressure on the Ex-Sportsman and he's thinking, "I've got to act in some way," in order to get himself out of harm's way.'

The Ex-Sportsman was not in a position to go head to head with Colin Smith unless he could get the green light from other Cartel bosses, so he was forced to bring in other backers. The Ex-Sportsman was more prudent than most of his contemporaries, hotheads like Kallas and David Hibbs-Turner. Though he was extremely violent, the Ex-Sportsman did not simply want to toss a hand grenade through Smith's door. If he was going to launch a hostile takeover, he wanted it to be as bloodless as possible. The Ex-Sportsman was a team player: he was sensitive to the fact that the Cartel was a corporation and no longer a street gang. He realised that killing Colin Smith would jeopardise the Cartel because they could potentially lose Smith's key contacts in Amsterdam and South America. Therefore, the Ex-Sportsman looked around the Cartel for potential allies. Who had a grudge against Colin Smith? In the end, he decided that he would have to go over Smith's head and talk to the Cartel's official boss of bosses, a shadowy Cartel overlord known as the Illegal Alien.

The Analyst: 'The question is: who would someone like Ex-Sportsman go to for that backing? Maybe someone he had been involved with before? Someone who had supported him previously?'

The Illegal Alien was an ex-British citizen who had swapped his nationality but was now living back in the UK under a false passport. A childless divorcé, he enjoyed fine wines and vintage champagnes, and he smoked like a chimney. Despite gorging himself on expensive restaurant meals, the Illegal Alien remained painfully skinny. A thick mop of black hair gave him a more youthful look than his 60 years. He hadn't been happy with Smith for five years or so, ever since Smith had allegedly 'bumped' the Colombians for £70 million following the assassination of Stephen Lawlor, Smith's former enforcer. Following Lawlor's demise, Smith had played a game of bluff and double bluff with the Cartel's main suppliers in Colombia: a dangerous game, and one that he'd won only by the skin of his teeth. The Illegal Alien was a powerful man who disagreed with upsetting the South Americans and thought Smith was getting too big for his boots.

The Analyst said, 'There are people who the Ex-Sportsman would have had associations with, people with whom he could have sat down. Who else could the Ex-Sportsman have relied on? People who could have been historical associates of Curtis Warren?'

In addition to the Ex-Sportsman and the Illegal Alien, there was another Cartel boss who had a grudge against Colin Smith. People with a motive to kill Smith were stacking up like £20 notes on a money counter. Smith's former boss Curtis Warren was serving a long prison sentence in Holland for drugs offences going back to 1996. As the storm clouds were gathering around Smith, Warren was coming to the end of his time. When he got out, Warren was expecting to reclaim his old throne. He was expecting Smith to hand over the reins of the Cartel – and the hundreds of millions of pounds that Warren had left in the business when he was jailed. Fair play was on his side, Warren argued. Warren had given Smith his big break, he reminded everyone. It was Warren who had allowed his then deputy to take the top job when he was put in jail. It was no coincidence that the Ex-Sportsman and the Illegal Alien were also allies of Curtis. Ever so slowly, almost imperceptibly, a conspiracy was building.

The Analyst said, 'All this suddenly corresponds to Curtis being due for release from prison in 2007 and wanting to come back to the UK. If you believe the hype at the time, Curtis had asked Colin whether he could come back to the UK. Colin said no, because Curtis was bad for business, because Curtis brought law enforcement with him. So does that clip Curtis's wings, in trying to re-establish himself, having been out of the running for ten years or more? Is Curtis's return something that Colin doesn't want?'

Of course, the Analyst was right. Curtis Warren was now infamous. Books had been written about him, documentaries had been made: even films were in the pipeline. Everyone from Interpol to the FBI knew his name. There was too much heat on him. There was no way he could come back to the Cartel and pick up where he left off.

There was also another reason why Curtis Warren couldn't come back: money. Smith was reluctant for Warren to come back to the UK because it would mean that he would have to give back his money. Before he went away, Curtis's fortune had been valued over £100 million. Some estimates said it was as high as £300 million. That was in 1996. Since then, the Cartel's money launderers had invested the cash in property portfolios, businesses and stocks and shares. Britain had also undergone a massive boom in which property had gone up in value by 100 per cent or more. Curtis's initial investments were now worth several times what they had been worth in 1996 – and had been 'washed' many times over. Since 1996, Colin Smith had been controlling a key part of Curtis Warren's assets.

The Analyst said, 'At that point, the key question is: does Curtis have the monies that people claim that he's had? It was claimed he was worth £250 million or more, so where is that money? By that time, the law enforcement had only found between four and eight million pounds of it. So where's the rest? The answer is: it was invested under other people's names, people who had probably exploited that money while he was away in jail. The bottom line was that the money that Curtis had had wasn't there. By this time, these people had built on it. It was a case of the Parable of the Talents.'

The Parable of the Talents is a story about a master who gives his servants a number of 'talents', a form of currency, before he goes away on a journey. On his return, the master is pleased to learn that two of the servants have invested their talents and his overall fortune has grown. However, Curtis

Warren wasn't happy. Certainly, his wealth had grown – but he couldn't have his talents back.

The Analyst said, 'In the Bible, two of the servants are given talents and actually make more of them, before they are given back to their master. In Curtis's world, someone may have said to him: "What you gave me was X, and I have made ten times X, but this is all mine now." In a nutshell, the assets that Curtis had controlled previously were now beyond his reach. He might have lost control of them. So then you have got to think that those people who have got control of his assets might have included Colin Smith, or at least his associates.'

In the summer of 2007, police learned that Curtis Warren had employed a well-known underworld debt collector called Tommy to wrestle his assets back from Smith and his associates. Curtis had told Tommy to start with the small debts, so that he would have some ready cash to play with when he got out of prison. Once Tommy had recovered the small ones, he could then move on to the bigger amounts. Tommy was a taxman who used to torture drug dealers. A decade earlier, he had been partners with George Bromley, whose assassination was described in *The Cartel*. In recent years, Tommy had fallen out of favour with the Cartel bosses. It was a great honour to be asked by Curtis Warren to recover debts.

The Analyst said, 'Tommy could have been running around early summertime trying to recoup very, very small debts from people as a bit of an enforcer and debt collector, to try to give Curtis some money, to try to get him up and running again. Would Tommy do that? It's probably within his make-up. He becomes involved in all of that. It's an intelligence picture, not an evidential picture. People are saying this is what's happened to Colin and why.'

Meanwhile, in Holland, Curtis Warren had successfully appealed against his extra sentence for drug trafficking. In a shock move, he was released from prison in June 2007. However, not everyone was happy to receive Interpol's former Target One. On the journey back home, he was refused a flight by EasyJet. Then he was escorted by armed Dutch police to a ferry terminal and was taken by ship to Harwich, in Essex.

Warren was met by a pal and driven back to Liverpool in a Lexus.

The big question was: would Warren try to depose his former deputy Smith and reclaim his throne? Immediately, the British authorities began to give him other ideas; they were trying to distract him from just that by making his life as difficult as possible. He was refused a British passport. When he applied to the Irish and Portuguese governments, he was also given short shrift. SOCA then took over the reins. They followed Warren's every move as part of a 'lifetime offender management' programme. An investigation called Operation Floss was launched.

CHAPTER 23

CONSPIRACY TO MURDER

2007

The conspiracy to assassinate Colin 'King Cocaine' Smith was now in place. All that was required was a man of action to make the final push. Someone who was used to taking part in complex criminal activities. Someone who was used to killing people. Someone who would benefit directly from Smith's murder to such a degree that he wouldn't have to think twice about it.

The Fraudster had been buying wholesale volumes of cocaine from Colin Smith for several years. He ran a profitable sideline selling on the gear to the Ex-Sportsman, and even street gangs lower down the food chain. Colin Smith liked having the Fraudster onside. He used the Fraudster to lean on creditors and rivals alike. Sensing Smith's weakness, the Fraudster had taken a few liberties. He ran up a £4 million coke bill with him. Every now and again, Smith would politely ask the Fraudster to settle up. Over the summer of 2007, the Fraudster had dodged the question by spending more and more time in Spain.

Now it was winter. Christmas was coming up. Everyone was running around collecting money that they were owed. Smith started making demands on the Fraudster. I want my money, he told him. It was a very dangerous request. You will have it by Christmas, Smith was told. A surprise was in store.

The coalition of the willing was now holding secret meetings and talking. The four main figures were the Ex-Sportsman, the Illegal Alien, the Fraudster and Curtis

134

Warren. And talking was all it was. Though the Fraudster was pushing for action in order to get Smith off his back, the others were more conservative. Curtis Warren especially had every right to be conservative. He was clearly angry with Smith. But did he want him dead? At the moment he had bigger worries. He needed money fast. He could not get access to his capital assets, so he needed a quick drug deal to get him up and running. He flew to Jersey to set up a drug deal.

Under SOCA's Operation Floss, on Saturday, 30 June 2007, SOCA called Jersey Police to tell them that Warren had been observed in Jersey with a Liverpool associate and Jersey resident called Taffin Carter. The pair had been driving around Jersey looking for isolated coves in which to beach a drug import from France. Drugs were three times the street price in Jersey compared with the UK or France, so Warren was expected to make a killing. Jersey Police started monitoring and bugging phone boxes and addresses linked to Carter.

A month later, Warren was arrested in St Helier along with seven others. He was charged with a conspiracy to smuggle £300,000 of cannabis into Jersey. For him, the war was over. He would no longer play an active role in the conspiracy to depose Colin Smith. However, some members of the Cartel speculated that during the brief period he was out of jail, Smith and Warren had put their differences aside and were talking about doing a big 1,000-kilo drug import from Colombia.

Meanwhile the remaining conspirators who were plotting to kill Smith refused to give the final go ahead. An extra ingredient was needed if they were going to act decisively. Something that would motivate them all. Something that would unite them.

In October 2012, a ship was making its way across the Atlantic from South America to Europe. Hidden inside was 1,000 kilos of cocaine: Colin Smith's cocaine. Some believed that Warren had a hand in setting up the deal. However, with Warren in jail, the deal was definitely under Smith's control. The load was due to land in Europe in the second week of November. Smith was aiming to offload the cargo at £40 K per kilo, generating a cool £40 million in revenue. The conspirators got wind of the shipment. If they could kill

Smith, install a new leader in the shape of the Fraudster and take control of the fresh 1,000-kilo batch at the same time, they would be £40 million richer. The money would come in handy. Like Ancient Roman emperors, the new court could legitimise itself by buying favours. Of course, the Colombians would be wary. The plotters planned to pay for the 1,000 kilos and keep them onside. They also planned to smooth ruffled feathers by reminding them that Smith had been the one who had turned them over after Stephen Lawlor's death a few years before.

On the continent, Smith's managers were busy. In Spain, Smith's number-one enforcer Paddy Doyle was given the job of organising the safe transfer of the load from the mothership to mainland Spain. Doyle had been doing deals on the side, some of which had gone wrong, but Colin Smith still had every confidence in him.

Doyle was being harassed by Turkish gangsters to settle an unpaid debt. But he brushed it off and focussed on the big one. If he could successfully land Smith's 1,000 kilos, he'd have enough money to pay off everyone. In October, the Irish police had received an intelligence report from Spanish police about a dispute that had arisen between two Irish citizens and a Turkish crime syndicate on the Costa del Sol. The Guardia Civil had identified the two Irishmen as Frederick Thompson and Patrick Doyle. Both had been warned by the Turkish gangsters that they would be murdered if they did not pay outstanding bills for a number of sizeable heroin shipments. Thompson is said to have given two fingers to the bearer of the message, while Doyle laughed and said that he would personally kill anyone who threatened him. He had serious business to attend to.

In Holland, one of Smith's lieutenants was making final preparations before the 1,000 kilos landed. Simon Cowmeadow, a fugitive British drug smuggler who'd been on the run for five years, was still a loyal Cartel functionary. The fact that Cowmeadow was on the run made him trustworthy in the eyes of the underworld. He wouldn't be doing any talking to the police and he'd always be grateful to Colin Smith for giving him a job. It was Cowmeadow's job to organise the transport. Once the gear was landed by Doyle, the plan was for Cowmeadow to move it up Holland by road. When the 1,000 kilos reached Amsterdam, he would oversee its safe storage. He was arranging a safe house where it could be stored and cut up and liaising with the transport bosses who would take it to England. Cowmeadow knew what he was doing. Smith liked him because he was a seasoned hand. In 2001, he'd been part of a £1 m Ecstasy-smuggling ring. With two others, Cowmeadow had been caught red-handed unloading an articulated lorry carrying 100,000 Ecstasy tablets at an industrial estate in Essex. Rather than face the music, he jumped bail and was later sentenced to 18 years in jail in his absence. Some of the gang regarded his arrest as clumsy. Cowmeadow wore it as a badge of honour, saying that he was a transport man through and through and he wasn't afraid to get his hands dirty. The raid had involved officers from the National Crime Squad, who had kept his gang under surveillance for weeks. The 40-year-old former plumber was also under investigation by the Serious Organised Crime Agency for previous drugs offences, which meant that his underworld CV stacked up.

It's not known whether Merseyside Police were specifically watching Colin Smith or his underbosses, such as Simon Cowmeadow, during the period of the 1,000-kilo shipment. However, what is known is that the police were playing a clever game. Merseyside Police certainly knew that there was heightened activity, and they were preparing for a number of eventualities. Prudently, they were putting the right resources in place, waiting for the moment that the Cartel made a mistake. They didn't know the full picture yet, but they knew enough to know that there was something big coming around the corner. Carefully, they got their ducks in a row, so that they could jump all over whatever it was at a moment's notice. That involved strengthening the links between the Analyst's team and his equivalents in SOCA – and police officers in different countries. It also involved building up finely balanced, multifunctional investigative teams containing detectives who were capable of getting to grips with small clues, others who looked at the broad strokes and others who kept it flowing along in accordance with the rules.

The Analyst said, 'It's not just a Merseyside-centric

investigation. I met with my equivalents in SOCA and we discussed high-level issues. You've people within the team whose responsibility it is to liaise with foreign police forces. There are officers on the team who talk about finer details with the police in Amsterdam and Spain, and officers whose roles lie somewhere in between. They are the compliance officers who fill in the forms and arrange the meetings with our foreign counterparts, and make sure that we are following the right procedure.

'You have always got to keep all three layers of the investigation – the strategic, the tactical and the operational – in sync. There are varying degrees of sophistication within this structure. But by investing time and effort into these processes continually, we felt that we were always ready for what was around the corner.'

It wasn't long before other police forces in the UK recognised that Merseyside Police were developing completely new systems and techniques that they wanted to copy.

The Analyst said, 'As regards other forces, I suppose everybody is learning, all the time. But Merseyside Police is good because we have made a commitment to tackling serious and organised crime, and have done that for a number of years, so in some ways we are ahead of the game.

'We were inspected by Her Majesty's Inspectorate of Constabulary a few years ago. I ran the investigation. We came out as a "Beacon Force", which is one that other people in other forces around the country would come to, to see how to do the job. That's because we've spent time and effort tackling serious and organised crime. If you go out to the Shire forces, they may not have that skill that we have developed.

'The only problem that they may have that is similar to ours is that of the "travelling Scousers", where people from our city are going to their patch to commit crime.

'The Shire forces don't see it like we do, because they are not used to it. We see this in context because we've got a lot of people in this city and a lot of crime goes on.

'Other forces will come and ask how we do deal with this, because our techniques have worked well. For instance, other forces are now trying to use organised-crime-group mapping, which is how we target crime groups, and set it up as a national business model. We are pretty good at crime-group mapping and targeting criminal groups. That's because we've got a history. Other forces are coming along now with no established protocols, no systems and processes. But they haven't got that history, but they've got to do it.'

CHAPTER 24

IRONED OUT

13 NOVEMBER 2007

For Colin Smith, the day began like any other. There's no nine-to-five in the life of an international drug dealer. No commute to the office. No structured work in the traditional sense. Like he did most days, Smith got up in the morning, took the kids to school and walked the dogs. Smith's five children were privately educated, as were most of the Cartel godfathers' kids. Around mid-morning, he went out to meet one of his mates. Along with his pal, Smith then went to a gym for a private karate lesson.

The Analyst said, 'He had a session there – £100 a time, not bad really. Then he went to another gym, called LA Fitness, on an industrial estate in Speke. After that he met another feller in the coffee shop of Borders bookshop and he had a coffee with him.'

Borders was a supermarket-sized bookshop on a retail park opposite Speke airport. It was ideal for an underworld rendezvous, as it had a coffee shop and was so huge it wasn't crowded. The coffee shop was at the back on a raised mezzanine, giving a good view of everybody coming and going.

The Analyst said, 'The feller he was meeting was over from Spain on a passing visit. So it isn't a coincidence that he meets this feller in Borders at noon or whatever time it is.'

The police weren't 100 per cent sure about the reason for the meeting. Was it connected to the 1,000 kilos of cocaine that was due to be beached in Europe any day now? Was this mystery visitor from Spain a messenger with important news? Most cocaine shipments from South America are beached on the Spanish coast before making their way to Amsterdam by road and train. Was the mystery visitor giving Colin an update? Had the Cartel received the satellite phone call from their man on the ship that let them know he was approaching land? Was Smith preparing his divers to go to retrieve his £40 million drop? Colin Smith never talked business on the phone. It was standard procedure for messengers to fly into John Lennon Airport from Malaga on EasyJet. The arrivals terminal was just a few hundred yards from where they were sitting in the Borders coffee shop. As Smith spoke, he could hear the planes on the flightpath above. All messages were delivered by mouth, by human courier. Or was the mystery man warning Colin that another plot was underway? Whatever the nature of the conversation, Colin remained unruffled and carried on with his day's appointments. One of his key appointments was at Nel's Gym, on a bleak housing estate in the middle of Speke. The gym was opposite a quiet shopping parade.

The Analyst said, 'He goes out and meets a number of people during the afternoon, then calls past at Nel's Gym late afternoon to try and speak to some people. But there's no one there. Or certainly, the people that he wants to speak to aren't there. He's certainly not going there to train at that time of day.'

Smith then went home for his dinner. He told his son to get ready to go out. His son played for Everton Academy. Meanwhile, across the city, Smith's arch-enemies were just getting in from work. The Analyst, the policeman who had devoted his career to bringing down the Cartel, was planning to have an uneventful evening. For 30 years he'd studied nearly every member of Britain's biggest crime group. He knew Colin Smith personally. Their fates had been entwined. As a young bobby, the Analyst had first encountered Smith standing on a street corner with a gang. Little did he know that tonight would result in one of the biggest investigations of his career. He got changed and was about to have his tea. He was just settling down for the night.

The Analyst said, 'So then Colin drops his son at footy.

Then, unusually, he gets asked to go back to Nel's Gym. This is not usual, because he normally watches his lad play footy: he was at the Academy and it means a lot to him. So, although it's out of character, he goes to the gym, for whatever reason: we don't know. Some people say he was just calling by to offer some financial support in setting the gym up. But the whole thing is caught on video, and when you look at the video he certainly wasn't there talking about how he sponsored certain parts of the gym.

'There's something else going on when you look at it all. When the gym was built, whoever did it put in a really state-of-the-art CCTV system. Every room in the gym has got CCTV on a multiplex system. The video doesn't capture sound, but the nature of the images point to a serious conversation. Several of the main conspirators are present. So you've got ten cameras all around the gym. And, spookily enough, the only camera that isn't working is the one that's outside of the gym, the one that covers the exit and the street. But inside you can see all of them: there's about ten people in the gym at the time. More importantly, you can see the whole set of interactions between them all. They are all just talking; there's no one working out. There were no arguments. But later we sent the CCTV footage away to experts. One is a specialist who looks at body language. The other is a psychologist who looks at how people behave. The bottom line is that you can see changes in people's behaviour as they are stood there in the gym.

'The group begin to trigger events. A number of people's attitudes suddenly change, until Colin Smith eventually walks out of the door to go to his car. The question is whether the trigger event that takes place is a phone call, whether someone within the group has received a phone call from a third party to say "everything is in place", to say that someone is now outside and all that we need now is for Colin to walk out.'

That someone outside was a young man known as Caesar, from the Toxteth area of the city. Though he was still young, Caesar was already an experienced hitman with several kills to his name. For a previous gangland assassination, he'd been paid £50,000 to murder a gangster at the back of a retail park in the Croxteth area of the city.

Caesar was sheltering in the doorway of a pizza parlour on the opposite side of the road to Nel's Gym, keeping a close watch on the door. He had been standing there for at least ten minutes, ignoring the taunts of the loudmouthed teenagers looking for trouble on the run-down council estate. At 8 p.m., the balding, sun-tanned figure of Smith emerged from the gym. Calmly, Caesar strode across the road, making no attempt to conceal his face, and drew his gun. The first bullet was to the back of the head; the second, to 'make sure', was into the stomach.

For the police, the significant fact was that the killer must have been a Cartel insider, otherwise he would not have been allowed anywhere near the venue. There were several very heavyweight gangsters inside the gym and some of them would have had their security with them. They would have been scoping the street for rivals and police. There might even have been lookouts on the street, waiting in cars and disguised as pedestrians. The hitman himself might have been playing the role of a foot soldier employed by the crew to be a lookout. He might have been a close associate of one of the men in the gym. He might even have been known to Colin. Colin might not have given him a second glance. Whoever organised the hit might have had some control over the local area in as much as they could have cleared the streets or warned away locals.

The Analyst said, 'Colin walks out and goes to the car and the gunman just walks up and kills him.

'The question is, if you are going to kill someone like Colin Smith, how do you bring a gunman into a place like Speke without causing suspicion? How is he able to stand outside a gym? Outside of a set of shops? A couple of the shops were open and there were people around. So the gunman cannot be a stranger, because the people will confront strangers. We know that Speke is an incredibly parochial area and that a stranger in Speke is most definitely a stranger. Don't forget the gunman must have been there for a period of time waiting for Colin. So for him to stand outside a gym, where it is suggested that a number of high-level criminals are meeting, and he's not confronted or challenged in any way, shape or form is very interesting.'

Caesar walked away from the scene quickly. Like Michael Corleone in *The Godfather*, he didn't run, so as not to attract attention. The Cartel's propaganda machine kicked in immediately. To cover Caesar's getaway, deliberate falsehoods were spread via the underground grapevine. The rumour was that the killer was an Eastern European gunman drafted in for the job who had been flown out of John Lennon Airport within an hour of Smith's death.

The Analyst said, 'The CCTV should have captured a recording of the murder. But it was the only camera in the gym not working. It was well planned. Whoever did it was very aware of policing methods.'

CHAPTER 25

MURDER SQUAD

14 November 2007

Within minutes of Smith's murder, the police investigation was underway. One of the first policemen on the scene was a DCI from the major incident team. One of his bosses was the Analyst. The next 60 minutes, known in police jargon as the 'golden hour', were crucial to finding the killer. Most of the vital clues must be gathered in the golden hour. Later, the forensics will start to decompose and witnesses will disappear.

The Analyst said, 'I didn't need to get my coat on and go out, because the golden hour was managed by my mate, the DCI on the scene. Immediately, I started to put in the phone calls to the relevant people on my team, because I knew what I would be walking into the following day. I, and the other members of the leadership team, knew what needed to be done: mopping the scene down, getting everything in place. We also had a duty Senior Investigating Officer in place – a Detective Superintendent – and a Detective Chief Superintendent. Between them all, they had the golden hour covered. This procedure came out of the Stephen Lawrence murder in south-east London. Forensically, it's the most important time. It's all about what you put in place to preserve the evidence at the scene. The greatest opportunity for forensics is within the first six hours.

'We ran a video camera round the scene, to capture all the cars that were there. We got CCTV from the gym and we found out who had been there. During this golden hour, you will have watchers – bystanders who come out to see what's going on. Later they starburst back into the community. Sometimes, the people who are responsible for the murder will come back to the scene because it's geographically quite tight. This has two meanings: first, statistically speaking, murderers are from the area or are familiar with the area that they kill in; and second, Speke is a very close-knit community, which means that the murderer will probably be known to locals. It's down to the natural curiosity of them and their associates: they want to know what's happening as a result of their actions. So we will ID them there and then and go looking for them later. You have got to ask yourself: how did the watcher know the incident had happened? Did they know it was coming? If you do it properly, this information will be crucial.'

The Analyst came into work at 6 a.m. the following morning and was one of the police chiefs who 'picked the murder up'. The immediate team was tight: one senior uniformed inspector, a CI and a DSI. But Merseyside Police no longer needed teams of officers to solve a murder, especially gang-related targeted killings. They had become experts in murder. The Analyst explained, 'We're not bad at this now because we have a lot of it.'

After a few days, the officers began to piece together the events leading up to the murder. Crucially, they learned about the tonne of cocaine that was steaming towards Europe. Surely the two events were connected. The mystery soon began to unravel. The police began to pick up fresh intelligence. Whoever was in charge of the load had got wind of his boss's murder. Significantly, he decided to abort the mission. Instead of beaching the 1,000 kilos as planned, he called off and changed course.

The Analyst said, 'The value of the importation could be £40 million: you're talking about a tonne of cocaine that cost £40 million. But if someone's on the ship, bringing it over, and he gets the phone call that says, "Colin's dead," that could have been the reason it wasn't landed. Instead, whoever was on board would have been a loyal associate of Colin's. You've got someone there, before it gets to Europe, saying, "No, don't do it." They would have contacted the distributors, either the Colombians or the Mexicans, and said, "We're compromised."

'So, what are they thinking now? Do you risk running the

importation as planned, when the most significant individual has now been killed, or do you say: "I think we need to sit on this. Don't compromise it." There's no point in putting it quayside, or at some other point in the distribution chain, because the Colombians' investment is then at risk. Whatever their cut of £40 million is, it's going to be a lot of money. They might have £15 million invested in that. Would you take that chance?'

For the conspirators, this news was devastating. The killing had backfired. One of the main reasons for murdering Smith had turned out to be worthless. The conspirators were banking on the windfall to fund their coup within the Cartel.

The Analyst said, 'If the importation doesn't take place, what are the consequences? Let's go back to the impact assessment. They thought that one of the benefits of killing Colin would have been filling the void in the power struggle, to take his position as the executive within the organisation, to be able to pick up the business but also to be able to take the £40 million, take it and say to the Colombians, "Sorry, we haven't seen it. Colin must have stolen it."'

Ironically, the plot to steal the £40 million of cocaine from the Colombians was based on an idea that had been Colin Smith's in the first place. The heist was a direct rerun of the trick that Smith had pulled on the Colombians in 2002, when Stephen Lawlor had been killed and Smith had managed to swindle a tonne of cocaine. Following the incident, Smith had managed to repair the damage because he was trusted. He managed to charm the Colombians into giving him the benefit of the doubt. However, the new conspirators had overestimated their ability to pull the same move again without raising suspicion.

The Analyst said, 'They hoped to say to the Colombians, "You need to build relationships with us, so we can restart the distribution network." They thought that they were going to establish themselves and get set up. But they lost the importation. Suddenly the £40 million is adrift and the payday hasn't happened. They've forced themselves into a difficult position.

'Colin may have been incredibly well respected, liked and trusted. But after they've killed him, they are not trusted, because they are not known to the Colombians. The South Americans are asking, "They have killed Colin Smith: can they be trusted?" Do the killers have the attributes Smith had to make that situation good? Those who tried to take over could have lost in the long run.'

In addition to the long-term consequences for the new Cartel bosses, there were also more direct considerations. The hundreds of people that made up Colin Smith's cell within the Cartel were hung out to dry. Dozens of drug dealers had been relying on Smith to feed them with the 1,000-kilo load. Now their payday had been snatched away at the last minute. Their boss had been wiped out. Confusion began to spread in the ranks. For the next year, cocaine supplies to the Cartel were disrupted. There was a drought.

The Analyst explained, 'All of those people who were being paid for Colin Smith's efforts . . .there were real consequences for them. Does that roll onto cocaine distribution for the next 12 months? Not only did they lose the importation, but now the whole infrastructure has got to be rebuilt.

'But who would agree to that, and at what level? If they did agree to this, could they have managed the consequences? I'm sure they have re-established themselves now, because a vacuum always has to be filled. But yes, at the time it sounded like a bad call for them.'

In the aftermath of the murder, meetings of senior Liverpool criminals were bugged by police. One meeting was recorded in the Marriott Liverpool South hotel, popular with Liverpool football players and close to John Lennon Airport. Those aware of the meeting's agenda likened it to a 'mini-Appalachian', a reference to a famous get-together of Mafia bosses in 1950s America. The comparison was telling. Merseyside Police had been tipped off about the mafia convention. A senior police source, who cannot be named, said, 'A lot of these heavy fellers checked in. One of them asked a manager to switch off the CCTV. Everyone expected Smith's allies to get revenge immediately. It was a nest of vipers.'

SOCA revealed that year that it had confiscated 89,000 kilos of cocaine, most of it from Colombia: a 20 per cent increase on the previous year. A SOCA source confirmed it was investigating Colombian involvement 'across the entire supply chain' of cocaine in the UK.

British detectives prepared to target Puerto Banús, a luxury suburb of Marbella from which Smith had flown before his murder. It is a popular foreign base for British cocaine dealers.

The Analyst said, 'The intelligence that you pick up about Colin Smith's life would suggest he was incredibly sophisticated in the way that he worked and well organised in what he did. In effect, he was the chief executive within his business. So you'd look at the people he associated with and ask what would be their motives for killing him. You look at the relationship between Colin and the Illegal Alien and find out where the Illegal Alien sat in that world and what influence he potentially had. What influence would he have with people in Merseyside and with people in London, as an example. Would someone like him have had to acquiesce to Colin's murder for it to have taken place? You're looking at a very sophisticated criminal underworld and you're almost considering the kinds of things that you usually only watch on the TV.'

CHAPTER 26

FALLOUT

18 November 2007

Exactly five days later and 500 km away, in Holland, the body of a fugitive British criminal was discovered in a scruffy suburb in the north of the capital. He'd been shot in the back of the head with a .38 handgun. At first, the Dutch *politie* identified the victim from his passport. They thought he was a 37-year-old man from Liverpool.

The detectives sighed knowingly: 'Not another one.' Their response was becoming all too common. British criminals were now the number-one foreign crime group operating in Europe's drug capital, and Liverpool criminals were the strongest and largest of what was becoming known as the 'English team'. They had beaten off competition from the Russian mafia, the Chinese Triads, the Jamaican Yardies and many more to become Europe's number-one drugs outfit.

The location of the crime scene should have given the detectives another clue. Zuiderzeeweg wasn't really a place; it was a big ring road connecting the northern and eastern parts of Amsterdam. This was really Nowheresville: just roads, a big bridge and a few logistics warehouses. Zuiderzeeweg was all about transport. Everyone who came here was on the move and passing through.

The passport that had been found on the body had been provided by the Cartel and it didn't take long for the detectives to establish that it was a false one. A few days later, Europol forensic scientists matched the fingerprints to a new profile. The real name of the victim was Simon 'Slapper' Cowmeadow, the 40-year-old ex-raver turned Cartel fixer from the Forest of Dean.

Cowmeadow's body had been found between 6.45 and 7.00 p.m. on an isolated country road 20 kilometres north of Amsterdam city centre. At first, it was rumoured that he'd been killed for grassing up several Dutch drug dealers who'd been arrested in the UK a few months earlier. But Cowmeadow wasn't a grass. Cowmeadow worked for Colin Smith as a general manager, specialising in transport and storage. The Dutch police, who had been criticised in the past for jumping to conclusions too quickly, were prepared to keep an open mind.

The mystery soon began to unfold. Unsurprisingly, the murder was soon being linked to Colin Smith. Cowmeadow was killed essentially because he was Colin's man and he had inside information about the 1,000-kilo load. Inside information he had chosen to use unwisely. Information that had got him killed.

Cowmeadow's job, before Colin Smith was killed, was to personally manage the landing of the 1,000 kilos into Europe. Full on and hands on, Cowmeadow was coordinating the final leg of the journey of the ship in which the contraband was hidden. He was in direct touch with Smith's other key players who made up the secret cell, including Paddy Doyle. Cowmeadow was also in touch with the most important member of the team: the man on the boat with a satellite phone. When the ship arrived off the coast, Cowmeadow was expecting a call from the satellite phone man to give the go-ahead for Doyle and his associates to launch the smaller boats and send divers to collect the 1,000 kilos out at sea. It was Cowmeadow's job, once he'd got the call, to make contact with Colin Smith for the final, last-minute authorisation.

Cowmeadow's problem was his loyalty. On 13 and 15 November, he repeatedly called Colin Smith in Liverpool to tell him that the ship was off the coast. Cowmeadow was waiting for the go-ahead and Smith's latest instructions, but there was no answer on the number he'd been given, presumably a mobile phone held by one of Smith's underlings. Cowmeadow did not know that Smith had been killed and that all communication had been severed. However, his criminal instincts immediately took over. Cowmeadow smelled a rat.

Meanwhile, on the opposite side of the fence, the conspirators who had killed Smith knew that they had to get hold of Cowmeadow quickly: to get him onside, to persuade him to join the new regime and to head him off at the pass. It was a race against time. They had to get hold of him before he had a chance to inform the satellite-phone man and the Colombians that something was up.

However, in the confusion, Cowmeadow refused to play ball. Instead he picked up the phone and called the satellite-phone man on the ship, instructing him to abort the mission. He told them that he didn't quite know what was going on but that Colin Smith was dead. The satellite-phone man told the captain of the ship to steam on. He then contacted the South Americans to inform them that he was holding on to the 1,000 kilos. Neither Smith's colleagues nor the conspirators were getting anything. He snatched victory from the jaws of defeat. The downside was that one phone call had cost the conspirators a cool £40 million – and Cowmeadow his life.

By staying loyal to his dead boss and betraying the new kings, Cowmeadow had signed his own death warrant. It was only a matter of time before they got revenge. Cowmeadow knew the predicament he was in; however, at the same time, he was confident that he could get out of Amsterdam. After all, he'd been on the run for 18 years. He knew all the moves: where to get false passports, and access to cash and safe houses. However, he underestimated the reach of the Cartel. Almost immediately, a contract was put out on Cowmeadow.

The Schellingwoude district is around one kilometre from where Cowmeadow's body was found. It was once a village, but the area now is dominated by a big suspension bridge that feeds traffic into north Amsterdam. Amid the caissons and concrete supports that jut out of the river, there is a depressing rag-tag array of run-down canal barges and half-sunk boats moored at the side of Zuiderzee. The area is popular with criminals and runaways, and there are plenty of drug-related shootings.

For the Analyst, Cowmeadow's death was more than the Cartel's reaction to a deal gone wrong. Long before, the new rulers had thought through every eventuality. For them, Cowmeadow represented more of a strategic threat: he was someone who had direct links with the Colombians and could have acted as a rallying point for Colin Smith's allies. According to the Analyst, the Cartel had long since decided to kill Cowmeadow. For them, it was just the logical conclusion to a long series of questions. For them, it was all about impact and risk assessment.

The Analyst said, 'Someone would have looked at Colin Smith's murder beforehand and said, "If we take Colin Smith out, what's the impact factor on the organisation?" At that level of criminality, if you took Colin Smith out of the Cartel, what would be the consequences? What's the impact factor, what's the risk? If he was involved in a large-scale importation, and you took him out at the 11th hour when a distribution was coming in and was ready to land – well, what would happen? Could the killers ride the storm? Could they take the importation themselves? More importantly, could they re-establish the organisation around that load, and who would they put in to fill the void?

'Or would it create a power struggle because there's now a vacuum? And is there going to be a problem? And if so, do you have to identify a couple of people around Smith as potential trouble makers? Who would have to be killed as well to prevent that power struggle taking place? Who would have to be killed to send a wider message to those who sat below Colin Smith? If other people are killed across Europe, would that quell any potential hostile takeover? If there was a conspiracy, then there could have been a murder in Amsterdam a few days after Colin's murder. That was Cowmeadow.'

Detectives began to search through Cowmeadow's history. They visited his last known address in the UK at the Coach House, Flaxley, in the Forest of Dean, from where he had disappeared on the day he was due to stand trial for smuggling Ecstasy worth £1.5 million into the country. They found out that he had picked up his first drugs conviction a decade earlier: in 1997, drugs with a street value of £12,596 were discovered in outbuildings at a house in Cinderford previously owned by Cowmeadow's grandmother. The haul included 341

Ecstasy tablets and more than half a kilo of amphetamine sulphate. Cash totalling £18,925 was also found under the stairs at the family home. Cowmeadow denied the heroin charge but admitted the other charges and was jailed for three years.

CHAPTER 27

LORD OF THE WINGS

2007

Meanwhile, in jail, Yael Feeney was fighting for his life. He decided that the best form of defence was attack, so he launched a number of pre-emptive strikes on potential enemies, even down to the lowliest drug addict. The drug addicts weren't threats on their own, but they hunted in packs and were often employed in gangs to carry out hits for powerful drug lords.

Yael Feeney said, 'I tracked down my enemies. You can be a well-known member of the Cartel, but that won't stop someone with money putting a price on your head and getting five or ten creatures to pounce on you unawares. You can be a Big Charlie Spuds, but if it gets out that you've been done in by bag heads then your reputation starts to decline very quickly. Before you know it, out of fear you're saying to the screws, "I'm not going out today; keep my door shut." I've seen fellers who can have a go crumble under the threat of being attacked in jail. People put money on their heads all the time. These big fellers can fight for England, but they can't handle the sheer ferocity of jail.'

Yael painted a dark picture of modern prison, where drugs are the currency and most prisoners spend most of their day hunting them down, keeping their eyes on the prize in a chaotic, anarchic environment populated by zombies, creatures and habitually violent gang-members.

Yael Feeney said, 'I was in jail in the south of England. As soon as the cell doors open, it's like a mini match letting out, like the crowds from a footy stadium pouring onto the streets. Everyone is screaming and running around in a mad way. That's all jail is: people running around for tackle. That's all you can hear: "Who's got gear?" Or, "Who needs tackle?" Or, "Where can I score?" In that situation, there's only one way to survive: you've got to become part of that culture. Not only that, you've got to dominate that culture. And you have to have the people who make up and run that culture around you. The creatures soon become your army. By that, I don't mean that you have to physically have the creatures around you as part of an entourage all day. But they have got to be at your beck and call to carry out work for you.'

Yael Feeney told how the adoption of a drug addict into the ranks of his gang became an open secret. Even the prison officer turned a blind eye to the practice, he claimed, in a bid to pacify the wider population and maintain the pecking order.

Yael said, 'The screws know that you're feeding five or six of these creatures. That means that they know you are paying five or six creatures in heroin. They know that's how you control your crew. But the screws want a quiet life – if people are smacked out of their brains, they'll sleep all day. So if you've got five or six of your creatures taking drugs all day, that's five or six less they have got to worry about. You only get peace in jail with drugs. Ninety per cent of jails are full of drug users.'

In jail, the heroin is not sold in wraps but in pinhead-sized amounts known as chicken eyes.

Yael said, 'That's all you hear about: chicken eye this, chicken eye that. Or, "Who's got any shine?" – meaning people need foil to smoke the gear on. If the public knew what went on in jails they would be horrified. The authorities couldn't publicise the scale of the problem: that's why the drugs issue in jails is rarely spoken about. Smackheads play on pity and ask their mums to send in a pair of £60 trainers. Immediately, they sell them for a £10 jaily – a jaily is four or five grains of heroin; it looks like a tiny bit of sherbet on a teaspoon – which is worth £2 on the outside. It contains £2 worth of heroin. So their families are being conned out of £58 for a smoke of heroin that will last a few seconds. When the dealers

156

are selling it, they say things like, "That's right from the Turk's arse – that's boss tackle."

'At the end of the day, I had replaced the army of bodyguards that I'd had on the outside. Don't forget that on the outside, my legitimate property business was still thriving. I had lads looking after my interests. I had more than 20 bodyguards. It's just that inside, they had no reach. Physically, I was cut off from them, even though they still worked for me outside. Some of my bodyguards and enforcers weren't prepared to get involved in my jail strife anyway. Therefore, I had to replace that power with something that I could use inside jail – and that was a prison army of creatures.'

For the first time, Yael had to mix with drug addicts. He even found one or two surprisingly OK. Yael was 'padded up' with a heroin addict who had stabbed his mother and slashed his own child during a drug-fuelled rampage. But he was gentle.

Yael said, 'In the run-up to when he was arrested, this lad had injected a lot of drugs. Then he turned to crack, and then when he couldn't get no stone, he went off his head. His mother was trying to calm him down, going, "It's enough, you've smoked enough crack – it's on top." Then a dealer arrived and started injecting. Suddenly he went mad. He smashed his mother up, smashed the dealer up and slashed his own kid four or five times. But inside, you couldn't wish to meet a nicer feller. When I left prison, I gave him all my tobacco. After all, he wasn't a "tabby" – someone who robs old women. He wasn't a knobhead low-level armed robber. He was just a victim of drugs.'

CHAPTER 28

ON WITH THE BODYCOUNT

2008

The new leaders of the Cartel began consolidating their power base. The first phase had involved killing Colin Smith. The next stage involved the assassination of operational manager closest to the £40 million cocaine load, Simon 'Slapper' Cowmeadow. However, despite their best efforts, they hadn't got to Cowmeadow fast enough and he had managed to tip off the Colombians that something was wrong. The 1,000 kilos had been snatched back by the South Americans just in time. The loss of the load was a big setback for the conspirators. They had been planning to use the cash from its sale to smooth things out with cells still loyal to Smith. With the load gone, the conspirators would have to stabilise the Cartel in a different way.

Phase two of the *coup d'état* involved wiping out Smith's allies before they had time to mount a counterbid for power – and before they had time to seek revenge. The first target was fugitive Irish wildman Paddy Doyle, whose job it would have been to help land the 1,000 kilos in Spain if the job had gone ahead.

The Analyst explained, 'Paddy Doyle was a family friend of Colin Smith's, and on occasion he visited the pub owned by Colin's father when Colin was there.'

Doyle had survived the first phase of the coup, but the new bosses weren't happy with him. He had kept out of the firing line by lying low in Spain. On Monday, 4 February 2008, just over two months after Colin's death, Doyle set off to visit another close pal of Smith's. Doyle was part of a group of Smith's former pals who were trying to garner support for a revenge attack on the Fraudster, who had taken Smith's place. Doyle was travelling in the front passenger seat of a BMW 4x4 driven by one Gary Hutch. Hutch was in a tricky position. He was related to the Monk, who was a long-term friend of the new rulers of the Cartel, and he had offered his support to them following Smith's demise.

Either way, the Cartel were determined to stop Doyle in his tracks. They were determined to stop the meeting between Doyle and the other Smith ally going ahead. However they planned to achieve that, it would have to be done carefully.

As Hutch drove the car towards La Cancelada, outside Estepona, they were ambushed. According to eyewitnesses, two men from a green car opened fire as Hutch's car drove by, the bullets smashing the windscreen and hitting the passenger door. Hutch crashed the car, and he and Doyle ran for cover. What happened next demonstrated a clinical, military-style ruthlessness on the part of the attackers. Whoever they were, they were determined to shoot smart: to kill Doyle, but to leave Hutch if at all possible. One of the gunmen singled out Doyle and began firing directly at him. At first, Doyle managed to get out of the jeep and tried to run away. But at least one of the gunmen, who wore no masks, calmly walked up to him and shot him twice in the head. In total, 13 bullets were fired at Doyle, who died at the scene. Meanwhile, a terrified Hutch crouched in terror and waited until the gunmen had left before presenting himself at a local police station.

The Cartel might have taken advantage of Doyle's growing unpopularity on the Costa del Sol, to persuade local crime bosses to kill him in much the same way that the Illegal Alien had rallied Smith's opponents in Liverpool to wipe him out. Yet the nature of the assassination led police officers in Spain and in the Guardia Civil to conclude that the gunman hired to do the job was Russian mafia; however, this was never confirmed.

A police officer in Dublin revealed that shortly after Christmas Doyle had been involved in a brawl with a young Russian man whom he severely beat up. Unknown to Doyle, the man was related to a senior Russian mafia figure. The Russian godfather was linked to the Cartel. He was delighted to lend a hand to the conspirators if it meant that vengeance could be exacted in a ruthless fashion.

The mystery deepened when, fewer than 24 hours after Doyle's murder, cocaine valued at about €9.2 million was seized by Spanish police in Estepona, close to the shooting. An Irishman was one of eight arrested. According to sources back in Ireland, the hit had also been OK'd by the Turkish *babas*, or godfathers, who Doyle had ripped off previously with his own direct boss Freddie Thompson. The two Irish criminals had decided to hold off on paying the Turks until they could generate much-needed funds. They'd been banking on money from the 1,000-kilo load that never appeared. Fewer than two weeks before his death, Doyle had been given a final warning, but he ignored it and met his inevitable fate.

Back in Ireland, Doyle's death was met with jubilation by his rivals. Doyle was probably the most violent and feared criminal during his time in Dublin and his presence was enough to deter the rival Crumlin gang from attempting to carry out attacks on Thompson gang members. The Crumlin gang had called a ceasefire because they were terrified of Doyle.

Doyle was just the latest in a long line of Irish criminals to end up dead on the Costa del Crime. The bodies of Shane Coates and Stephen Sugg, leaders of the notorious Westies gang, were found in a concrete grave in Alicante less than a year after they fell out with a violent drugs gang. Drug dealers Sean Dunne and John McKeown also went missing in Alicante and are presumed dead.

Money laundering was great news for drug dealers – but only when they were alive. When they were 'taken out' in gangland killings, suddenly the process became a nightmare for the families they left behind. Few assets were owned under their own names. Nothing could be recorded on a will. For the spouses and siblings trying to sort out inheritance, money laundering got very messy. Some members of Colin Smith's family got busy trying to unravel the complex network of companies, certificates and heavily valued word-of-mouth transactions that Colin Smith had been involved in. They tried to stake a claim to a £70 million share of one business. The Analyst said, 'The family talk about that because that's part of the battle over the estate. They are still in probate.'

Meanwhile, the murder was proving an investigative boon for the police. Through an ironic twist of fate, Colin Smith's death had allowed the police a rare glimpse into the secret world of the Cartel without the need for costly and intrusive surveillance. For the first time, the police were given permission to step inside – with the permission of known criminals. Some members of the Cartel began cooperating with the police out of a sense of loyalty to their former leader.

The strange situation had come about at the behest of Smith's family and friends. The law-abiding members of the family were determined to find out who killed Smith. The police told them that the only way they could do this was if Colin's inner circle cooperated with them. That would mean senior Cartel drug dealers who were still secretly loyal to Colin Smith sitting down with officers and telling them all about Colin Smith's dealings. That would require a bit of give and take on both sides. The police would have to promise not to prosecute anyone who spoke to them; the criminals would want a certain degree of immunity and trust, so that no one would find out. An agreement was reached, and some of the Cartel's longest-serving drug dealers began to do the unthinkable: talk to the police. From the information obtained, the police were able to map out the hierarchical chart of Colin Smith's part of the Cartel.

Others steadfastly refused to talk to the police. One former enforcer and close confidant of Colin Smith emphasised the link between Smith and Curtis Warren as the major cause of friction before Smith's death. He believed that it had been a row over money that had triggered Warren's wrath. The enforcer revealed how Curtis and Colin Smith had initially gone into partnership over the 1,000-kilo load. However, the relationship deteriorated and Smith may have wrestled control of the 1,000 kilos out of Warren's reach from the outset. It remains unclear as to exactly what happened.

The enforcer said, 'Curtis and Colin had set up this big deal with the Colombians. They had both agreed to put up the money, each putting up a proportion of the 1,000-kilo

161

load. But when the time came to pay for the parcel, before it had landed in Europe, possibly even before it had left South America, Colin refused to give up the money. That caused a lot of tension. He refused to give Curtis the money, and that was very unusual, as Colin was known as a straight-player. It's not clear whether that meant Curtis lost his stake completely and Colin took over. The evidence for the fact that it was unusual for Colin to mess around about money is that very few people had issues with Colin. Of course rivals like Carli Sleevey had issues with him, but Colin didn't have as many enemies as he could or should have had, bearing in mind that he was the main man in a huge drug-dealing business.

'After the fall out, Curtis asked the Illegal Alien to go to see Colin, but still he wouldn't hand the money over. Then someone asked for him to be scrubbed out before the drugs landed.

'The Fraudster definitely did not pull the trigger, because he was in the gym at the time. The shipment got landed, but it never reached the Fraudster. But I don't know whether it was divvied up, smashed up, left or what. It's very much unfinished business.

'The Illegal Alien is a very patient man; he doesn't do things today or tomorrow or next week. He does things next year and the year after.'

Another two murders were carried out that were directly related to the demise of Colin Smith: those of Paddy Doyle and Simon Cowmeadow.

The Analyst said, 'You might look into it and actually find out there are some more murders. In total, four people were murdered in the wake of Colin Smith's death. One was Paddy Doyle, who was a family friend. He used to go in their pub. He was killed in Puerto Banús. There were some more murders.

'It all goes back to the fact that there was one tonne of cocaine and £40 million at stake. Then the fact that Colombians or Mexicans said, "We don't need to land this. I think we need to sit on it." The conspirators would have stood to make a lot of money. The loss of the importation meant the big payday didn't happen.'

The increased tension, particularly along the Costa del Sol, triggered numerous other, unrelated shootings. A struggle for power was underway. Players were vying for position in the new order. In one incident, a Liverpool gangster was gunned down in Spain. Then, in revenge, a Liverpool security boss, once described in court as a 'premier league' criminal for being part of a 'Yardie hit squad', was gunned down on 24 September in Puerto Banús. The man was shot five times in broad daylight by a lone gunman in front of dozens of witnesses: in the eye, the groin, the pelvis, his right leg and his right arm. Police immediately said they believed the attack was a 'settling of scores' related to drug trafficking.

The police began to draw up a list of suspects in relation to Colin Smith's murder. Suspect Number 1 remained the Ex-Sportsman, who had been at the meeting at Nel's Gym but fled after the shooting. The police discovered that his family-run security firm was no more than a front for contract killings, protection rackets and a drug-distribution operation. Suspicions increased when the police found out that the Ex-Sportsman and Illegal Alien had been associated with each other in the run-up to the murder. Then the police found out that Smith and the Illegal Alien had fallen out six months before. The police believed that the Illegal Alien was unhappy with Smith because he had badmouthed one of his associates.

Suspect Number 2 was a British man known as Cagey, a drugs baron based in Amsterdam who believed Smith and the Fraudster had been behind a failed hit on him two years ago as well as the deaths of several associates.

Suspect Number 3 is a former member of a rival gang, his motive, bitterness at the way Smith did business.

CHAPTER 29

SURVEILLANCE

2008

The murder of Colin Smith triggered the biggest threat to the Cartel's long-term future in 20 years. The disruption it caused weakened the organisation. At the same time, the police were finding out much more about the inner workings of the Cartel than ever before. The police realised that with the Cartel on the run, there was a unique opportunity to attack it further. In a bid to kill off increasingly large parts of the Cartel once and for all, the police went ahead with a massive push. Their secret weapon was surveillance. Since 2000 and the introduction of the RIPA, the police had had the legal powers for deeper, more intrusive covert surveillance than ever before. But when the law had been brought in, they had lacked the technology to implement it. Now, just eight years later, with the rapid advance of cheap microchips, the Internet and various forms of wireless technology, those systems were now available at a price the police could afford.

The Analyst explained, 'The two main types of surveillance are directed surveillance and intrusive surveillance. Part 2 and Part 3 of RIPA deal with this. Directed surveillance is following people. Intrusive surveillance is bugging people.'

RIPA gives public bodies the powers to carry out surveillance and investigation and to intercept communications. It was introduced to take account of technological changes, such as the growth of the Internet and strong encryption, utilised by crime groups and terrorist organisations. RIPA can be invoked by government officials specified in the act on the grounds of national security and for the purposes of public safety, detecting crime, preventing disorder, protecting public health or in the interests of the economic well-being of the United Kingdom.

The Analyst said, 'The law is a wide-ranging tool, but the skill of using RIPA is about cherry picking the most appropriate form of surveillance for the job in hand. It's also about keeping ahead of the game. Our criminals are not restricted by money, which gives them an edge. If they think that they are subject to surveillance by the police, they can have their vehicles scanned for tracking devices. They are not naive. Therefore we've got to have national groups of people working for law enforcement who make and test equipment. They evaluate the complexity and covert nature of the products available on the market. Then they make them available to law enforcement. There are some incredibly sophisticated pieces of equipment that you would never suspect of being a surveillance device.'

The first question a good surveillance officer should ask is: 'How can we outwit the criminals?' Despite the new opportunities that new technology offered, the best results still came about by putting devices in cars and houses. The venues were the same, but the quality of recording improved and the devices were rarely discovered. The goal also remained the same: to gather and exploit private information. Every police surveillance team was guided by an authorising officer. The post usually went to a superintendent in the force. The Analyst took up the job in 2005.

The Analyst said, 'Every piece of covert policing would come to me, and I would authorise it if it was legal, necessary and proportionate. The sensitive issues, such as serious crime and terrorism, need to go to the chief constable. We've achieved a lot because some of the material was fantastic. If suspects go back to their houses, they will assume that the houses are bugged. But, such is human nature, they will forget about it after a day. So in the first 24 hours we might get nothing at all, but maybe later on, people will start speaking freely because the idea of a bug drops off their radar and they don't see it as a threat any more. The technology is out there to capture all this, but it all depends on the environment we have to work in.'

Covert surveillance was not a magic bullet; in order for it

to succeed, the RIPA squads had to be supported by traditional policing. The continued use of informants to help direct surveillance onto targets was crucial. Everything still went back to the question: do people still talk to the police? However, better surveillance helped to increase the effectiveness of informants by bringing an element of verification into the process, and it also helped the police to become less dependent on every word informants said. For instance, once an informant had helped identify a target, the police could record the target's conversations completely independently of the informant, who did not have to be present. This gave the police a lot of freedom and meant that they no longer had to rely so much on using assets such as participating informants or potential witnesses.

The Analyst said, 'People will still speak to law enforcement and provide intelligence. But it's what you use it for – you can't use it as evidence, but it will help you to do other things. It still goes back to being a good investigator and being shrewd in using what you've got, exploiting opportunities and being one step ahead of the criminals.'

The flexibility and low cost of new technology allowed a degree of trial and error when looking at big drug dealers. The officers could scatter bugs among various safe houses and they were able to increase the number of lower-level gang members they could feasibly handle in one operation. Trying out as many of those opportunities as they could became routine. Even if only one paid off, the investigation got the benefits. Not every one paid off, though. The senior officers had to rise to the occasion. They had to improve their management skills so that the organisation of an investigation worked well.

The Analyst said, 'It's not like on the television where the surveillance team sit down the road with a handset and talk into the radio and assume no one sees them. The people we were up against were really switched on to surveillance, so as far as your traditional surveillance teams went, there was a danger of compromise.'

Surveillance no longer had to be a person sitting in a car. But keeping one step ahead of the Cartel became crucial. Predicting what might happen next meant that the most unlikely places and situations could provide surveillance opportunities. RIPA meant that the status of surveillance squads increased, but the ones with the highest success rates were those that kept traditional investigation at their core so that they could build a case which would win in court.

The Analyst said, 'You might be getting material off a listening device, but you have still got to ask the basic questions: who associates with who? Why? What else do they get involved with? When did they meet previously? What sort of documentation have they got to connect themselves to each other? For instance, you might ask of a couple or business partnership: did they jointly apply for a mortgage together? If so, the traditional method of building a case will be able to pick that up. It's about the organisation of intelligence so that leads get followed through. All the time, you're proving conspiracies, building the whole case, looking at factual evidence.'

Telephone evidence became the most popular form of surveillance. Criminals made life difficult for the police by swapping numbers and changing phones. But in the end it was the ingenuity of officers and the size of police operations that overcame the problems.

The Analyst said, 'In all fairness to law enforcement, they are not thick. A drug dealer might have an organisation of 100 people, but there are 4,700 here at Merseyside Police. Our organisation is much bigger and that makes us much more effective. A cartel might not have to pay tax. A drug dealer might not have to worry about budgets, and there are advantages they can exploit. But that said, law enforcement does all right. For all of the Cartel's evasiveness, we became increasingly aware of what was being planned and that there were prearranged meetings taking place.'

CHAPTER 30

THE JUG

2008

Yael Feeney had been sent to jail. Bubbley Shalson was also serving a sentence. David Hibbs-Turner was now in jail. They were all deadly rivals. In addition, a number of drug dealers who hated Yael were lifted for murder and drugs. It wouldn't be long before their paths crossed. Yael began to make preparations to deal with the threat.

To survive in jail, Yael Feeney needed to get a 'firm' of hardened criminals around him. There was only one way Yael thought he could do this. For the first time in his life, he decided to deal drugs directly. The big problem was recruitment. Jail wasn't like the underworld outside on the street, where loyalty could be bought with a combination of money, status and a strange form of criminal honour. In jail, drugs were the key to nearly everything. Yael figured out that he could use a stash of jailies and chicken eyes to tempt smackheads to join his gang and stay. Heroin was the currency he used to pay his gang members and keep everyone in line. Heroin was the only way to maintain and increase power.

Yael Feeney said, 'I've never sold drugs in my life. I'm not a two-bit criminal. I was a well-known organised-crime figure who had international links. On the outside, I wouldn't be seen dead with drugs. It was small-time. I was faced with a dilemma: either I sharpen up or go under. Either I forget all about all these morals that make you draw the line when you are living a normal, free life outside jail, or I get killed or seriously injured. This was the law of the jungle, and I either had to become part of it or crumble. Drugs would become as key to my survival as food, water and shelter. The race was now on: I had to get a bit of tackle in and quickly get some creatures around me. Once I had a bit of gear in, I could put my team in place. Then I knew I could take over the wing – and no one would fuck with me.'

Yael arranged for an 'eighth' of heroin to be smuggled into jail. An 'eighth' is drugs shorthand meaning an eighth of an ounce, which is equivalent to 0.125 oz or 3.6 g. Yael used a female drug courier to bring in the first batch.

Yael explained, 'Using my mobile phone, I phoned one of my people on the outside. They bought some gear, an eighth of an ounce, or an "end", as it's called, because it's literally the end of a block. Then I arranged for them to meet a girl I knew. The gear was wrapped inside a johnny or a balloon. She put the gear up her fanny or in her knickers. Then she would come up to the prison for a visit.'

Yael fixed it so that the drug-carrying prostitute visited one of his 'creatures'. For the purposes of the rendezvous, the couple pretended to be boyfriend and girlfriend. The mule was 'scanned' by prison officers, but the drugs were never found because they were secreted inside her body. Once inside the visiting room, the girl would go to the toilet and switch the package from her vagina to her mouth.

Yael said, 'Then they kissed and she passed it over to my creature with her tongue, and that's that. I now had £3,000 of heroin to start building my little empire.'

Outside on the street, an eighth of heroin is worth £150. But inside jail, the same amount is worth 20 times as much. Yael began to set up drug-smuggling visits every week. The weak link in the chain were his own creatures, who were sent to collect the heroin from the mule during visits. They were desperate drug addicts who wouldn't think twice about turning Yael over. If given the opportunity, they would try to steal the drugs they had just collected, even if they knew it would result in a severe beating. In order to prevent this, Yael insisted on observing every handover from the prostitute to the creature. Yael watched the meeting from a neighbouring table in the visiting room.

Yael said, 'Every time my punter went on a visit, I'd have

to book in on the same session and see the handover with my own eyes, so that the creature couldn't blag it later on and say that he hadn't received it. Afterwards, I would escort the creature back to a cell. If he couldn't spew it out there and then, then I'd wait until he shit it out and he'd have to wash the bag and then give it to me.

'The eighth means I'd end up with 3.6 g. But because I knew the dealers, I got over the odds, slightly more, at 4 g. That eighth had cost me £150 out there on the street – in jail that's worth £3,000, so I was making 20 times as much in profit.

'Once I'd got my four grams in, I then got it bagged up. That involved going to someone I trusted, a lad who was on the gear but hadn't got a heavy habit and wasn't like your typical creature. I'd get him to make it up to 100 jailies. Jailies are the standard unit in which heroin is sold in prison. Each jaily costs £10 and weighs 0.04 g. My jailies were slightly bigger than others. That meant my return would be 100 times £10 – £1,000.'

In order to attract punters, Yael made his jailies slightly bigger than the competitors' and didn't dilute his heroin. He said, 'I was in a very big jail near London. I made sure that I gave fat ones out. My gear was also better, so the punters started queuing up. It meant that I'd fall out with the competition, but it's dog eat dog, so fuck it. After a week or two, I had achieved my aim: I'd got a circle of creatures around me who were now on my payroll. They were in cells close by, so I could shout at them in their pad of a night: that was the way I gave my instructions out. I'd shout things like: "I need you to go to this pad tomorrow and collect some gear." Or, "I need you to go and slice such and such and cut him up." Or if someone was acting up and not paying his bills, I'd say, "I need you to go get someone on the outside who can go and torch his car and knock his bird out." Decent lads had reach outside.

'Remember – I was still running my legit property business from inside and I could have asked my enforcers to do things like knocking people out or spraying up a house with a machine gun. But I didn't want to mix the two worlds. I had to be disciplined about keeping jail and normal life separate.

I didn't want any of my outside enforcers getting involved in my jail life.

'But you need to be able to have power on the outside, because in jail you fall out with people all the time because you're selling gear. However, it's frustrating, because sometimes you can't do your enemies in jail. For instance, one time I had trouble with a fellow inmate. I couldn't get to him in jail, so I decided to attack his wife outside jail. One of my creatures hired someone outside using a mobile phone and I told them to follow his bird to school and knock her out outside of the school. Another time, I told them to attack the wife of another drug dealer. I said, "Go and squirt them with washing liquid and say to them next time it'll be battery acid. Tell your feller to keep his mouth in jail."

'It's like a guerrilla war every day until you get established. Then, once everyone knows you're the boss, it's happy days.'

Yael went out of his way to recruit the vilest, most despicable petty criminal drug addicts who would literally do anything for a quick fix.

Yael said, 'We want the lowest of the low: creatures who will carry out extreme violence for 100 quid worth of gear. It's a risk that you'll get grassed up by them because by their nature they are untrustworthy scum. But, at the end of the day, there is insurance against this, and it's not from them, it's from the system. It's quite simple: the screws know what you're doing. They know that you are dealing drugs. But if your wing is quiet, then they let it go – because drugs are the thing that is keeping everyone quiet. It's like an unspoken agreement.

'I was number one on the biggest wing in the prison. There were 400 cons on our wing and I had it boxed off 100 per cent. The grass didn't grow without me knowing about it; I had more influence than the governor. They knew I had a phone. But I created a pecking order, and everything ran like clockwork: there were no fights unless I started them, and the screws were safe. When it came time for me to ship out to another prison, they didn't want me to leave, but I had to, because by that time there was a price on my head.'

CHAPTER 31

PRISON WARS

2008

After a few months, Yael's success at taking over the wing started to cause resentment amongst rival gangsters. In another prison, Bubbley Shalson had also become a big drug dealer. This prison was home to the main enforcer of his then arch-enemy David Hibbs-Turner. Hibbs-Turner was on a separate wing, so they never saw each other. But Kallas was now running Hibbs-Turner's gang on the outside. Suddenly the gang war was reignited inside jail. Although Kallas was free, he managed to spread it around the jail that he would pay to have Bubbley Shalson slashed and killed.

Shalson said, 'I'm nothing special. I was just a drug dealer from Toxteth. But I had a bit of arse, I could have a go. Plus I had the backing of a Somali crew who would hack you to death. When you've got a bit of a name, people always want to take it off you. The old enemies started to come out of the woodwork. Kallas and Hibbs-Turner had allies in jail. Hibbs-Turner was in a different jail, but one of his enforcers was in the same one as me. He wasn't on my wing, but he could get to me. It's not like on the outside, when you can simply jump in your car and confront these people. You're stuck on the wing, and there is treachery all around you. Rival creatures would walk past and whisper, "You're getting it in the yard, ching ching," meaning you are getting slashed. Then they'd run off.

'The screws told me that there was £10,000 on my head, put up by well-known drug dealers from the outside who wanted to swill me with boiling water and cut me up.'

Secretly, Kallas had paid for one of his enforcers inside the prison to remove a metal part of a frame and file it to a sharp point so that it could be used as a knife to kill Shalson. Just to make sure, a second attacker was paid to turn a plastic handle into a skewer to poke out Shalson's eyes and stab him in the kidneys.

Shalson said, 'Even though my jail was hundreds of miles from Liverpool, I had a good network of informants, so I quickly got wind of the plots against me. One of them had filed a toilet brush handle to a blade: it took him a whole day.

'As always, I took pre-emptive action. I ran into the kid's pad and with my steel toe-capped boots, I knocked fuck out of the toilet-brush man and his accomplice with the knife. I ran in while they were still in bed, stoving their heads in with a fucking big tin of fruit. Tin cans are an excellent weapon in jail, especially old-fashioned fruit tins that will only open with a tin opener. Tins of tuna and beans that you can get with a ring pull that you can open yourself just burst on impact. I only ever used the big, industrial-sized tins. They were like my weapons: I treasured them. Anyway, I smashed their fucking heads in. Me and my mate got the toilet brush from underneath his pillow, and from the back of a bag under the other bed, we retrieved the knife.

'When I got back to my cell, the screws came to see me and told me to "calm it down". One of them said, "We know what's going on, Bubbley, but if it gets to the governors, they will just ship you all out." But once everyone knew that I was willing to stove them in with a catering tin of Baxters soup or mixed fruit, they backed down for a while.'

However, Kallas was determined to kill his enemy in jail so that he would never get out alive and pose a threat to him again. Kallas ordered more attacks – and instructed a hitman to shoot Shalson's sister.

Bubbley said, 'I got shipped onto the lifers' wing. I'd arranged for my enforcers on the outside to bodyguard my sister and mum 24/7, but when the prison authorities found out, they didn't like it, because it was leading to violence at visiting time between my lads and my enemies, who were there visiting members of their crew in jail. I got asked to go and see the governor. He said, "Your sister is having to be escorted to the jail with a cavalcade of cars. This is causing a disturbance." To prove it, he showed me CCTV of two gangs outside fighting. One was trying to get to my sister and attack her, and the other was my gang trying to protect her.'

Something similar was happening to Yael Feeney. Kallas's gang was targeting his 30-year-old daughter, who came to visit him near London.

Yael's daughter's minders tried to insulate their charge from the attacks. On one occasion, she walked through a crowd of fighting men, oblivious to the fact that Kallas and Sidious's brother Kaim had been waiting to ambush her outside the prison. Kaim was a big player in David Hibbs-Turner's gang.

Yael said, 'I was eventually taken to see the governor. He said to me, "We'll create a file on you and use it to bring disciplinary action against you. You'll end up getting sent to Cat. A and losing what privileges you have."'

From now on, Yael would have to box clever. He would still have to attack his enemies and protect his family, but he'd have to do it under the radar. If he ended up getting moved out of the London jail to another prison, his lucrative drug-dealing business would collapse and he'd have to start all over again in another jail. A truce was struck.

Yael said, 'I ended up agreeing to a ceasefire with my enemies. We made contact with each other and he said, "Before we came inside, you let a few shots off at me. I've let off a few shots at you. Now you've had a go at my people and I've had a go at yours. I'm looking at life in jail now; I can do without this headache going on any further."'

However, there was no such truce offered to Bubbley Shalson. He was still looking for an opportunity to attack Hibbs-Turner's underboss, who was safely insulated on another wing. However, another drug dealer known as Moab W. also declared war on Bubbley.

Bubbley said, 'In jail, most of the people are in there for drugs, GBH woundings and shooting people. They are hardened criminals who have never been to church in their lives. But, mysteriously, once in prison, they find God. However, this is not because they want forgiveness. Again, it's all to do with drugs: going to church is a good way to meet contacts from other wings so that you can do deals. They all go to church of a Sunday to pass tackle because the wings are all integrated there. The screws only bring dogs in there now and again, but we'd get tipped off anyway so it didn't matter. But as well as using this to sell drugs, I knew I could use it to get at this Moab W. and his gang.'

To get to the church, all of the inmates from other wings had to walk past a workshop where Bubbley was working. Shalson prepared to ambush Moab W. and his underboss. He said, 'I'd recruited an inmate to attack Moab W. and his mate as they went to church. The guy I chose was a lifer who'd been given 20 years for killing a drug dealer. I paid him six jailies: that's £60 worth of heroin in prison, worth about £3 in real terms. We planned to do it as they were coming back from the church. That was because at the Mass they'd have taken the gear that they'd bought and would already be high as a kite and more vulnerable.

'One of their gang was called Stretchy. As he came past the workshop, I banged him out and sent him flying off the side of the landing. It broke his jaw. Then these creatures I'd paid, including the lifer, just ran in and attacked them, jumping all of them.'

The attack was devastating for Moab W., his underboss, and their external boss, Kallas. In retaliation, an ally of Moab W. went after Bubbley himself – and this time they wanted him dead. To counter, Bubbley threatened to have a home-made grenade, known as a pineapple, thrown at Moab W.'s house.

Bubbley said, 'One of Moab W.'s gang phoned me and said, "We're putting serious dough on your head now. You are dead. This time you will not get away from us." They put another five grand on me: £5,000 is a lot of money in jail, so I knew I had to act fast before creatures started taking up the contract. To counter that, I got Moab W.'s bird's address. This time I phoned him, mobile to mobile, in prison and said, "I will put a hand grenade through your bird's window. I will kill your whole family." At that time, my gang on the outside had these "pineapples": Chinese fireworks that go 1,000 m high. We wrapped a two-litre can of petrol around it and bingo: that was ready to go through the drug dealer's bird's window. Just being exposed to the noise would have been enough to kill his newborn baby.

'There was another variant: four fucking thundercat fireworks stuck on a can of petrol, which would blow a house up.

'He knew I would do it. Over the phone, I warned: "I will do life for you." Later, one of his underlings phoned me up. It was Sidious. Sidious wouldn't let it go, because he was still fuming: he was blaming me for shooting up his mum's house. He said to me: "I owe it to you for pebbledashing my mum's house and ruining her quiet life." She couldn't get to sleep after that.

'I said the same thing to him: "I will pineapple your house all day long, right through your window."

'At first, they said that they'd wait until I got out. After that, it went a bit sick. It went to the extreme of getting their little brother: he was only 10. Someone who was loyal to me sprayed up Sidious's ma's house when he was on the couch with the baby.'

CHAPTER 32

WAR ON DRUGS

2008

Meanwhile, back in the real world, the wheels of justice turned, indifferent to fear or favour, grief or pleasure. Merseyside Police was busy investigating the gangland murder of Colin 'King Cocaine' Smith. Britain's number-one anti-drug cop, the Analyst, was the senior investigating officer on the case. One Cartel godfather smiled when he heard that the police were determined to find the killer. He said, 'Whoever killed Colin Smith did the police a favour: they won't want to spend too much effort finding out who murdered one of the biggest gangsters in the country. The busies won't be losing a lot of sleep over that.'

But he was wrong. The Analyst was determined to do things right, to plough just the same resources into the hunt for Smith's killer as he would into the murder of a non-criminal. It was not his job to determine who got recourse to justice and who did not.

Merseyside Police officers visited Smith's grieving family at home, seeing his mother and vowing to find out who killed her son. Witnesses were the key. Just as they would in any other murder investigation, the police persuaded the family to help publicise the crime in the *Liverpool Echo* in the hope that it would spark someone's memory or trigger a guilty conscience into coming forward. The odds were low, but the Analyst was not going to leave any stone unturned.

In June 2008, seven months after the murder, a man was questioned by Merseyside Police and five addresses were given.

The suspect, believed to be an on–off chauffeur for Smith, was arrested for conspiracy to murder but later released without charge. The police were rattling the Cartel's cage to see what fell out.

One of the people the police thought could shed some light on Smith's murder was his brother John. John Smith was then in jail serving a sentence for the Channel ferry heroin conspiracy, but if he thought he was going to get any breaks from Merseyside Police or special treatment because he was grieving then he was mistaken. John Smith was hit for a £600,000 asset-recovery bill. John Smith, then 47, had been the mastermind behind a gang who posed as booze cruisers to bring cocaine into Britain from Holland on passenger ferries. But now police wanted to seize his houses in Allerton and Marbella – and the stacks of cash he'd moved from UK bank accounts out to Spain.

John Smith might have been able to help the police to find his brother's killers, but the Analyst was not in the business of doing deals. Smith was told that he'd get five years slapped onto the thirteen-year prison sentence if he didn't cough up the assets the police were trying to recover. Four members of his crew were also ordered to pay back nearly £150,000 between them. DCI Mike Jones, head of the North West Regional Asset Recovery Team, told the *Liverpool Echo*, 'Not only are some individuals in the process of selling the family homes to satisfy the orders, but also it will stop the proceeds being reinvested into further drug dealing on Merseyside.'

Meanwhile, things were looking bad for another Cartel big shot. This time it was Yael Feeney, a respected combatant in the arena of the Cartel. Yael Feeney might have arrived at a truce inside prison, but outside, his set-up was disintegrating. His frontline was collapsing. Yael's business partner branched out on his own.

In addition, Yael's enemies were now sophisticated enough to mount a smear campaign. Sidious got his underlings to write to the companies who had done business with Yael Feeney, such as property companies. Some of them were legitimate businesses with rock-solid reputations that didn't realise that their client was running the business from inside prison. They would be horrified to learn that Yael had committed money-laundering offences.

Yael's daughter, who was now running the family business, had tried to limit the damage to those businesses' reputations by closing down Yael's old company and renaming it. However, when the companies they worked with found out, courtesy of a black PR campaign, they dropped Yael like a hot potato.

Much of the mischief making was emanating from Yael's old enemy Kallas, who was laughing from his sunbed in Spain. Kallas was now running his own drug cell in Marbella, a charter granted to him by the new rulers of the Cartel, including the Fraudster, who had a soft spot for Kallas. The Fraudster wanted Kallas to look after the Cartel's interests in Spain and make sure that no one tried to avenge the death of Colin Smith. Kallas was ideal for the job. It didn't matter whether he was on the streets of Norris Green or Nikki Beach; if trouble started, he would pull out a gun and start shooting. In the sweltering heat of August 2008, Kallas and members of his crew were at a bar along with two Iranians. A fight broke out and a British man was shot. It is not known whether Kallas pulled the trigger. Nothing might have come of the shooting, but the two Iranians ran to the UDYCO, the arm of the Spanish police that combats organised crime. This was a potential nightmare for Kallas and the new regime. If he were charged, there would be no end to the trouble the Spanish police could give them. They'd been waiting to get a grip of Kallas for a long time and this was an opportunity to get into the Cartel. The Iranians grassed up Kallas. He was arrested one month later, and things weren't looking good.

However, Kallas had the best lawyers money could buy. Instead of keeping him in Spain and trying to get a conviction, the Spanish police threw in the towel almost instantly. Miraculously, he was let off and sent back to the UK under 'provisional liberty' until the case was investigated further. Kallas was getting a reputation for beating cases and giving the authorities the runaround.

In Liverpool, Kallas's crew were misbehaving as well. Notorious gangster Daniel Gee had just turned 28 but was running around like a teenager, shooting at anything that moved. By rights, in the new order in which teenagers ruled,

Daniel Gee was getting too old for combat. But Gee was convinced that he was invincible, making the same mistake that the old guard had made. He began to treat the teenage gang members with disrespect, as though they were street rats for whom he held no fear.

One day, Gee began a feud with a local family. Gee began to bully them and make death threats, not caring whether he upset the family's 16-year-old son. On New Year's Day, Jamie Starkey 'copped for' Gee outside a pub and shot him at point-blank range. Gee survived, but swore revenge. Starkey was hailed as a vigilante who had stood up to the drugs Mr Big. The court sentenced him to seven years, and he served three and a half before being released in September 2011.

Meanwhile, a blast from the past suddenly appeared on the scene. An ex-Cartel boss called Kaiser began turning up in Liverpool. Kaiser had shot to power 20 years earlier, in 1988, when he'd been part of the firm that smuggled 1,000 kilos of cocaine from South America to Liverpool, via Amsterdam, for the first time. Kaiser had been partners with a man known as Scarface, who had sailed a small yacht packed with the drugs across the Atlantic.

The partnership had long since dissolved and both men had gone their separate ways. Still, they had never been caught. Since Curtis Warren had been arrested in 1996 and then their South American contact Lucio a few years later, they had distanced themselves from the Cartel. Scarface had set himself up as an independent smuggler, covered by the double life he led as an English country gent in the south of England. Kaiser had been more adventurous. He had ripped off a Turkish heroin gang for £50 million and fled to South America, where he traded shipments of cocaine like a commodities broker.

Now he was interested in getting back in the game and returning to Liverpool, so he slipped back into the city. At night-time, he took part in 12-hour-long crack cocaine sessions, some of which went on for a week. On one occasion he blew £40,000 on rocks. But money didn't matter; he was worth tens of millions of pounds.

One day when he needed some cash he went down to London to pick up a few kilos of drugs to sell. One of his pals said, 'Big Kaiser lives in Colombia, but he comes to Britain to smoke crack cocaine. That's a holiday for him. He orders £100 worth each time. Smokes £400 worth over a night, but he's done 20 to 40 grand in on some sessions that have gone on for weeks. A few days ago, he brought three kilos back from London to sell to pay for his holiday here. He drove down there and put the three kilos in the boot of a car. Then he handed over the keys to a kid who works for him and got him to drive it back to Liverpool. Kaiser came back on the train. He's not stupid; he let the lad drive back and take the risk while he put his feet up.

'He had the Turks off for £50 million. He's been shot, all in the side of his body. But he's still going strong. He bought ships to smuggle things here and there. He's still got lots of places in Amsterdam that he uses. Even though he's a big player, he's still not afraid to get his hands dirty. In 2010 or 2011, he got nicked on the way to kidnap someone.'

Meanwhile, the Cartel began road testing a new product. As a result of the war in Afghanistan, the price of heroin fluctuated and its quality was uncertain. Heroin was getting a bad name. The Cartel decided to revamp heroin's image and relaunch it with a stronger version aimed at its core market of hardened addicts. Kids were no longer interested in buying heroin. They'd watched their mums and dads screw up, and now heroin was seen as the mark of a victim. To inject some life into the maturing market, some Cartel bosses began smuggling in pure opium. Trusted dealers were given 100 g sachets of opium to test out on their punters. However, the trial didn't go well. It was far too strong. Without exception, everyone who took it either overdosed, fell over and injured themselves or wrote off their cars in traffic accidents. The opium was abandoned immediately.

CHAPTER 33

DISRUPTION

2008

The rise of the foot soldier meant that street gangs were the new force in organised crime. A decade earlier, the door-security firm had been one of the building blocks of the Cartel, but this way of doing business had been destroyed by the gun-toting new kids on the block. However, the US-style street gangs weren't having it all their own way. Just as they had largely defeated their enemies and were about to take over the Cartel, they were outflanked by a surprise surge from the biggest gang of all. Merseyside Police poured huge amounts of money into reducing gun crime and anti-gang activity. The Matrix units had free rein. Huge police manoeuvres, such as Operation Sphere and Operation Neon, put whole areas on lockdown. Disruption tactics were redoubled. Education was made a priority. Merseyside Police commissioned a play called *The Terriers* to tour schools to show the downside of guns and gangs. So vital was the link that the Matrix squad helped to fund the project. Other organisations chipped in money, including Liverpool DISARM, Liverpool Unites, the Rhys Jones Memorial Cup Trust and Liverpool Football Club. Astonishingly, gun-crime figures began to fall. The force had the highest success rate in the country in reducing firearm incidents. Prosecutions soared.

The Analyst said, 'Take disruption: it's not just about investigation; it's also about disruption and reduction. *The Terriers* was reduction by education. In other forces, they will have a firearm discharge and investigate what happened and might or might not get a result. But we used intelligence-led policing to tell us who exactly had access to guns and who was likely to commit gun crime, so we could get there to disrupt them beforehand.

'Disruption also gave us evidential opportunities. It was all about being broad-minded – it was no longer just about working in the clues. We didn't settle for a simple reactive investigation in the hope that would tackle the gangs. Still, the scenes of gun crime, such as the deposition sites, might throw up evidential opportunities, to point the way to the suspects. But when we get to the suspect, we might use technical equipment. So we started to use proactive techniques to support the reactive investigations. It's not one-dimensional any more; it's a multilayered approach to tackling criminality. That's why Merseyside Police have become good: because of the way we work.'

Following the murder of Colin Smith, the police watched to see what would happen. There was a chance that the problems associated with the Fraudster and the chaos caused by the gangs would scare away many distributors, especially wholesale buyers from the regions around the UK who'd come to rely on the Cartel. Gangs in London, Manchester and Scotland came to the Cartel for hundred-kilo batches of heroin and cocaine because they couldn't be beaten. Even going direct to Amsterdam and Colombia was more expensive than going to Liverpool, because the Cartel had invested in the trafficking infrastructure, such as transport, safe houses and distribution, and a network of back-up services, such as security and money laundering. The Cartel had already paid for much of this: they were sunk costs, so they no longer had to factor these costs into the price at which they sold the gear.

However, after Colin Smith's demise, the landscape would change. Would the Cartel lose its competitive edge?

The Analyst said, 'Liverpool is not unique, because drug distribution goes on everywhere. But with the likes of the Smiths and the Warrens at that real hierarchical level, the question for buyers was: should they do traffic in the drugs themselves or should they tap into this national distribution network? If you become a trusted associate, you have an opportunity to tap into the distribution. So if you buy 200 kilos from that network, you're helping to cut down the cost. Instead of getting a kilo of cocaine for 34 K you might get it for 32. It's economies of scale. You buy more, pay less. By staying with the established network, you're able to buy cheaper.'

CHAPTER 34

THE TEQUILA CONNECTION

2009

In 2009, the Mexican cartels declared Europe their number-one focus. The same year, President Felipe Calderón of Mexico sent one of his best men to London to counter the threat. Eduardo Tomás Medina-Mora Icaza was made the ambassador to the UK. Medina-Mora was eminently qualified: for the previous three years, between 2006 and 2009, he had served as Mexico's Attorney General, the country's number-one crime fighter, responsible for the investigation into and prosecution of federal crimes. In effect, Medina-Mora had been in charge of the Mexican government's war on drugs. The post had come with its own 100-strong air fleet of Gulfstreams and Learjets, many of them confiscated from drug lords, and more than 50 helicopters used for drug-crop eradication. Medina-Mora had overseen a restructuring of the fleet to make it airworthy and ready for battle, and he had also ordered 30 new Eurocopter helicopters for surveillance and interception.

In London, Medina-Mora bolstered his team not with helicopters but with diplomatic staff who understood the world of counter-narcotics and intelligence gathering. These experts included a similarly minded deputy called Ariel Moutsatsos, a former journalist who had worked as Deputy Director of Intelligence and Senior Adviser at the Office of the Attorney General in Mexico.

In 2009, the Mexican drug cartels were celebrating their 30th anniversaries. The Mexican drug cartels were founded in 1979 by former Mexican Judicial Federal Police agent Miguel

Ángel Félix Gallardo, known as the Godfather. He created the Guadalajara cartel, which throughout the 1980s controlled all illegal drugs in Mexico and the trafficking corridors across the Mexico–USA border. Gallardo started off by smuggling pot and opium into the USA and was the first Mexican drug chief to link up with Colombia's cocaine cartels in the 1980s.

After 30 years of solid growth, it was no surprise that Mexican drug cartels had come to dominate the wholesale drug market, controlling 90 per cent of the drugs that entered the United States. But the arrests of key leaders, particularly in the Tijuana and Gulf cartels, led to increasing drug violence as cartels fought for control of the trafficking routes. Analysts estimate that wholesale earnings from illicit drug sales range from \$13.6 billion to \$49.4 billion annually.

Several prominent cartels dominate in Mexico, but it is likely that one of the smaller, more maverick crime groups, rather than one of the more well-known cartels, such as the Sinaloa, is the one that makes contact with European groups, such as the Liverpool cartel.

In 2009, the Los Zetas cartel was celebrating its first decade in business. In 1999, a Gulf cartel leader hired a group of 31 corrupt former elite military soldiers, now known as Los Zetas, who had deserted from two elite Special Forces groups of the Mexican army and began operating as a private army for the Gulf cartel. The Zetas were instrumental in the Gulf cartel's domination of the drug trade in much of Mexico and have fought to maintain the cartel's influence in northern cities following the arrest of their main leaders.

Medina-Mora said, 'The Zetas are, or were, the operative armed faction of the Gulf cartel. The Zetas were essentially security: hitmen who had military-style training and could use arms in a sophisticated manner. The Zetas were not historically involved in logistics, marketing or finance. But they spun off into trafficking drugs and started making shipments from Colombia to the US directly. This is an emerging approach by this group.'

The Sinaloa cartel was the best-known group in Mexico. It began to contest the Gulf cartel's domination of the coveted south-west Texas corridor following the arrest of a Gulf cartel leader in March 2003. The 'Federation' was the result of a

2006 accord between several groups located in the Pacific-facing state of Sinaloa. The cartel is led by Mexico's most-wanted drug trafficker, Joaquín 'El Chapo' Guzmán, whose estimated net worth of US$1 billion makes him the 1,140th richest man in the world and the 55th most powerful, according to his *Forbes* magazine profile.

Medina-Mora said, 'It wouldn't be logical for the Sinaloa cartel to send drugs to Liverpool. That's because they mainly sell to the US and are more orientated towards the Pacific than the Atlantic.'

The Gulf cartel has been one of Mexico's two dominant cartels in recent years. By 2009, the partnership with the Los Zetas hitmen was dissolving and both groups engaged in widespread violence.

La Familia cartel was a major Mexican drug cartel based in Michoacán since the 1980s. In 2009, a counter-narcotics offensive by Mexican and US government agencies resulted in the arrests of at least three hundred and forty-five suspected La Familia members in the US, and the death of one of the cartel's founders.

The Tijuana cartel was targeted in 2009 when DEA 'Wanted' posters pictured many of its leaders. Tijuana is one of the most strategically important border towns in Mexico, and the Tijuana cartel continues to export drugs even after being weakened by an internal war in 2009.

The Juárez cartel controls one of the primary transportation routes for billions of dollars' worth of illegal drug shipments entering the United States from Mexico. Since 2007, the Juárez cartel has been locked in a vicious battle with its former partner, the Sinaloa cartel, for control.

By 2009, the Mexican government's drug war was paying dividends. Rather than face the army, many members of the cartels headed south to set up operations in neighbouring countries.

Medina-Mora said, 'There are reports from cartels that Mexicans are going down to Central America because Mexico is no longer a safe haven for them. That's because in Mexico we are enforcing the law. The Mexicans go to places like Guatemala.'

Prior to 2009, the Mexican cartels' attempts to establish a

foothold in Europe had failed. The drugs were coming in piecemeal, carried by mules, rather than in 1,000-kilo loads like the Liverpool gangs were used to.

Medina-Mora said, 'In Spain we have seen Mexican mules, or mules employed by Mexicans, but it's nonprofitable and the volumes involved are negligible. In 2009, the Mexicans declared Europe a target market. Since 2005, the volume of drugs exported to Europe have been increasing. Since the mid 1990s, when the Florida route was closed down, Central America has become the conduit. This is a multinational operation; it's not necessarily only Mexican. Of course, the people who are killing people in Mexico are Mexican. Distribution in the US has been mainly carried out by Americans. There is no evidence of drugs from Mexico going anywhere else other than the US, where there is a much larger market compared to Europe, with better margins too. There is some evidence of US-to-Europe activity. It's volume that is the key to being taken seriously in this market.'

Coca cultivation in the Andes, which has decreased by 28 per cent over the past decade, continued to drop in 2009, largely due to eradication efforts in Colombia. World cocaine production fell by between 12 per cent and 18 per cent between 2007 and 2009, the United Nations Office on Drugs and Crime (UNODC) figures showed. Meanwhile, the market for cocaine, worth an estimated $88 billion, is shifting towards Europe. It is severely destabilising countries in West Africa as well, the report said.

The number of cocaine users in Europe has doubled over the last decade to about 4 million people, who consumed about one quarter of the global production in 2008. North America remains the world's biggest market for cocaine and is valued at $37 billion. However, the European market appears to have almost caught up and is now worth $34 billion.

The highest prevalence of cocaine use on the 'old' continent was found in Scotland (at 3.9 per cent), and in England and Wales, and Italy, at 3 per cent each. In each of the SEE countries (members of the South East Europe programme, an EU-run club of 16 states in south-east Europe aiming to promote trade and strategic links), it was lower than 1 per cent. It was

0.9 per cent in Croatia and 0.8 per cent in Montenegro.

The events several thousands of miles away in Mexico might not have affected the business of the Cartel, except for several important developments. First, within a few years, the Mexican crime groups would have a big influence on the price and quantity of much of the cocaine shipped to Europe, even if it was smuggled from other countries, such as Colombia, such became their power in the global market. Second, the Mexican drug barons took a strategic decision to actively target Europe as a secondary market following the saturation of the US market. Third, within a few years the Cartel would also find itself in the position of needing a new cocaine supplier. The big question was: would the two groups do business with each other?

CHAPTER 35

GLOBALISED CRIMINALS

2009

Despite the attacks on their prestige, some of the old-guard Cartel godfathers continued to prosper. They reacted to the setbacks they faced by rolling with the punches and adapting. They did not want to fight the younger generation and neither did they want to get trapped by the increasingly internationalised police operations. Instead, they decided to rise above the milieu and become what sociologists were calling 'globalised criminals'.

Some members of the Cartel were now wealthy enough to become 'global citizens' in their own right. Increasingly, they distanced themselves from Liverpool and the UK and orientated themselves internationally as regards employment and investments. Freedom to travel and cultural 'pluriformity' were their new attributes; using private planes paid for by tax loopholes, drug dealers acted like international bankers flitting between finance capitals,. Much of the study into this new class of criminals was done by sociologists such as Saskia Sassen, a Dutch-American scientist who specialises in globalisation, population movements and crime. Sassen describes a culture of expats who feel at home anywhere in the world and defines criminal expatriates as people who settle in other countries for unlawful reasons. It was as though the phenomenon of the 'travelling Scouser' had evolved to another level. (The 'travelling Scouser' was a term adopted by Merseyside Police to describe migrant criminals from Liverpool, particularly drug dealers and thieves, who had a higher propensity to commit crimes in other regions and countries. Several factors had been identified that caused Liverpool criminals to push crime across borders, including 'opportunities of transport' afforded by the city's industrial transport links, the maritime heritage and their expertise in handling contraband. Other reasons have also been put forward, including the talkative nature of Merseyside criminals, the success of Liverpool FC in Europe and their ability to network in prisons.) These criminal expatriates are different from foreign nationals who simply end up abroad somewhere and become involved in crime.

Between 2002 and 2008, researchers in Holland studied 25 cases cracked by the National Crime Squad there. The researchers found nineteen criminal cells, each involving between four and twenty members. They were all Brits. Six cases involved Dutch criminals in Spain. All involved in narcotics. A lot of the cases were similar. A typical example of a crime involving a British criminal in Amsterdam is a man who was murdered after his sister stole drugs from a British drug dealer in Spain. It was not uncommon for a single crime to have connections to several countries simultaneously.

The new findings showed how the landscape had changed since the 1980s, when an inquiry by a Dutch parliamentary committee found that of eight foreign crime gangs in the country, none of them were British. However, they had found a Dutch group who were importing hashish via Cyprus, then handing it over to a UK gang. This became a foothold for the UK criminals, and their presence in Holland had grown ever since.

Later, the Dutch police watched the British gangs emerge. After a spate of murders, they set up a team to investigate English-speaking crime groups comprising some 150 individuals. Some were involved in reasonably professional, large-scale exports to the UK, Scandinavia, Australia and the US. Tens of millions of pounds had gone through currency exchanges. By 2009, the British criminal in Holland had one of two roles: broker or co-working manager. Brokers set up the deals, although there were different types: 'dependent' brokers functioned as outposts of the Cartel in Amsterdam and their living expenses were paid for. They enjoyed an open relationship with suppliers, who were allowed to go over their heads to Cartel bosses. 'Independent' brokers, on the other hand, were middlemen. The Dutch traced one who offered a consignment to the Brits, but while he was waiting for an answer, they offered it to a Lithuanian gang. Independent brokers received instructions from the Cartel bosses and acted for several clients at once. They tried to keep suppliers and buyers apart but typically got 1,000 euros' commission per kilo.

Co-working managers supported brokers by supplying transport, packaging and security. They are freelancers and receive a small fee. In Amsterdam, Brits of ethnic origin started to trade with their own nationalities. Dutch criminals supplied synthetic drugs. Everyone dealt in hash. It was interesting to note that British criminals did not invest in Amsterdam in the same way that they did in Spain. They shied away from buying long-term properties, building residential blocks with profits, and opening businesses. That's because they mainly saw themselves as transient 'fixers' whose role and circumstances might change at any moment. In addition, they viewed Holland as a mature economy in which they could see little return. The social fabric of Holland was seen as 'too complex' and on a level with Britain where high levels of bureaucracy and state monitoring and strong local customs were concerned. The Cartel viewed Holland as an equal, where Spain was still considered a poorer country with an inferior and less intrusive government. Most of all, the Cartel bosses wanted to lie low and didn't feel comfortable setting down permanent roots in Holland, as it might leave them exposed to Dutch police and other international gangs.

Instead, both the Dutch and Cartel criminals preferred to set up HQs in Spain and fly back to the Dam for business. Like diplomats or the managers of major companies, these high-flying Dutch and British criminals resided in luxury and engaged in constant international travel for business purposes. Once a few dealers had settled in Spain, the network snowballed because of what sociologists call the 'family and friends' effect: the pull of a surrogate network.

The British and Dutch criminals had different skills. The Cartel was good at finding brokers in established smuggling networks. The Dutch in Spain were good at establishing completely new networks from scratch. The Dutch were driven by the lure of establishing beachheads in international drugs markets; entering the supply chain early ensured enhanced profits.

CHAPTER 36

JOINT ENTERPRISE

2009

No one within Merseyside Police knew more about the Cartel than the Analyst. Now he turned his attention to studying the new generation of gangs. He came up with several theories to try to explain their violent and erratic behaviour.

The Analyst said, 'A whole number of issues are to blame. One of them is the downturn in religion, which is exemplified by shifts in cultural behaviour, such as shops opening on a Sunday. There is also the fallout from really violent interactive video games on Xboxes and PlayStations. They desensitise kids to violence. We only have to go back to the Bulger murder: The murderers, Robert Thompson and Jon Venables, were part of that generation who made up the next wave of organised criminals. They were brainwashed by violence and so were many of their contemporaries. Someone dies in a film like *Die Hard* and there are no consequences to it. No one considers the emotional connection between violence and someone getting hurt. Socially, these people are not strong enough. They don't give a damn about the consequences of their actions. If they assault a police officer, it's by the by.

'Take America. Around 100 police officers were killed in the USA while doing their job. The big question is: what's the change in society that lies behind that? What's changed people's attitudes? For instance, you might ask: do people now see policing as a threat?'

The Analyst was also convinced that prison wasn't working in the way that it was meant to. Instead of curtailing crime, jail was promoting illegality by acting as a real-life social media network, as it connected criminals from around the world.

The Analyst explained, 'In the 1980s, it was the phenomenon of the "travelling Scouser" that enabled criminals to form links with criminals abroad and start importing drugs. Today, that's changed: it's through the prison system. And it all starts with the justice system. When they're arrested for crime, they know that we, the police, have got to act within the constraints of the law. We've got to do everything properly. The criminals see this as a chance to play the system, and they use it to minimise the impact of the sentence. Should they go to prison, they see it as a chance to re-educate themselves.

'A good example of that happened recently, when we found that criminals from Merseyside were stealing cars in the UK, breaking them up and shipping them out to Gdansk, in Poland, where they were sold by a Polish crime group. That had happened because a group of Liverpool criminals had been in prison with a group of Polish criminals and they started doing business together when they got out. Building and developing relationships in prison is adding value and enhancing organised crime in the UK to a great extent.'

Merseyside Police continued their drive to punish the old-guard Cartel dealers by confiscating their assets. Several years after he was convicted of smuggling 593 kilos of cocaine, Edward Jarvis was ordered to pay back £800,000. His wife, Alison, tried to convince the court that her life of luxury on the outside was paid for by her husband's underworld associates. But the court heard that when her only income was supposed to be benefits, Mrs Jarvis spent up to £5,000 a month on foreign trips, and in Harvey Nichols and Harrods, while living in the family's luxury five-bedroom house.

The Analyst hoped that the fear of having their money confiscated would deter the younger generation, but the gang members didn't care what happened to them or their money. They weren't rational when it came to economics. Like crime robots, they killed and maimed on autopilot, saying little before, during or after. Their code of silence wasn't enforced, like the Mafia's *omertà*. It was a default setting, a natural state of being.

The Analyst: 'The younger lads today have the attitude: "You don't tell anyone anything." That's something that has changed; in the past, criminals loved to talk.'

In the old days, only a few years previously, experienced officers like the Analyst were experts at getting serious criminals to give them intelligence. The process was long and tortuous, but by going step by step, the Analyst knew he could get his charges to talk. Of course, at first they were adamant that they wouldn't tell the police anything. But the Analyst could get the villains' respect by convincing them he had encyclopaedic knowledge of the scene.

The Analyst said, 'If you could talk of their world with a degree of authority, then the suspect would talk to you as an equal. If you had the local knowledge, they would open up. It would end up as a conversation as opposed to an interrogation. In that way, you could pick up some really good stuff. But you couldn't underestimate them. Sometimes they had a hidden agenda. They like undermining their own rivals, because it takes the attention away from them. You could get a lot of valuable information, depending on the way you treated people. If you treat them fairly, with a degree of professional courtesy, then you could still have banter with them. People want to talk to you.'

But the new gang members maintained an unnatural silence, like soldiers shot down behind enemy lines. They treated the police like a hostile force. A good example involved the gratuitous murder of a 16-year-old army cadet who'd been visiting a youth club. Joseph Lappin was a model teenager, but he got caught up in a war between rival gangs and was stabbed to death in a case of mistaken identity. A ten-strong mob had jumped Lappin without any provocation. The police knew who had done it. James Moore was a textbook tearaway who was convinced that he was above the law because no one would talk about him, make statements or grass him. In 2007, he had been given an ASBO for terrorising his neighbours and local businesses. Despite repeated breaches of the order, the police couldn't do anything because of a lack of witnesses. Moore threw golf balls at moving cars, harassed a couple until they were driven from their home, smashed windows at another local's flat, and revved car engines at high speeds. Moore relied on gangs' tight lips to get through the day. Arrogantly, he flouted referral orders and supervision orders imposed by the courts to punish him and rein him in. Moore was not locked up, despite breaking the law almost monthly from the age of 13 and breaching 45 orders. When he stabbed Joseph Lappin, he expected to walk again.

The Analyst said, 'The Joseph Lappin murder was a good example of the change in attitude, and how the young criminals refused to talk to the police. There were ten people involved in the attack. We knew that one person had killed Joseph Lappin, but no one within the gang would tell us.'

Instead of letting it drop, the Analyst tried something new. He'd been studying the new gangs for several years now and came up with a simple but radical solution. If the suspects thought of themselves as a gang, if they sought sanctuary within it, then he would treat them like a gang. No longer would he see them as individuals. He would prosecute them as one.

He said, 'In the end we charged them with a joint enterprise murder, meaning that they would all go to jail for the killing if convicted.'

The legal concept of joint enterprise was all about looking forward. No longer could a gang member arrogantly hide behind a wall of silence. If at the time of the offence a person who was part of a gang knew that the gang were going to have a fight, and reasonably suspected that their group was going to cause serious harm to someone but then did nothing about it, then that person could be charged jointly with murder. The joint enterprise tactic had the effect of putting pressure on the peripheral gang members, who might not be directly involved in a stabbing but could and would protect the person who'd done it, simply by saying nothing. However, faced with being treated as one, they suddenly became scared that if they didn't speak out they could get as many years as the leaders, such as James Moore. Now they started talking. Eventually, the police were able to entice the defendants to turn on each other, in what's known in the legal trade as 'a cut-throat defence'. Moore was singled out in court and sent to jail for 17 years. The judge praised the police, but criticised the 'remarkable leniency' which had allowed him to get away with everything but murder for years before.

The Matrix squad hoped that in addition to joint enterprise, their new strategies would pay dividends too. As well as hitting key impact players hard, they now wanted to show them a way out of crime as well by offering them access to education and jobs. Social workers, the job centre and other agencies were roped in as part of a new 360-degree approach to criminality. New methods of data handling were also introduced.

The Analyst said, 'Organised-crime-group mapping involved bringing together all of the information we had about a particular type of crime. If it was gun crime, we would map a certain area based on history, using gun-crime figures, prosecutions of gun-crime offences, investigation, disruption and reduction.'

Academics hoped that Liverpool's increased prosperity in recent years, during the Blair–Brown boom, would also help, in particular that the good money would push out the bad. Liverpool has undergone an urban renaissance recently, with new public infrastructure and major economic upturns. Employment increased by 12 per cent in eight years, between 1998 and 2006. More than 24,000 new jobs had been created during the good times. However, just when the future was looking bright, disaster struck and wiped the slate clean. The banking crisis led to a massive recession.

CHAPTER 37

POLITIE

2009

Amsterdam was home to at least 20 international crime gangs. The worst included: the Russian mafia; the Albanians; the Balkan gangs; various 'gypsy' coalitions from Eastern Europe; several rival outlaw motorcycle gangs, including the Hell's Angels; the Chinese Triads; various Caribbean Yardie outfits; the Turkish Connection; Egyptian cannabis suppliers; representatives of Colombian, Venezuelan and Mexican drug cartels; Israeli mafia; the remnants of the IRA; Bulgarian hit squads; the US mafia and the Italian mafia – not to mention drug buyers from every surrounding country. The crime map, pored over by the tired officers of the Amsterdam *politie*, looked like the route planner of a major international airline. However, one nation had gained supremacy over them all: the Brits. UK criminals were now the number-one international drug traffickers in Holland. Within the British contingent, one group dominated: the Cartel. The Brits were now target number one for the Amsterdam police. The 'English team' were leading the charge not because they were the most violent or the biggest, but for a number of other mundane reasons. First, they were 'traders', as defined by the Dutch police, underworld businessmen who were only interested in buying and selling the end products: they ruthlessly stayed clear of processing and production. The other competitive advantages were self-evident, for example: they spoke English, the international language of business; Britain and Holland were geographically close and had good motor links and sea lanes;

the Brits had been in Holland since the 1960s; they could mingle with the huge number of obsessive Brit drug and sex tourists; they had better access to forged identities; it was a key destination for on-the-run Brit criminals; and, bizarrely, they were trusted by landlords and estate agents and could rent and buy houses without much problem.

The middle-aged Cartel bosses had been successful at corrupting legitimate businesspeople in Holland – especially lawyers, estate agents and bankers – to form an underground network where money laundering became a massive enterprise. Amsterdam's white-collar professionals preferred to do business with the Brits rather than with the other mafias, who also dabbled in prostitutes and people smuggling.

By 2009, billions of euros' worth of cannabis was being grown in Holland, so much so that Police Commissioner Max Daniel said, 'Cannabis is a threat to our democracy.' The Cartel had been prudent and in the early 1990s, when it realised that skunk was more profitable than Moroccan solid, it had invested much of its money in illegal cannabis farms.

The Dutch police formed a special Joint Investigation Team (JIT), an investigative body specifically designed to bring together different organisations to combat the growing problem of British criminals operating out of Holland. The main contributors were SOCA, Amsterdam *politie* and the Dutch equivalent of the FBI, known as the National Crime Squad. Two British police forces found themselves working with the Dutch JIT more than any others in the country: the Metropolitan Police in London and, of course, Merseyside Police. The structure was part of the 'protocols' that the Analyst had been talking about.

The seasoned Dutch police officers who served on the JIT did so anonymously for security reasons, referred to by their service number only. Officer 120499 is known by his number for security reasons. He said, 'We are dealing with the upper class of criminals. In some cases, detectives and higher-ranking officers have been threatened. For that reason, we only use numbers on reports.' British criminals in Amsterdam are not afraid to go after the men who want to put them behind bars. He is a tactical investigator for the Quick Response Unit. His colleague Officer 17154 is an information specialist.

SOCA sends over information, mainly intelligence from the UK, on notorious British criminals believed to be operating in Holland. Officer 17154 collates the information and sucks in more data from his sources to build up a better picture. Some of his best information comes from beat officers on the front line in Amsterdam's streets. They are now specially trained to lock onto British criminals in the street, quiz them and establish their ID.

If a suspect is found, the case can be pursued and a British criminal can be located to an address, then the information is passed to Officer 120499. His 'hit and run' team will then organise the arrest, often involving the Dutch police's heavily armed SWAT team.

The Quick Response Unit deals with serious and organised-crime 'emergencies' in Amsterdam, such as kidnapping, shootings and drug busts. The information flow between British and Dutch police goes both ways.

In 2009 and 2010, 87 British criminals were arrested in Holland. Most of them were sent back to the UK for trial. SOCA is Britain's main national crime-fighting organisation, but it relies on officers, information and intelligence from regional forces who can track local criminals to Amsterdam. Merseyside Police and the Metropolitan Police provide most of the Dutch leads to the JIT. Put simply, the vast majority of British criminals in Amsterdam are from one of two cities: Liverpool or London.

Officer 120499 said, 'A lot of the British criminals we have to deal with are from Liverpool. It's not so important for us where they are from: to us, they are just British criminals and we have to find them all the same. But we do get a lot of information about Merseyside crime groups in Amsterdam. As long as we can catch any criminals, it's not important where they are from. SOCA in Liverpool send us a lot of information. What's happening now is that we can actually see them. British criminals have always been in Amsterdam, but now, because of the JIT, we have more information about them. If I'm driving home and I see an English licence plate on a car, I stop and make a note of it. Uniformed officers are also more aware today. Amsterdam is a big distribution point for drugs to the UK.'

Like the Analyst, Officer 120499 believes that drug crimes basically grow out of simple advantages. The attraction of Amsterdam is simply 'transport opportunities'.

Officer 120499 said, 'It's because it's easier to transport drugs over water than through the air. At Schiphol Airport, we have 100 per cent checks on all risky cargoes. "Risky" might apply to a destination that we know is associated with drug trafficking, such as the Dutch Antilles, which has strong trade links with Venezuela and Mexico. That means that gangs use the ports instead. Drugs are sent from the ports to the UK at Amsterdam and Rotterdam, the latter being the biggest port. You only need to find a small container to transport drugs. Often, if a big consignment is going through, the criminals will give away something small: that means they will arrange for some of the cargo to be found by police, as a decoy. This happens all the time. Belgium and Antwerp are also used.'

In addition to transport, the Cartel find Amsterdam efficient as a base of operations because there is a criminal infrastructure already in place, with a long and established heritage. A ready-made network of trusted 'facilitators', as they are known to the police, cater for every whim, like a service industry dedicated to making life easy for the Cartel. These facilitators are fixers and middlemen who supply everything that a crime group needs to get in place before it actually starts selling contraband: accommodation, safe houses, cars – the basics of life and business.

Jack Vanderwyk, who runs the Amsterdam Gangland website, said, 'Liverpool gangsters in Amsterdam are extremely well organised and far more violent than the Moroccans, Chinese, or Turkish factions have ever been. These groups control their own markets, while the Liverpool lads are trying to expand theirs.'

CHAPTER 38

KALLAS

2009

By now, former Cartel leader David Hibbs-Turner had made himself so at home in jail that he'd almost forgotten about getting out. Hibbs-Turner was two years into a long stretch for conspiracy to murder his rival Michael Wright, not forgetting a concurrently running sentence for running a massive drug operation. Inside, Hibbs-Turner's conflict with Yael Feeney had ended in a truce. However, his war with rival drug baron Bubbley Shalson had turned into a long-running war of attrition. Both bosses slogged it out in a bid to become the daddy. Shalson was also fighting another war with a jailed Cartel gangster called Moab W.

The situation outside wasn't much different. The trail of destruction that Hibbs-Turner had left in his wake was still clogging up the courts. The legal process was moving slowly, taking up the valuable time of both police and prosecutors. Hibbs-Turner's drugs cell was so big and complex that it was still unravelling after two years of serious court action. Fourteen of Hibbs-Turner's gang had weaved their way through the system between 2007 and 2009.

Last up in the dock was the man who symbolised the new face of the Cartel, the criminal with a dark history moulded by what Tory politician Iain Duncan Smith had dubbed 'Broken Britain'. Terence Riley was the grown-up urchin who'd found James Bulger's dead body back in 1993. In court, his lawyer tried desperately to use his traumatic childhood to defend his role in the multimillion-pound drug operation.

Louise Santamera told the court, 'He has seen things which no young person should have to see. Of course, finding James Bulger's body on the railway line, without any counselling, was bound to have some effect on such a young person.'

But the excuse didn't wash. The prosecution said that Riley had had a leading role in the drugs ring, willingly following his boss, Hibbs-Turner, into his dark world. The police gave no ground. The prosecution had no truck with Riley's attempt to blame his ills on society and a lack of proper treatment. They said that the £4 million worth of drugs that they had seized was just the tip of the iceberg. They reiterated that Riley's gang, most of whom were collectively already serving more than 150 years behind bars, were 'armed and very dangerous'. Hibbs-Turner had been jailed for life, with a minimum of 37 years. The jury agreed with the prosecution's version of events. Riley was jailed for 11 years.

The police were determined to keep on going. Total war had been declared on the new generation of gangs, a strategy the police hoped would strangle their power at birth. After finishing with Hibbs-Turner's core gang, officers now went after anyone and everyone who'd been associated with him. They pushed through prosecutions on affiliates and subcontractors. The allied Grizedale Crew, who had been a powerful drug-dealing gang run by the Gee family, were now being dismantled piece by piece by the police. Three members of the Grizedale Crew were put on trial for the murder of an 18-year-old hoodlum called Tony Bromley, who had been chopped down from behind with a machete after being chased through the streets of Anfield by two attackers on a motorbike: standard gang activity. The murderers were found guilty and sent to prison. Tony Bromley was the son of an infamous Cartel drug dealer and torturer called George Bromley, who had also been murdered, in 1997. Dad George had been known as the Taxman, but his chilling reputation failed to protect his children. George's other son, George Bromley Jr, hadn't fared much better. He'd hit the headlines a few years earlier after terrorising Liverpool captain Steven Gerrard.

In 2009, Kallas celebrated his 30th birthday. He was no longer a rooting-tooting 20-something upstart wanting to take on the world. His criminal record was impressive: he'd clocked up fifteen convictions, four jail sentences and triggered literally dozens of police investigations.

However, at 30 his youthful exuberance showed signs of mellowing, at least in some respects – particularly business. Kallas now took negotiations seriously and was interested in sticking to deals, not ripping off his colleagues. He also sought to settle disputes without resorting to violence instantly. Reluctantly, the upper echelons of the Cartel had allowed him into their ranks. Following Colin Smith's death and the destruction of his key operators in Amsterdam and Spain, the Fraudster had bestowed lucrative territory on Kallas. He was granted a big franchise in Spain, where he and his ragtag crew of street urchins took over a large villa on a Spanish holiday estate and turned it into a frat house for international drug dealing. Kallas was the Fraudster's new main man in Spain, keeping everyone in line with sporadic acts of *Goodfellas*-style violence.

Occasionally, Kallas came back to Liverpool. You could take the boy out of the gang, but you couldn't take the gang out of the boy. Instead of being low-key, he insisted on starting fights in bars just like the street hoodlum he'd always been. In September 2009, Kallas and another maturing member of his gang visited a swanky bar called Palm Sugar Lounge in Liverpool One, a huge state-of-the-art retail development that symbolised the city's new image. The legacy of the city's year of being European Capital of Culture might have still been tangible, but for Kallas it was all window dressing. Instead of settling down for a cocktail and a bottle of Cristal, he picked a fight with the doormen and started throwing chairs around. He didn't look like one of Britain's biggest drug dealers. He threw a punch at a bouncer before launching chairs at security staff while terrified passers-by fled to safety. Another member of Kallas's gang hurled a ceramic ashtray towards staff. Kallas and his Croxteth Crew pal were sentenced to six months behind bars. Astonishingly, the judge suspended the prison sentences for two years because of the pair entering early guilty pleas. Money had bought the kind of legal firepower most criminals could only dream about. Kallas was given a slap on the wrist and was ordered by the judge to stay indoors. However, his lawyers argued that even that was too harsh.

They asked the judge if their client could be excused from the order for the last and first day of every month – so he could leave the country to answer bail on a separate charge in Spain relating to the shooting of a British man at Nikki Beach a year earlier. It was international legal ping-pong and the only winner was the criminal. As he left court, he pulled up his jumper to disguise his face. Despite his notoriety, Kallas was still a hoodie at heart.

Not all drug dealers were part of the Cartel. There was still a healthy population of 'independents', a breed that had been identified by the Analyst and by the sociologists who had studied the market in Amsterdam. A good example was former soldier Matthew Perry, who transformed his home into a cocaine-mixing factory. Matthew Perry, who had served in the Balkans and was later described in court by a judge as 'bright, intelligent, articulate, worldly', was found with 2.5 kilos of 75 per cent pure cocaine at his rented home. His cottage industry was basically a packaging plant – complete with hydraulic press and 46 kilos of cutting agents – ready to dilute drugs. It was a new trend based on the plentiful availability of the adulterant benzocaine. Lads could make a living by simply adding benzocaine to cocaine and making extra profit. Perry was jailed for six years.

Benzocaine is used legally as a dental anaesthetic and gets users high if snorted or injected. The powder had been flooding into Britain because it was made cheaply in China and sold over the Internet. Now SOCA warned that benzocaine was a dangerous drug in its own right, cheap enough to spread fast amongst younger users. It wasn't long before crack dealers discovered that benzocaine could be 'cooked up' and 'washed up' to form crack cocaine-style rocks.

Poncho had been part of the Cartel cell that had smuggled the first 1,000-kilo load into Liverpool. He said that the widespread use of adulterants was killing off the market for drugs, because dealers pushed too hard to make extra profit. Terrorism and increased police pressure were also factors in the market's decline. Poncho said, 'The cocaine market has gone down because all of the big fellas have been nicked or shot. Terrorism has made smuggling awkward. The agendas have changed, leading to low-quality cocaine, which punters are not buying. A £35,000 kilo is cut with a quarter of a kilo of benzocaine, then re-pressed and sold for £50,000. One kilo of brown is cut into six kilos. I know I used to do this. For example, I bought two kilos of paracetamol from a wholesaler for £40 and heated it up in a Pyrex bowl until it turned a light brown like heroin. Then I mixed it with the real heroin. The difference is that today it's done on a massive scale with hardly any real drugs.'

Some dealers simply got rid of using real cocaine altogether and used benzocaine to make fake crack. It was a win-win situation because benzocaine cost next to nothing to make yet yielded a staggering 8,000 to 10,000 per cent profit. One dealer made £50,000 worth of fake crack from just £500 worth of chemicals.

CHAPTER 39

THE DAM

2009

The Cartel found Amsterdam safe and welcoming, according to the Dutch police officers who made up the JIT anti-Brit crack squad. The job of the Tactical Investigations wing, the Dutch police unit that spearheaded the JIT, was to do the opposite: to make Amsterdam harsh and hostile. More than 200 nationalities have settled there, and the native Dutch are tolerant. British criminals started to arrive in Holland during the 1980s and continued to settle throughout the 1990s and 2000s. At first, the Cartel workers living in Amsterdam found that if they stayed under the radar and didn't fall out with each other, few outside their own circle would even realise that they were criminals.

During the early years, the dealers only had to take simple measures to stay one step ahead of the law: disguising themselves as tourists, for instance. Meetings took place in the bars off Dam Square, such as an Irish pub on Paleisstraat, a subterranean chintzy, wood-lined theme pub. The Irish pubs got a reputation for being 'clean but crap'; however, there the Brits didn't stand out and they could eat full English breakfasts and roast dinners all day long. Other favourite meeting places included a faux Bavarian *bierkeller* at the posh end of Dam Square, close to the ornate £150-a-head Reflet restaurant and the Grand Hotel Krasnapolsky. Inside the darkened Euro Pub, drug dealers met contacts under the red neon lights, or sat outside at the wicker tables. The venue was convenient for the Mr Bigs higher up the chain, who refused to go in but

THE DAM

allowed their foot soldiers to hold the meetings on their behalf. They preferred to wait in a nearby upmarket hotel or eatery well off the tourist trail, so messages could be ferried to and from the 'workers' taking part in meetings in Dam Square very quickly.

The venues were excellent for criminal activity, the police discovered, as they were also easy to find for the newly arrived scallywags that often make-up the rank and file of the Cartel. Often the new arrivals were criminals who were on the run from police and rival gangs back home in the UK. Consequently, the apprentice Cartel dealers needed to adapt fast. They needed places to meet that were centrally located. They hadn't found their feet yet, so it was convenient to hold meetings at obvious places that everyone could find. Criminals felt reassured that the meetings took place in public places. Often the Cartel reps were meeting gangs from Eastern Europe, representatives from biker gangs, such as the Hell's Angels and the Outlaws, and 'gypsy' traffickers from Romania and Bulgaria, all of whom could be violent and unpredictable. The Hell's Angels control much of the transport from Holland to the UK and are also involved in firearms. A bohemian coffee shop became another a favourite for Cartel foot soldiers; Irish pubs on Warmoesstraat were also good. The Cartel workers are invariably simple creatures with unsophisticated tastes who more often than not behave like lads on a stag do than international drug dealers. Of course, none of the owners of these establishments, nor the staff, knew that illegal activity was going on inside their premises.

Amsterdam is also close to the UK, and this is the big advantage for British criminals. One Cartel hitman and drug dealer known as the Moviestar said that he preferred doing deals in Holland, as opposed to Spain and Portugal, because it was within driving distance of Liverpool. The Moviestar was a career Cartel hitman who'd killed more than ten marks. From the age of 14, the Moviestar carried out his targeted killings. The first one happened in London when he assassinated a Turkish drug boss. He went on to carry out several more, including at least three in Amsterdam.

The Moviestar said, 'I was on the run from the police in Britain so I ended up in Amsterdam. I liked it because I could get someone to drive my kids over from Liverpool to meet me and it would only take a few hours door to door. It was also easy for me to blend in, especially if you moved out of the centre of Amsterdam to smaller towns like Haarlem, where there was a big ethnic community, so you get lost amongst the Turks and the Caribbeans.

'We never used to shop in Amsterdam, because we suspected Merseyside Police or their Dutch liaisons had the Marks & Spencer staked out. Nearly every major Liverpool drug dealer shopped in there, because they missed home. We started driving out to M&S shops in other towns and then we settled on Haarlem.

'Holland is also an easy place to live: there are lots of sports going on, so on your day off you can go rally driving, or scuba diving or get a martial arts lesson – I got into all three.'

The international community welcomes the British, according to Dutch police. One of the 'problems' is that the Dutch are too friendly with other nations, more tolerant than most – there are over 200 nationalities in Amsterdam. By staying under the radar, not falling out with anyone, paying the rent on time and not getting involved in other forms of crime, such as robbery and fraud, some UK drug dealers have stayed in the Dam for years without being noticed. The facilitators, who act as letting agents providing safe houses, are prepared to take cash payments. According to the Dutch police, the fixers have been key to the Cartel's success. Usually the fixers are Dutch nationals, more often than not a single individual who has personally been involved in crime. In prison, they have made contacts with British criminals, identified their needs and realised they could make just as much money from being a 'fixer' for a cash-rich Cartel as from being actively involved in crime.

For instance, by renting one property, the facilitators get the standard one month's rent up front as a fee. On average, that is 1,000 to 2,000 euros. But the British tend to like bigger houses – newer and more luxurious properties that cost more. They pay bonuses for houses with garages, that are either underground or connected to the property, so that they cannot be seen unloading contraband from their cars. So these properties are even more expensive and are a rich vein of specialist income that has been mined by the fixers.

Many of the Cartel employees want a second, totally separate safe house from their main residence specifically to house contraband, or a second property that could be used by their criminal associates. The high demand for extra safe houses meant that fixers could make even more money. Amsterdam police have also noticed that the British criminals tend to move around more frequently than criminals of different nationalities do, so the fees keep coming. They claim that the role of Amsterdam's small army of fixers in helping the Cartel grow and do business cannot be underestimated.

Officer 17154 explained, 'There are no rules relating to letting agents. You don't need a permit to operate as one, or to rent a property, like you do in other major capital cities. The fixers stay away from smaller properties, because that type of building tends to be regulated, because they are made accessible for poor people. As far as the police are concerned, the facilitators are good starting points for investigating British criminals. If we follow a facilitator then he will lead us to a British criminal.

'For instance, one of these facilitators was a car-rental company. One day it reported a car missing. We tried to find the car, but then that turned into an opportunity to focus our attention onto the company itself. We investigated it and then we found ourselves on the trail of some UK drug dealers. These companies are magnets for criminals. In a lot of car-rental places, if you pay a little more, you can pay in cash.

'In a similar situation, we looked into a corrupt housing agent and we found a property linked to a suspect in a killing.'

By using painfully simple investigative policing, such as following fixers, the Dutch police have arrested several high-profile Cartel dealers and their associates. Peter 'Fatso' Mitchell was an Irish drug dealer with close links to the Cartel. He had hidden out near Liverpool while on the run. After being shot in Spain, he fled to Amsterdam to lie low. SOCA wanted him badly, and it didn't take long for Amsterdam police to flush him out. Officers traced Mitchell through a housing agent.

Officer 17154: 'We were checking a housing agent and found Mitchell. We found him visiting a property that we'd already linked to another big drug dealer.'

Mitchell and a number of other foreign nationals were watched as they came and went from the estate agency. The police had wanted Mitchell for years. He was a close friend of Brian Meehan, who was serving a life sentence in connection with the murder of journalist Veronica Guerin. When stopped by the JIT's Tactical Investigations police posing as routine traffic cops, Mitchell handed them a false passport. A second man in the car produced a passport that belonged to Mitchell's brother. They were asked to step out of the car, but within seconds Mitchell had pulled his companion back inside and sped off, pursued by detectives. Mitchell drove the car up one-way streets at speeds of up to 100 kilometres an hour; two guns were allegedly thrown from the vehicle and later recovered.

Officer 17154 added: 'He got out and we chased him. He eventually stopped and we found him. A gun was lost by one of the criminals during the chase. He ran to get rid of the gun.'

The career criminal was arrested and charged with possession of two guns. He had more than 8,000 euros of cash in his pocket. However, he was later cleared on a technicality: the elite cops who'd first stopped him had posed as traffic police, which was against procedure. Despite the setback, the Tactical Investigations unit weren't bothered. The message was now clear. Amsterdam was no longer a soft touch for drug dealers.

On another occasion, increased cooperation between the Dutch and Britain's SOCA led to the arrest of three Britons who were plotting to take at least two people hostage over a Cartel drug deal gone wrong. The UK nationals had 'extremely violent reputations', according to SOCA. Nine people were eventually pulled up in Amsterdam, including four Dutch citizens and a Colombian. Three firearms were seized in the investigation.

The Joint Investigation Team also became good at following the money – and there was certainly a lot of money to follow. By 2009, nearly 20 per cent of the GDP of the European top 15 member states was dirty money that had been laundered by criminal gangs. Between 2 and 4 per cent of the world's total worth was estimated to have come from criminal sources. The Cartel were still relying on hawala bankers. In 2009, two money washers were jailed after meeting in a Tesco car park to launder more than £300,000 in cash through a Bradford money sender.

In Liverpool, numbers of a different kind were worrying the economists. The ranks of the gangs began to swell as large numbers of working-class males were thrown onto the dole and joined their underclass pals in gangs and crime. In Norris Green, the Bowly, a subsidiary of the Strand Gang, was made up of out of work builders and factory workers. By July 2009, the credit crunch was hitting home. There were 21,536 unemployed people in Liverpool, a rate of 7.6 per cent, compared with a national average of 4.1 per cent. Like always, the Cartel were hovering, waiting to take advantage.

CHAPTER 40

NICKY AYERS

2010

Justice-wise, Kallas was living on borrowed time. By rights, he should have been in jail in both Britain and Spain – simultaneously. His life was becoming a tangled mass of international warrants, bail applications and new police investigations popping up from nowhere like court summons. This was police disruption writ large: determined and focussed harassment and interdiction of Kallas by coordinated law enforcement on a pan-continental scale. Admittedly, the charges didn't relate to massive drug dealing, but as part of the new disruption policy, Merseyside Police were settling for anything and everything on Kallas, settling for Level 1 crime, such as the affray outside the Palm Sugar Lounge in Liverpool during which ashtrays and chairs were thrown, in a bid to keep him under pressure and off their manor. However, by paying his top-end lawyers well and by paying off witnesses and intimidating them, Kallas was tap-dancing through the raindrops. He was still walking the streets and telling everyone how it was.

By now, Kallas was earning millions of pounds, but he couldn't help getting involved in petty disputes: it was his nature; the gang mentality still ran strong within him. When he should have been comfortably strolling around the golf courses of southern Spain or sitting in his mate's yacht in the Med, Kallas was bouncing round the streets of Liverpool like the rooting-tooting super scally he was. His old enemy Nicky Ayers was out of jail after serving a six-year sentence for drug smuggling into Jersey. It was only a matter of time before an excuse was found to lock horns. Some of the opportunities for guerrilla war were provided by the holy grail of gangster sport: Sunday league football.

Sunday league football had long been established in inner cities, but violent behaviour often surrounded the matches, such as boxing, martial arts and shooting. Grudge matches between rival pubs had turned into arenas where disputes were settled. The sidelines were filled with rows of police vans and anti-riot cops instead of the supporters. Armed response vehicles were parked in nearby streets just in case they were needed.

In March 2010, Kallas went to war with drug dealer Nicky Ayers. Ayers wasn't in Kallas's league, but he could give him a run for his money. The problems between them had started a few years earlier, when Ayers had been a contender for Kallas's title of top dog of the new generation of teenage killer. Ayers had the balls to have rivalled Kallas. But as he was jostling for position within the new gang scene, Ayers was cut short in his prime. Six years earlier he had been one of the most feared figures amongst the new leaders. But in November 2004 he was thrown in jail unexpectedly after being caught in connection with 3,875 Ecstasy tablets and 30 kilos of cannabis on its way into the island state of Jersey. Now that he was out, Ayers got stuck into the two things he loved most in the world: footballs and gangsters. He became manager of the Western Approaches FC, a footy team run out of a Norris Green pub frequented by some of the city's most feared underworld extremists. However, the pub also had a more glamorous clientele, including Wayne Rooney's dad and, occasionally, the area's most famous scion himself. Sometimes, Ayers combined both of his passions at the same time. Twice he was linked to incidents where guns were pulled at Sunday league football matches.

Then an incident occurred which seemed to sum up the cold, cruel code that the new generation lived by, one that seemed more at home in a Nazi death squad than on the streets of Britain in the new millennium. The act was barbaric and brutal in the extreme. The use of a mobile phone to exacerbate the pain felt by the victim exemplified how new technology was being used to bully remotely, to transmit suffering over a distance so that the impact was multiplied.

One spring day, Kallas decided to track down Ayers and chop him up so that he wouldn't have a chance to fight back. He chose a samurai sword for the job. He knew where to find Ayers. The footy team Ayers managed, the Western Approaches, had an important fixture with another pub called the Britannia VNC. Kallas stormed into the pitchside changing rooms in a bid to strike Ayers unawares. A fight ensued, but Ayers and his brother escaped. Several members of Ayers's gang joined in the fray. One of them fired a gun at Kallas from a white Transit, to cover Ayers's escape, before fleeing the scene himself.

Soon after midday, the area was swamped with police. Witnesses told officers that shots had rung out from the white van in the car park, but thankfully no one was hit. Crowds that had gathered on the fields hoping to watch an under-12s' football match on a neighbouring pitch were dispersed. The referee chose to abandon the game: a decision that was becoming all too common. Gang warfare was affecting the community directly.

As usual, Kallas was arrested on suspicion of affray. As usual, he was questioned. As usual, he went through the motions: a 'no comment' interview. Then, as usual, he was released on police bail. Members of Kallas's gang immediately plotted revenge on Ayers. They couldn't find him, but they did spot an acquaintance of his walking his dog and watching a Sunday league football team. They believed the dog owner to be the member of Ayers's gang who'd shot at Kallas from the white transit van, enabling Ayers to escape. Kallas's foot soldiers stopped the car, dognapped the one-year-old black and white Staffordshire bull and sped off. Later, they phoned the owner and told him to listen. The gang tied the animal to a post. Then they poured petrol on it. Then, laughing like hyenas, they set the dog on fire, forcing the owner to listen to it scream in pain as the flames engulfed it. Later, the dog was found burned to near-death on a playing field. Residents ran to help the dog, but a vet had to put her down because the burns were so severe. Angry residents labelled those responsible as 'not human'.

Police launched a full alert, staking out that weekend's amateur football matches to stop any reprisal attacks. The dog's owner was arrested on suspicion of having the gun used in the shooting. He was later released on bail.

Meanwhile, Merseyside Police were determined to keep up the pressure. Increased resources were ploughed into post-conviction measures, such as asset recovery, in a bid to squash Cartel members out of existence. Terence Riley, who as a boy had discovered the body of murdered toddler James Bulger and later turned to drug dealing, was given another 18 months on top of his sentence after failing to pay back £30,000 of his ill-gotten gains.

Even if villains were already inside, the police still attacked them voraciously, loading them up with extra charges in a bid to make sure they never got out. It was now total war. The reasoning was simple: if the police could annihilate the current generation of villains, there was less risk of them corrupting younger people. The police wanted to break the cycle of generational crime.

In 2010, then 28-year-old Andrew McIntyre was leader of a street gang called the Baker's Green Boys. He was already in jail for armed robbery, but the police weren't happy. They went after a conviction for drug dealing to keep him there, and bingo! They managed to get a whopping 23 years added to his sentence. He was also found guilty of running a firearms business from prison, using smuggled mobile phones. The drugs conviction was very important. The sale of green skunk cannabis was now becoming the staple of street gangs' business, whether the Cartel bosses liked it or not. Teenagers could become extremely rich without having to rely on the patronage of a godfather to serve them up with imported cocaine, just by selling the less profitable and more readily available homegrown skunk cannabis. This represented freedom for the street gangs. The *Liverpool Echo* reported that DI Bill Stupples of Merseyside Police's drug support team said that cannabis was now the 'ATM for organised crime'.

Despite having the upper hand in the gang war, Kallas kept up the hunt for Nicky Ayers. Less than a month after burning one of Ayers's dogs alive, Kallas's gunmen found their man. They tracked him down to a house linked to a family member.

When Ayers appeared at the address just after midnight, a gun was fired at him at close range. At least three bullets hit home into the victim's body.

Almost immediately, Kallas was pulled in and quizzed by police. But, as usual, he said nothing, answering questions with a barrage of 'no comments', 'no replies', yawns and snarls and was, as usual, out on bail again within a few hours.

Instead of lying low, Kallas continued to wage war against his enemies. This time it was a local boxer called Lee Siner who'd upset him and his henchman Sidious. Sidious had split up from his starlet girlfriend, who had by then told the newspapers that he'd been beating her up for years. Sidious was angry. One night, he and Kallas masked up and ran into a restaurant where their new enemy Siner had been spotted eating a meal. Sidious hit Siner with a metal car lock and Kallas piled in with his trademark samurai sword. Sidious got eight and half years in jail. Kallas went on the run to Spain and Amsterdam.

An underworld source said, 'Kallas is on his toes in Holland. He got off after an incident involving a samurai sword in a restaurant. Lee Siner wouldn't say nothing to the police when he was quizzed even though he was injured quite badly, so he wouldn't give a statement naming Kallas. Hence Kallas got away with it again. There's no benefit for the police in getting a warrant, or even getting him back from Holland, because they haven't got enough evidence. If they brought him back, he'd be out on bail and back on the street here. While he's on his toes, he's somebody else's problem. There's no end in bringing him back.'

This was now the tacit policy of Merseyside Police with regards to its most dangerous key impact players: to let them leave the city until the police were certain of a conviction. No more disruption. No more 'no comment' interviews. No more bail. They would give Kallas enough rope abroad, let him think that he was safe. They would wait until they got him on a big one and pot him off for 40 years.

CHAPTER 41

THE COFFEE SHOP CONNECTION

2010

Over the past 15 years, the Russians, Albanians and Yugoslavs had assassinated a string of Amsterdam-based godfathers. Despite this, when asked who they thought the most ruthless gang was now, the Amsterdam police were clear. It was the British.

To know their number-one enemy, the Amsterdam police began profiling British criminals in the same way that the FBI profiles serial killers. In Amsterdam, the Joint Investigation Team have taken to studying the lifestyle patterns of Cartel drug dealers to make it easier to identify and catch them, right down to the specific types of property that the Cartel dealers choose to live in. Ten or fifteen years ago, the drug dealer's property of choice was a large, isolated dwelling in the countryside, more often than not within the commuter belt surrounding Amsterdam, so it was close enough to get in and out of the city for meetings, but far enough away so as not to attract heat from the police and other rival gangs. A good example was the kind of HQ that Curtis Warren chose when he set up base in Holland in 1995/1996. The Cartel drug lord chose to live in a converted barn hidden within a rural village called Sassenheim. The outhouses were used to accommodate criminal associates, guns and drugs. Warren had chosen the property because it was surrounded by miles of flat land that he could survey constantly using binoculars and telescopes. However, the reasoning wasn't always 100 per cent logical. Warren might have been surveillance-aware, but he wasn't socially aware. He never stopped to think that the presence of around ten hardened criminals from the north-west of England, who liked prostitutes and fast cars, in a middle-class area of a northern European country, might arouse the suspicion of well-heeled neighbours. It did, and in 1996 the property was hit by a SWAT team who found piles of guns and drugs lying around like furniture.

But in 2010, the Cartel's new generation preferred new-build, self-contained flats in big developments where they could get lost in the crowd. The tactical team's Officer 17154 said that nearly all of the British criminals they had arrested in recent years had lived in new apartments in big residential complexes. The reasons were simple. They liked to feel they were getting lost in the crowd, living like young men would in a city – it was what they were used to back in the UK. However, the densely populated complexes were deceptively private and ideal criminal safe houses. In the day, most other residents were at work. In the night, they kept themselves to themselves in their flats. The communal spaces were always eerily quiet. Drug dealers could move contraband from underground car parks to their premises in private lifts and fire escapes. This information might seem mundane, but it helped to profile the new generation – and it helped the SWAT teams to plan for more urban raids involving fighting in a built-up area.

In Amsterdam, the swift actions of the JIT and close cooperation stopped a gangland massacre from taking place. Two rival factions of the Cartel had fallen out and the two Mr Bigs in charge of the gangs were planning to kill each other. A Liverpool criminal called Paul Woodford was in charge of one side, and he was accompanied by an associate called Marcus Swan. Intelligence linked the crew, which included a total of four Merseysiders, to an underworld feud that had long been simmering back home in Liverpool. The gang were planning a string of executions across the Dutch capital. However, SOCA found out about the lot and tipped off the JIT.

Officer 17154: 'We intervened quickly and found the weapons that they were going to use. Paul Woodford was "most wanted" – there was a European Arrest Warrant out for him – and he had a criminal history, so we knew that we had

220

the right man. But there were others in the apartment who we didn't know as well. As usual, they had lots of false documents on them. They weren't using their own names on their passports and driving licences, and they were really good ones. During the raid, they were really calm, especially a man called Marcus Swan.

'At first, Swan thought he was going to slip through the net. I almost felt sorry for him – he stupidly thought we didn't know who he really was, but SOCA had sent me a picture of him earlier. We'd got the intelligence from the UK, so I had ID'd him immediately but didn't say so at first. As we were looking around the apartment, I think they knew that we knew. But it was good for them: instead of being on gun and conspiracy charges, they would have been facing murder charges. If we hadn't found them first, then later we would have found the corpses of their victims.'

Luckily, the success of the case had rested on good intelligence from the British police, along with solid paperwork in the form of a European Arrest Warrant (EAW). On another occasion, the Amsterdam police found a senior Cartel killer by accident.

'Often, it's just luck,' continued Officer 17154. 'We might just stumble on a British criminal when we get called out to deal with another incident, such as a domestic. That happened recently: we got called out to a man who had been beating up his wife. It turned out to be an Englishman who was wanted in the UK.'

The scenario was textbook disruptive policing, the kind that Merseyside Police had been banging on about for years. Level 3 international criminals almost always let themselves down by indulging in Level 1 crimes. That isn't to trivialise domestic violence; it's merely to point out that international drug dealers were criminals through and through who would just as easily get involved in assault and theft as cocaine trafficking because they had criminal minds. But one thing was for sure: Amsterdam police believed British drug dealers were as ruthless as the Russian mafia and the Turkish Connection in the way they killed people.

Officer 17154 said, 'Most of the Brits we go after are already wanted criminals. They are in Amsterdam with a purpose, and it's all about drugs. The disputes between them revolve around territory, shipments and ripping each other off. For instance, in this case the man we picked up for domestic violence was also wanted in connection with the murder of an innocent man. The victim had a sister who was involved in drugs. A load of drugs went missing. The criminals came to his house, but the sister wasn't in, so they killed the brother to make their point.

'I think the British criminals are ruthless. That said, if they know that we know who they are, then they will be ruthless in coming after us. The same thing would happen to us: they would kill us. It's especially a great hazard for the uniformed cops. When one of our guys turned up to the domestic violence incident, they were attacked by the man – really abused – just because he checked the suspect's ID and the man was backed into a corner. It turned out he was a convicted murderer – and one of Liverpool's most wanted. If you back them into a corner, they will kill you. They trust in false documents, but once that stops working, they turn to violence.'

The Joint Investigation Team have to be cautious. Sometimes they have to play soft in order not to provoke the wrath of Cartel drug dealers. They let the criminals' lies wash over them, using a kind of stoical indifference as a disengagement tool. Other times, they play very hard and call in a SWAT team to stop any messing around.

Officer 17154 said, 'Sometimes we arrest a British criminal and we know who he really is, but we don't let on. We say, "If you are saying you are such and such, then you are such and such." It's not worth challenging them, because we know they will be violent. It's a case of: get them back to the station and then confront them within a controlled environment. Of course, if we get the SWAT team there, we can do the checks there and then. The SWAT are really good and fast. If we think the area needs a tactical team, then we go to the public prosecutor and argue that it's much safer if the SWAT team make the arrest.'

CHAPTER 42

DYLAN PORTER

2010

In August 2010, Dylan Porter was finally released from prison after serving 11 years of a 21-year sentence for heroin dealing. He was still very bitter, blaming his former fellow dealer Cagey for grassing him up. The episode had given him a pathological hatred of police informants. During his time in jail he had stayed clear of the Cartel's two most notorious 'snitches': John Haase and Paul Bennett.

Dylan Porter said, 'In jail, I never went near Haase and Bennett. I stayed well clear of them even though we were in the same nicks on occasion. Even before I went inside, when I was at it, I stayed away from that rat bastard Paul Grimes. I didn't know he was a grass.

'I was grassed up by a lad called Cagey. On the day I got out, lo and behold, he was waiting for me. I shook his hand and looked him in the eye and I knew he was the grass. I didn't hold back. I said, "How come you left me to rot?"

'He said, "I got nicked with Curtis and got three years."'

Cagey was referring to a drugs plot involving Curtis Warren for which he had been charged and sent to prison. But Dylan wasn't looking for excuses.

Dylan said, 'I probed him again. "But Cagey, you haven't even sent me a stamp when I was in jail, or even been to see my bird, to see if she needed anything." I wanted compensation. "Have you got any dough on you now?" I asked him. Cagey emptied his pockets and handed over a few hundred pounds.

'Now I don't do no graft cos I'm too scared of losing my

kids. Of course, in the first few days after I got out, all the lads came round to see me, throwing money at me, trying to tempt me into doing deals with them, wanting me to get back into that life. You've got to remember, I'm still very useful to them, basically for two reasons: first, because I know people all over the world and throughout the prison system. Those are still useful contacts for them to buy gear from and sell to. Second, I have served a long prison sentence and not said a word to the authorities, so everyone knows I'm staunch. They are very valuable commodities in that world. If I wanted to, and my wife gave me permission to leave home for six months, I could get off somewhere, start doing graft again and make millions.'

Crucially, Dylan made contacts in the world's number-one emerging market for cocaine: Brazil. Huge amounts of cheap cocaine paste are smuggled into the country every year. Brazil is boxed in on its western border by the four biggest cocaine producers on Earth: Colombia, Venezuela, Peru and Bolivia. However, as outlined earlier, the trade is increasingly controlled by the Mexican drug cartels who have migrated from Central America to South America to dominate producers and traffickers. The point is that much cheaper cocaine can be bought in Brazil and shipped to the UK.

Dylan explained, 'I could go and see a mate of mine in Brazil, and then there are some Americans I know. Through them, I could throw a parcel over to Spain and make fortunes. But now I would never dream of doing that. I can't risk going back to jail, even for ten or twenty million. Me being in jail had a bad effect on my kids. While I was away, my lad got kicked out of school when he was 13. He had nothing going for him. But now I'm back, it's a different story. He's doing great again. He's got a job as a joiner, up at 6.30 a.m. every day, and he's got a girlfriend. My little daughter is in drama school. It would be impossible to keep that happening if I was to go back to jail. I have to be there for my family – and that is the greatest deterrent against crime.'

CHAPTER 43

IRISH EYES

2010

By 2010, the cooperation between Amsterdam police and British forces had reached unprecedented levels. SOCA not only shared intelligence with the JIT but also its best officers and latest technology. A whopping 23 British fugitives were arrested in 18 months, many of them paid-up members of the Cartel. In Amsterdam, the Cartel was on the run. They no longer felt relaxed in the city that houses the world's international stock market for drugs. To keep up the pressure, in a bid to turn the attack into a full-scale rout, the cross-Channel cop alliance launched a new raft of guerrilla tactics. The Dutch and UK officers felt confident enough to mount random stop and searches on Amsterdam's streets, to let the British criminals know that they could no longer feel safe wandering around disguised as tourists. SOCA brought over its latest hand-held wireless devices, which could check fingerprints, passports and criminal records on the spot.

Officer 17154 said, 'We started to take the fight to the British criminals by literally going looking for them in the pubs. SOCA have got an electronic fingerprint reader – the SOCA officers come with us – which can identify in real time by scanning a suspect's fingerprints on the spot in a bar. The information is then beamed back to the UK. It takes 60 seconds to get a result, so if we get a match with a wanted man, we can arrest him there and then.

'We've also got a mobile passport reader, which scans the

barcode on a UK passport and beams it back to the UK Border Agency, which then tells us whether the information is correct or whether the passport is forged.

'The operations are effective, but there are weaknesses. As far as suspects are concerned, it's only voluntary, so we cannot order people to give us their prints if they don't want to. But sometimes that doesn't matter: they'll agree to go ahead anyway in order not to arouse suspicion. In any case, the point is that it is very visible policing, so everyone in Dam Square knows that we are now checking them out. We are not passive.'

Like London, Amsterdam is home to crime groups from all over the world. The Chinese Triads are there in force, but the police rarely see them in public, despite officers knowing that they are involved in human trafficking. The Albanian mafia are much more visible and make no secret of the fact that they are involved in human trafficking, dealing cocaine and prostitution. The Amsterdam police describe the Albanians as 'hostile' in that they fight viciously with each other and are ready to shoot first and faster at other outside gangs. Then there are Turkish crime groups and Moroccans who have been in Amsterdam for 40 years or more and supply cannabis to coffee shops and far beyond.

Amid the United Nations of crime, there are the Dutch crime groups. The local mobs have produced several low-key godfathers over the years. Three of the main players were shot and killed in the 1990s and early 2000s by Yugoslavian gangs. Unusually, the native Dutch criminals don't mind international criminal gangs muscling in on their turf. Nor do they want to control the hierarchy citywide, unlike British criminals back in Britain, such as those involved in the Cartel.

'We are tolerant as a people,' said Officer 17154, 'and that is reflected in the nature of our criminals. If an Albanian or Turk gives a Dutch criminal two kilos of coke, then the Dutch guy says, "We are now friends." They agree to work the territory together. They are cooperative and disapprove of disagreements because it prevents the smooth flow of things. We don't have gangs in Holland, except in the south-eastern part of Amsterdam. Everything is about cooperating with each other.

But the British are completely different. The British and the Dutch criminals have totally differing views on how to run things.'

The relaxed nature of the homegrown Dutch mafia has allowed the Brits, particularly the ambitious leaders of the Cartel, to take over. The British love hierarchies. Their aggressive, intrusive and competitive attitude is a reflection of the 'Anglo-Saxon' model of capitalism in which they were brought up. Anglo-Saxon economies are free market economies that encourage individualistic bargaining, with less cooperation and more of a 'dog-eat-dog' approach. This type of capitalism is prevalent in English-speaking countries and the USA. European countries have tended to opt for social market economies, also known as Rhine capitalism and welfare capitalism. This type is characterised by more collective bargaining, cooperation and stability, and less speculation. But the big problem for the police is simple. For the most part, British criminals look like well-off western Europeans. They don't look like the rough, tough Albanians or Russians, and they know how to blend in to their surroundings, like chameleons.

Officer 17154 said, 'The British always want to play the biggest part in an organised-crime network, and in Amsterdam they have succeeded. They get involved in their operations more than other gangs, and they are involved in everything: money laundering, killings, drugs, weapons . . . They are higher up the ladder than other gangs, but they are difficult because you can't see them. Our relationship with SOCA is unique; that is what is helping to fight them. We don't have that bond with any other country, except Turkey. The British police bring their legal requests and information to us. They request that we do some investigating, and we do it because we respect the UK police, we know what they are telling us is correct and we know this because the British police are successful at fighting crime. The fact that the British criminals are here in Amsterdam in the first place is testament to the success of the UK police at driving them out of their own country and giving them nowhere to run. So they come here. The British police really do try to catch criminals, which is not always true when you look at forces from other countries.

SOCA show more determination: it's that simple. Therefore we want to help.'

Officer 17154 added, 'You only have to look at a case of Paul Woodford, the Liverpool guy who we arrested for guns. He was one of six criminals from rival drug gangs from Liverpool, who were arrested in Amsterdam, where they wanted to fight matters out. In their dwellings we recovered three automatic rifles, a revolver, a pistol and ammunition.

'Half of the drugs on the streets of Liverpool are from Amsterdam, and the Amsterdam police have the Liverpool gangs, who are building up their empires in the city, as one of their top targets.'

John 'the Coach' Traynor was a 65-year-old Irish career criminal who'd been on the run all over Europe for 15 years, on and off. Traynor had fled Ireland in 1995 after being linked to the assassination of Irish journalist Veronica Guerin. Traynor was old-school rough; he smoked and drank heavily and sported worn-out tweed jackets. A good all-rounder, Traynor managed to stay on the run because he had money coming in from bearer-bond fraud, prostitution, drug smuggling and money laundering. Though he had links with the Irish National Liberation Army, Traynor had better contacts in the Cartel in the UK and Amsterdam. After first spending time in Spain and Portugal, Traynor ended up in Amsterdam in the mid 1990s. However, it wasn't long before he was picked up. In 1997, he was arrested by the Dutch police with Brian Meehan, who had ridden the motorbike when Guerin was killed. The police were forced to release Traynor without charge because of a lack of evidence. The *politie* were angry and vowed to get him again.

By the late 2000s, there was renewed interest in Traynor as the level of cooperation between British and Dutch police continued. SOCA announced a zero-tolerance policy to criminals that were on the run from the UK and hiding in Holland. An outstanding arrest warrant for Traynor dating back to 1992 was resurrected. He had absconded from Highpoint Prison while serving a seven-year sentence for a big fraud.

SOCA had also picked up intelligence that Traynor was

hiding out in Amsterdam. He'd been heard on wiretaps talking to Cartel drug dealers on the phone. In Amsterdam, Traynor was acting as a Mr Fix-it for expat Cartel mobsters. He regularly met the Scousers in Chinese restaurants in the red-light district.

More information had been gleaned from a previous Dutch–UK operation the year before. When Irish criminal Peter 'Fatso' Mitchell had been arrested in 2009 because of his connection to an underworld property agency, the Dutch and SOCA had continued to investigate the people around him. Mitchell wriggled out of the charges on a technicality, after claiming that the officers who had 'routinely' stopped him for a traffic offence were in fact JIT specialist cops disguised as beat cops. But it didn't matter: British police knew that Mitchell would lead them to Traynor. And he did. It was just a matter of time before the police joined up all the dots from the wiretaps and the Mitchell case and closed in on Traynor.

SOCA put a man under surveillance who they thought was Traynor, but they couldn't identify him for sure. In addition, they couldn't just pick him up on a hunch, as that would be against Dutch law. Instead they waited for him to make a small mistake, which would give their officers an excuse to check his fingerprints on the spot with a handheld fingerprint machine.

On 24 August 2010, Traynor was driving through the Amstelveen area of the Dutch capital without a care in the world. He was stopped for a traffic violation: once again, an example of a disruption tactic, stopping for a Level 1 offence in the hope of bagging a Level 3 suspect. However, the Dutch police had to be doubly careful that they didn't break any rules, as the example of Mitchell slipping away had demonstrated. So they had to sit back and wait until normal cops stopped him for genuine reasons. In days gone by, Traynor would have been given a ticking off by the traffic cops, but now they were trained to routinely check whether driving licences were fraudulent. It turned out that the convicted fraudster was using a driving licence in the name of a well-known Amsterdam-based Dublin-born drug dealer. Then when Traynor's prints were sent back to the UK for on-the-spot verification, it gave a positive ID and he was arrested.

Officer 17154 explained, 'That's how we got the old guy John Traynor. In 1997, we'd let him go. We found him back again in 2010 and picked him up under an EAW. We get a lot of information through wiretaps. A lot of the people talking are from Liverpool – you hear the accents. We recognise the accents because some of the officers from SOCA are from Liverpool and also talk like that. Though SOCA is a national police organisation, it's the SOCA officers from London and Merseyside that are our main contacts.'

It turned out that John 'the Coach' Traynor was carrying the driving licence of a close associate of Peter 'Fatso' Mitchell. Astonishingly, during a follow-up search of Traynor's Amsterdam apartment, Mitchell himself was found lounging in the living room. Garda and criminal sources said that Traynor had been travelling regularly between southern Spain, Amsterdam and Brussels to organise large-scale cannabis deals. Security sources said that the owner of the driving licence was a trusted associate of Mitchell who forged a close relationship with 'the Coach' during their self-imposed exile.

Merseyside Police were determined to close down another of the Cartel's communication networks. The 'easy graft' phenomenon, whereby Cartel criminals would jump on a budget flight to Holland to meet other drug dealers at football matches and parties, was well known. SOCA were tipped off and went to work on it.

Officer 17154 said, 'By doing this, we hope that we're disrupting big smuggling networks, but we don't get any feedback. With SOCA, we keep an eye on the movements of British criminals coming over to go to football matches and parties. Then we try to find out if they are travelling on false documents. We single them out for more attention, which we hope will snowball into an investigation that leads to an arrest.

'We also work with SOCA in Rotterdam, the Hague and a couple of other places where there are major investigations. The UK criminals have one or two connections in these places. A lot of the drugs traffic goes by train, car, boat and air. The British collect their cocaine, heroin and Ecstasy together in

Holland, and then put it together in groupage. They use mules and Dutch transport to get the drugs back to the UK, through Belgium and Rotterdam mainly. But one thing is true no matter where: the Brits want control from A to Z.'

CHAPTER 44

THE FARLEYS

2010

Paul Merkelbach was a typical Dutch villain: laid-back, accommodating, unaggressive – but he also had great contacts for buying Class A drugs who weren't too stressful to deal with and who he was prepared to share with anyone who cared to buy. Merkelbach wasn't even a proper drug dealer. Until recently he'd been a sewer pipe repairman who spent his days getting his hands dirty in underground tunnels. But he had fallen onto hard times. Now he got his hands dirty in the underworld, and he was good at it.

It wasn't long before he came into contact with representatives of one of the most secretive and professional cells within the Cartel, run by a couple of brothers known as Ian and Alan. Ian Farley was 43 and Alan was 38. They weren't young enough to be members of the new generation of gang members, but they weren't quite old enough to be part of the old-guard godfathers. They were kind of in the middle, combining the best and worst of both worlds. On the one hand, they were extremely violent and unpredictable and not afraid to take on the new generation. On one occasion, when a young pretender had tried to blackmail a rich friend who enjoyed their protection, they dealt with him violently. But the Farleys had also learned wisely from the old hands. They were very low-key. The only hint to their hidden wealth was a Mercedes C-Class with an '09 plate, driven by Alan Farley. But even that purchase was well thought through. It wasn't exactly a standout car where he lived, in a suburb called Crosby. Unlike many of their rivals, the Farleys didn't flash the cash and rarely brought trouble to their own door through violence and guns, which they used sparingly but effectively behind the scenes. They left others to show off in Prada puffer jackets, £100-a-head meals were avoided and fancy hotel meets were frowned upon. Trademark tracksuits were the name of the game. Gyms were used as offices, and they ate at a cafe in Anfield owned by their mum. They plotted deals in local pubs with names like The Arkles and The Devonshire.The Farleys were known as 'blenders': they mixed in so that they looked like typical unemployed 30- or 40-somethings. But behind the facade was a serious organised-crime gang being run like a professional business.

To the Amsterdam police, the Farleys were textbook British criminals. Instead of subcontracting the transport of heroin back to the UK to a third party like the Hell's Angels, which was becoming increasingly popular, they insisted on controlling shipments from A to Z. Instead of using the big ports like everyone else, they insisted on using boutique boats and small, off-the-beaten-track harbours. Instead of using a loose arrangement of gang members to ferry parcels, they used a single highly trained, highly trusted courier called Malcolm Lewtas. Everything was tightly controlled.

Detectives believed the Farleys were bringing £2 million of heroin into the country from Holland every fortnight. Though they had got away with grafting for 20 years, they had done so because the police had not been sophisticated enough to catch them. In addition, the Farleys had been clever enough to hide their crimes well. However, now the new scientific approach of Merseyside Police was sensitive enough to pick up the crime footprint they left behind. Police applied a simple technique to gauge how badly the Farleys were affecting the community. The system was called 'organised-crime-group mapping', which gave Cartel gangsters and gangs a score based on the amount of harm they caused within communities. The Farleys came out near the top of the Merseyside map. Under old legislation, they would have been classed as Level 3 criminals: top crooks with international connections and influence. No matter what it took, the Farleys would now have to go. The computer said so.

The police were particularly determined to bring them down. First, officers despised their arrogance. The Farleys thought they were so good that they were untouchable. Second, they were slippery. For more than 20 years, the force had known that the Farley family were up there with the leaders, but they couldn't arrest them. They had defeated police tactics time after time. Their criminal sophistication made it a waiting game. The police took years to work out how they were doing business.

What made it so frustrating was that the Farleys left virtually no criminal footprint. Like most second-generation Cartel bosses, they were clever and did not overtly display their wealth. The money was well hidden. They understood that violence acted like a mini-recession: it sent profits plummeting. They were not stupid and therefore not an overtly violent gang. Surprisingly, the Matrix firearms team couldn't recall a single gun discharge that could be linked to the Farleys. The brothers worked against the police like a terrorist cell. If they saw their people bringing attention on themselves through their activities, be it driving stupidly or being involved with guns, they put a stop to it. That was the nature of modern organised crime. The Farleys were part of a new breed who were aware of disruption. Everyone paid their car tax, stopped at red lights and didn't park on double yellow lines.

In 2009, officers launched Operation Hadley and found out how the Farleys were bringing in drugs from Amsterdam. Shipments were concealed on small boats that were sailed into small harbours. If contraband came by road, it was transported by shady small-time haulage companies that drove along back routes and A roads.

In August 2010, the police in Holland and on Merseyside got wind of a ten-kilo shipment of heroin that their Dutch contact was about to send to the UK. A joint UK–Dutch police operation kicked in. With the assistance of the UK Border Agency, the police were able to trace the package from the moment it left Amsterdam and was taken to Rotterdam before making its way to Britain. The Farleys sent their courier Lewtas down to collect it once it was in the UK. The plan was to sail the shipment from Rotterdam in a small boat to complete the drop-off at Ramsgate Marina. The police took the decision to intercept the parcel in Holland and keep it as evidence, but to do it in secret so as not to alarm the Cartel end. Inside a sports bag, officers in Holland found ten kilos of heroin split into half-kilo bags. Lewtas arrived in Ramsgate as planned to collect a delivery that had already been intercepted by Dutch police. Instead, he was arrested. Back in Amsterdam, the police raided the home of the ex-sewage worker and found another 30 kilos of heroin, which police said would eventually have wound its way to Merseyside. The drugs had a purity of between 60 and 62 per cent.

Lewtas was jailed for seven and a half years for his role as the courier, while Merkelbach was given eleven and a half years. Both the Farleys got fourteen years each.

Merseyside Police were now considered the number-one police force in Europe when it came to investigating drug criminals. They were so good that a new, higher level of classification was being used to describe their capability.

Level 4 grading was part of the Professionalising Investigation Programme (PIP), a standards-raising venture to introduce best practice into forces. PIP trained police officers whose role involved them conducting or managing investigations. Level 4 involved those officers who could handle critical, complex and protracted investigations. The honours fell to senior ranks, such as Heads of Crime, Detective Chief Superintendents and Assistant Chief Constables.

The Analyst said, 'We have officers who have passed the Professionalisation of Investigation Procedures. They brought out a Level 4, which is the strategic coordination of those types of investigations. It's about managing a reactive investigation – for example, a murder hunt – alongside a covert operation. We have proved we can do this over and over again.

'Take the drugs operations into Hibbs-Turner. That was running at the time of the Michael Wright murder. If I was running a murder investigation, I wouldn't normally have access to the covert operation. But we had the experience to be able to bring both strands together. It's how you harmonise them: what's intelligence and what's evidence, and asking yourself, "How do I use both?"'

The pressure was taking its toll on some of the old guard,

such as one of the founding members of the Cartel who had been a close confidant of Curtis Warren and had been involved in huge drug deals. But these days he was trapped in a swarm. The police were on his case and the young gangs were threatening to overrun him. He folded under the stress. He became a heroin addict.

Dylan Porter said, 'After I got out of prison, I saw him – I couldn't believe it. He's on methadone and is just waiting to die. It's crazy how his life has come full circle, from dealer to user, from big shot to no mark.'

After he was released from prison, Dylan wandered the streets in disbelief, amazed at how things had changed since he'd been gangster number one. There was no hierarchy any more. No order. No respect.

Dylan said: 'It's like a stand-off, because everyone has got guns and no one backs down. No one can bully anyone in this city any more. No one can say that they are in charge or that they are going to get the graft organised. It's like anarchy.'

To illustrate the situation, one day Dylan was intimidated by a ten-year-old gang member who treated him as his equal.

Dylan said, 'I was out of prison and enjoying my freedom. I went for a walk in the park. A lad called Little T, who is ten, came up to me and my son in the park and said, "What's happening, lad?" But he wasn't talking to my son: he was addressing me. He was only ten, but he was itching to kill someone. It was frightening.

'If I had money now, I'd move out of Liverpool. I try to keep my kids away from gangs, but the proper feral ones are hard to talk to. Because I got such a massive sentence, people think I'm a big thing that I'm not. People think that I can take on the gangs like I'm a big vigilante or something. One woman came to see me who was getting pressure off the gangs. She wanted me to have a word with one of these gang members, who was looking for revenge after a shooting. But I'm on licence for ten years. It does me head that people think that I've got this big reputation.'

Despite the change in structure and leadership, Dylan Porter said that the Cartel was still flourishing: 'The Cartel is still going. Amsterdam is on top, but they have still got Spain right off. Spain is now key to drug smuggling in Europe, and if you can keep hold of that then you're still top dog. They have managed to stay prominent over there: not because the gangs are killing more people or because they're taking more risks. It's just for the same reasons why they were successful 40 years ago when it started. It's just because they're basically gypsies by nature. They're travellers, in the sense that they relocate quickly. There's no Mr Big any more; it's just loads of different firms doing their own thing. In Spain, there's loads of Russians and Irish, but people still go to see the Scousers if they want gear. There's big firms from Leeds, London, Ireland and Manchester, so the Russians and the Scousers are not prominent in the sense that they've got a monopoly. But the group from Liverpool have been established longer, since at least 1991 in Spain, so people will go to them for work. At present, there's a Huyton firm in Spain that people go to for weed and charlie.

'But it is true that the Scousers are falling out with each other. That is to do with the new generation. They are disruptive and they will shoot first, not knowing that the police will hit their transport to punish them. But the police in general will never stop drugs completely – because you can't stop smuggling, whether it's any commodity: sugar, booze, tobacco. Heroin will die out: young people laugh at the older generation for taking it. I know a 68-year-old workie who snorts it on the way to work like it's going out of fashion. But they are the only people who are taking it now.'

CHAPTER 45

NATIONAL SECURITY

2010

Strategically, the big question was: what direction would the Cartel take now? Clearly, the business wasn't growing as well as it should. Revenue streams were being impeded by a combination of better law enforcement, the disruptive influence of the new gangs and the weakening of key territories, such as Amsterdam.

For the authorities, a big fear was that in response the Cartel would radically change their business model to kick start growth again. Yet the biggest fear of all was that the Cartel would start forging direct links with the Mexican drug lords, in much the same way that they had done with the Colombians in the late 1980s. It seemed like a perfect fit. Collectively, the Mexican cartels were now the number-one crime group in the world. They dominated the export of cocaine from the Americas to Western markets, such as the US and Europe. In December 2010, the Spanish government remarked that Mexican cartels have multiplied their operations in Spain, which had become cocaine's main entry point into Europe.

The link-up between the Cartel and the Mexican mafia looked like a good fit on paper. The new leaders of the Cartel, such as Kallas and the Fraudster, were extremely violent and ruthless – not to the same extent as their Mexican cousins, but they were both cut from the same cloth and were up for new ideas. Both crime groups were led by younger, more ambitious criminals from the new generation. However, there was no official word on a union. Certainly, there was much speculation that the Mexicans and the Cartel were talking and it was known that the Mexican cartels had switched their focus from the US market to Europe. However, the Mexicans' representatives in Amsterdam and Spain were still Colombian and Venezuelan. To place their orders, Kallas and the Fraudster still had to deal with the South Americans. The Mexicans might have taken over production in South America, but they insisted on keeping the old sales force in Europe.

Ambassador Eduardo Tomás Medina-Mora said that there was no evidence of links between the Mexican crime groups and Liverpool crime groups: 'Not from our side anyway,' he said. 'It's total rubbish. Yes, of course Europe is an emerging market for cocaine. But there are two very important markets for cocaine at the moment. Number one is Brazil, because of geography – it's close to production in South America – and because of the rising incomes of its people and relatively weak law enforcement. The coca paste is taken into Brazil; it is not refined into its chloride derivative. In Brazil, it is turned into crack cocaine. They have huge problems related to crack cocaine.'

The cocaine trade is based around volumes, Medina-Mora said. In order to make cocaine trafficking pay, producers have to grow and export thousands of tonnes per year. That means they need access to thousands of hectares of agricultural land that can be sowed now and remain cultivated for years, so as to pay for themselves. That means the land must be cheap and free of any immediate plans for development. In Colombia and Peru, there are still vast regions with a sparse population. Brazil is different. Medina-Mora said, 'It's not impossible to grow coca leaves in Brazil, but there is huge demographic pressure on the land, so that's why it's imported from neighbours.'

Medina-Mora also said, 'The second-largest emerging market is Europe: it's now a target market for drug traffickers. The simple explanation is price. It's all about opportunity cost: how much you pay for the product, and the number of obstacles in between the producer and consumer. Of course, distance is a problem for South America to Europe. But US consumption has essentially levelled off. There's a more noticeable reduction in total volumes. Cocaine has been displaced in the US by other stimulants, such as methamphetamine. Opiate consumption has also picked up and use of marijuana is increasing. Street prices in the US have varied significantly, as new obstacles have been put in the way, such as better law enforcement, and cooperation between Colombia, Mexico and the US. There have been more seizures on the route from Colombia to the US.'

The number of seizures in Central and South America is a direct result of the amount of cooperation between governments and the sharing of intelligence. In 2007/2008, seizures in Mexico far outnumbered those in Colombia. But by 2009/2010, seizures in Colombia increased because Mexico shared intelligence. This was partly to do with the fact that some Mexican criminals had moved south. The Mexican government had been able to identify them and pass the intelligence to Colombia, which could in turn identify the criminals on their own turf.

Medina-Mora explained, 'In the border area of the US, the price of cocaine is $28,000 per kilo, within the wholesale market. The price increases when it gets further into the US, but not dramatically. However, in Europe, the difference is remarkable: the price of a kilo is around 45,000 euros. You get a higher margin in Europe; however, the volumes aren't considerable. For that reason, it's not the main market, but the traffickers can get additional income from marginal sources. It's a much lower margin than in Brazil. But Europe is a most attractive market because it's a young market. Consumption levels are comparatively low. The purity is much less than in the US.'

The low consumption levels, low purity and high price make Europe the number-one growth market for drugs on the planet. It is the continent with the most potential for profit. Top experts used the statistical system of 'prevalence' to find out how common cocaine usage is within a population over a certain period of time. Prevalence is defined as the total number of cocaine users in the population at a given time, or the total number of cases in the population, divided by the number of individuals in the population. Unsurprisingly, cocaine prevalence is higher in the US, probably because of its higher quality, which attracts and keeps users in the market.

However, Medina-Mora added, 'There's a very high prevalence in Spain also: it's the number one per capita consumption in Europe. Prevalence is linked to availability and peer pressure, which boils down to "how cool is this".'

The high usage in Spain might be because the country is the first port of call for cocaine landing in Europe and a large amount might subsequently filter into the local market. But from a marketing point of view that means it's worth targeting Britain until the levels reach that of Spain.

For the Cartel in Liverpool, the growth of the Mexican drug gangs seemed academic. It was thousands of miles away and there was no easy way of getting in touch with the drug lords who mattered. But suddenly, this began to change. According to a Cartel enforcer, British gangs began to meet representatives of the Mexican criminals in Spain, Africa and, of course, Amsterdam. The representatives weren't Mexican nationals, but they claimed to be selling cocaine that was under Mexican control. The first tentative steps were being taken.

CHAPTER 46

THE HUB

2011

The scene looked like the hunt for Osama bin Laden. Shadowy figures in blurry luminous green glided across a night-vision monitor. The buildings behind them sank into total blackness. Heavily armed special forces troops moved in slowly on the property during the early hours. Their polycarbonate body armour gave them the appearance of futuristic warriors; their state-of-the-art assault rifles, bristling with telescopic sights and grenade launchers, were slung into the firing position. They waited for the order to storm through the doors and windows. Then . . . Bang! A flash! The door went in! Soldiers shouted orders to get down!

But this wasn't a Taliban bolthole or an embassy siege. This was a suburban apartment complex in Holland next to a boating lake. The target wasn't an international terrorist but a 'solja' of a kind himself. He was a skinny British criminal with a shaved head who looked like numerous other gang members. In February 2011, 24-year-old Sean Devalda was arrested in Vinkeveen, a small town 18 miles from Amsterdam and famous for its lakes and watersports. Devalda's 1,500-euros-a-month yuppie apartment was raided by the Dutch police's SWAT team. The door was blown off by explosives.

Devalda was wanted for armed robbery. He was just another UK criminal on the run in Holland, but it wasn't the calibre of his criminality that was important: it was the wider propaganda message that his arrest heralded. This was a communication from the Dutch authorities to the UK underworld: Amsterdam was being closed down for business. No matter how big or how small you are, we will come to your door in the middle of the night and take you down.

In addition to noting the fact that British criminals were getting younger, the Dutch police noticed another big change: British drug dealers were evolving. Today they were not so much concerned with smuggling 1,000-kilo loads of cocaine direct from Colombia under their own steam. The new generation of gang members who were taking over had started out as distributors and wanted to remain so: 'Let other gangs bring it in – we just want to trade it.'

Officer 17154: 'British criminals have certain characteristics, which might not be exciting, but they are part of their nature. British criminals tend not to have their noses in the coke, and that means they don't busy themselves with coke laboratories. They are not interested in processing chemicals and so on. They are traders, pure and simple. We see the British criminals as being above the people who own the actual coke labs. The Brits are above the processors in the criminal food chain. They are buying and selling the end products and not getting their hands dirty. The guys who actually make the stuff in the coke labs are Albanians, Yugoslavs or the Turkish, for instance. These non-UK traffickers operate as independent crime groups who themselves import. In Amsterdam today, the British are traders. They try to act as an invisible hand, guiding events from behind the scenes. We see the British cars coming and going from the garages where the coke labs are hidden. Of course, the British are still importing and exporting as well, but that's hard to see.'

The new faces of the Cartel had turned themselves into quick-turnaround, high-volume middlemen: stack 'em high, sell 'em cheap. Of course, they could do the same thing back in the UK on a smaller scale, but why bother when in Holland you could trade in bulk, like a commodities broker on an exchange. If you got caught in the UK, you would receive a heavy sentence; however, in Holland, the outcomes favoured dealers, who got a comparatively lighter sentence for a larger volume of coke – if, by chance, you were caught in the first place. By being so successful in the UK, Merseyside Police had effectively displaced Cartel crime to Holland as villains fled the 20-year sentences that were routinely being handed down at home. In addition, the multimillionaire godfathers were terrified of the Assets Recovery Agency.

Officer 120499 said, 'We have more British criminals living in Amsterdam than any other crime group. Criminals from France and Germany don't tend to stay here and settle down here. They come, do business and then go. British criminals stay because the jail sentences are so light in Holland. If you are caught with one kilo here, it's six months or a year in jail, depending on the circumstances. For one kilo in the UK, it's up to seven years and an unlimited fine.

'The British are not really trouble in a violent sense, because they are higher up the food chain. There are shooting incidents involving the English and Albanians, but it's a lot of work to find out what's behind it. Most of the time, British criminals remain invisible. They are generally between 30 and 50 years of age. They are often older, more mature criminals who have contacts. This means they can introduce other British criminals, and, for that matter, foreigners like the Albanians, to the key players they need to do business with in Amsterdam. They tend to have served a few years in prison back in the UK, then after release they go abroad and end up here. It's a safe haven where they can make a living. When we come across them, they try to be nice guys. They don't act suspiciously at all; they don't want to do anything that draws attention. They only get a little nervous when we approach them, and they know that we know their real identities, or that we simply know they are criminals. But they also know it's hard for us to establish their IDs, or search their vehicles without good reason, or search their property without a warrant.

'But now we have trained our uniformed officers to check the ID of English people routinely, to put their details through the system immediately to see if they are wanted. We can check their details in the UK. From the time it's rung in off the street to the time the UK takes to get back to us, it can only be a matter of minutes – if it's within office hours, that is. We get our uniformed officers to make a report of who was in a particular vehicle that was stopped, then we can find out which known facilitator was behind the car: that is, who has rented the car to them. We find phone numbers. It's disruption, to make them nervous.

'Now I think it's easier to go to Spain; there's too much heat here. Someone has just been arrested in Spain who was wanted here by British police. Sometimes the British criminals kill people – themselves, Albanians, even the Dutch – but when that happens, it involves a lot of drugs or money.'

In Britain, the penalty for possession of cocaine is an unlimited fine and up to seven years in jail. A conviction for trafficking or producing coke is more severe, carrying an unlimited fine and/or life in prison. The way that police forces in the UK deal with drug offenders varies by region. In some cases, a person caught with a small amount of the drug will be cautioned and not arrested. Often, incarceration for use can be avoided by checking into a court-approved cocaine rehab programme. When a drug case does get to court, some jurisdictions are more likely to impose a substantial fine or send the offender to prison.

CHAPTER 47

BAD BEHAVIOUR

2011

Superscallies Kirk Bradley and Tony Downes were typical of the new generation. Both of them were 25. Both of them had skinheads and wore black North Face jackets. For two years, both of them had thrown hand grenades at rivals and shot them up with automatic weapons. The pair went on trial, accused, alongside four others, of being part of a 'criminal team' who used guns and grenades in a two-year 'campaign of violence' against underworld rivals. One of their stashes included an Uzi sub-machine gun, a Browning pistol and a Colt 45, as well as ammunition and hand grenades. The Uzi was one of several seized from gunrunner Steven Greenoe, the ex-US marine who had flooded Merseyside with weapons before he and Liverpool-based accomplice Steven Cardwell were jailed.

When Bradley and Downes were finally caught and put on trial, they cared little. They simply arranged for an armed gang to spring them from the prison van on the way to court. Following standard procedure for criminals, both of them went on the run to Holland. However, both of them were soon captured. The process of finding fugitives in Amsterdam now worked like clockwork. It was almost like shooting fish in a barrel. The police could barely contain their delight.

Ian Milne, Head of European Operations for SOCA, said, 'Like his partner in crime Anthony Downes discovered only a few weeks ago, there is no such place as a safe haven. Kirk Bradley was shocked when officers burst through the door of his luxury apartment in Amsterdam. He had no idea we were on to him.

'Joint working with Merseyside Police and the Amsterdam police has led to the capture of these two violent and dangerous individuals. They are now back behind bars where they belong. This shows that criminals who flee to other countries are not beyond our reach.'

Arno Julsing, Chief of Detectives for the Amsterdam police, said, 'What a successful arrest. The collaboration with our British colleagues has so far been fantastic. Together we have managed to apprehend many dozens of dangerous criminals in the last couple of years. Our approach works and we have found that the number of fugitives hiding in Amsterdam is decreasing. Our message "Amsterdam is not the place to be" has apparently been heard. Those who still don't get it will be traced, arrested and handed over to the British authorities.' The icing on the cake was the fact that both Bradley and Downes were given life sentences.The court heard that the men presided over a 'guns for hire' organisation that carried out contract violence for money.

Meanwhile, drug lord Curtis Warren lost his appeal against some of the evidence used to convict him when he had been arrested in Jersey for a £1 million drugs plot. It had been three and a half years since he had been arrested as he walked along the Channel Island seafront and was later jailed on the strength of wiretap and conspiracy evidence. Warren, who was now 47 and residing in Belmarsh Prison with Islamic terrorists and south-east London's finest, vowed to take his case to the European Court of Human Rights in Strasbourg. His solicitor said he claimed he was being victimised 'because of who he is rather than on the reality of the situation'.

No one could ever accuse the Cartel of not being inclusive. In June 2011, a one-legged father of ten called Vincent Graham was jailed for seven years after pleading guilty to conspiracy to supply Class A drugs. Graham was one of the new generation of independent dealers who had looked for alternative smuggling routes. Amsterdam was getting too hot. Graham had focussed his attention on Africa. Through a Nigerian contact, he was able to get a link up for cocaine from South Africa and open up a supply line. It was a good example of how everyone was becoming more flexible as the old hierarchies broke down. The only problem was the police were getting nimble as well. The job was given to the North West Regional Organised Crime Unit, known as Titan, who surveyed Graham rolling up to do deals in a fleet of flash £35,000 cars.

In Spain, a Cartel smuggler was busted by police after more than £500,000 of cannabis was found stashed in his car. The trafficker was due to board a Plymouth-bound ferry with 171 kilos of cannabis. In Liverpool, a little semi-independent heroin-smuggling firm masterminded by a Liverpool University graduate was jailed for 100 years. Akbar Bukhari was convinced that he would stay below the police's radar by using the Cartel's contacts to smuggle heroin without quite being a full-time member. The former business student used Cartel contacts in Amsterdam to get heroin to Liverpool, where he was partnered up with some local distributors. Bukhari kept the operation at arm's length by doing business in Birmingham, but he got involved in the minutiae by keeping detailed accounting records of sale-or-return transactions. SOCA found the evidence more than helpful when he was caught red-handed during a handover.

An old-school Cartel godfather was facing a retrial after he joined up with a young gang to defeat his rival. However, they went beyond his orders and attacked his rivals with grenades. During the trial of the godfather, the court heard that half of the grenade attacks in the UK had taken place in Merseyside: seven out of fourteen. The case was an example of what happened when the old crime families admitted out-of-control 'youngsters' into their ranks. One of the grenade attacks was orchestrated from prison, and a bomb was left outside former Liverpool manager Kenny Dalglish's house by mistake.

Then came the mysterious case of Brett Flournoy. The background to the case involved senior Cartel members who were desperate to find a smuggling route from Brazil. Brazil was now one of the biggest cocaine markets on the planet. The South American boom economy was the second-biggest importer of Mexican mafia-controlled cocaine. The Cartel had not yet established direct links with the Mexican cartels, but they were prepared to do the second-best thing – buy cocaine from Brazil. Some of the test runs went well, and the Cartel managed to get several parcels muled in by foot-soldier couriers. The Cartel then tried to recruit a cannabis grower called Thomas Haigh, who lived on a remote farm in Cornwall. Haigh didn't want to get involved, despite feeling obliged because he owed the Liverpool drug dealers thousands of pounds. Two Cartel enforcers – Brett Flournoy, 31, and David Griffiths, 35 – were sent down by furious bosses. Haigh believed that these Liverpool bosses, who had ordered the men to look after him, had links with the IRA. Haigh claimed the bosses were part of an IRA-linked gang that 'ran' Liverpool's drugs trade. Later, the Garda investigated the case. They found that Haigh's theory was partly right. The Garda said that the gang who tried to recruit Haigh was a Cartel cell linked to a mixture of Dublin- and Limerick-based associates, some of whom were ex-IRA.

But when Flournoy and Griffiths got there, a group of Hell's Angels were waiting for them. The pair were shot. Their bodies were thrown in a van, burned and crushed with a digger, then buried. The case was very murky and highlighted the growing role played by biker gangs working both for and against the Cartel. The market was breaking up under pressure from young street gangs, and 'independents', such as outlaw motorcycle gangs, were rushing in to fill the vacuum.

The case reignited interest in the links between the Cartel and the IRA. The Irish police confirmed that there were members of one well-known family with both IRA and criminal links in south inner Dublin that had links to drug dealers in Liverpool. These links went back for at least two decades. John Gilligan's name also came up during the investigation. Gilligan's gang was infamous in Ireland; it had become well known after the shooting of Veronica Guerin in 1996. As a result of this case, Gilligan's gang was broken up. Gilligan and several members of his gang relocated to Holland and started doing business with the Scousers in Amsterdam.

More bad news was on the way. The old-school middle-aged godfathers were falling like flies. Nine Cartel bosses were jailed for a record-breaking £4 billion cocaine-smuggling plot.

Astonishingly, the smuggling operation had been run from a phone box in Liverpool city centre, which the police eventually bugged to foil the plot. Greying 55-year-old Liverpool-based crime boss Paul Taylor had joined up with a Turkish Connection heroin boss called Mehmet Baybasin to carry out the importation. The gang planned to smuggle the drugs from South America by sea, hidden inside tins of fish and wooden pallets. Taylor got twenty-two years and the Turk got thirty years. Ten other gang members received sentences of nine to twenty-three years each, while twelve more accomplices were given lesser terms.

The capture was a huge blow for the Cartel. The old guard had seen it as a last throw of the dice in a bid to re-establish themselves at the top of the pyramid, but an international partnership of police had joined up to defeat them. Baybasin and Taylor had been drug-trafficking fanatics who talked of little else. SOCA listened and watched. Merseyside Police, the Police Service of Northern Ireland, and police partners in South and Central America all helped to break up the network.

Yet the big shot traffickers weren't the only people under pressure. A whole family of notorious drug sellers who ran a 24-hour dial-a-dealer service on the street were closed down. The operation was run from top to bottom by a well-known crime family who formed a cornerstone cell of the Cartel's street-distribution system. Thirteen members of the Whitney clan and their associates were sentenced to a total of 82 years behind bars following a long-running undercover police operation. Merseyside Police described their network as a 'drugs cash-and-carry business'.

CHAPTER 48

THE AMBASSADOR

2011

If the Cartel and the Mexican mafia did decide to forge closer links then it would undoubtedly give a massive boost to the cocaine trade in the UK. Again, the reason is simple, as explained by the concerned Mexican ambassador Eduardo Medina-Mora: volume. The Mexicans could increase the amount of cocaine shipped 100-fold by simply switching to containerisation.

At the moment, the standard load smuggled into the UK from Venezuela is 1,000 kilos. Put simply, this is because the Cali cartel and its neighbours still traffic drugs in a traditional way – the method known as 'break bulk', which refers to the way that items such as bananas and other commodities are transferred in boxes and bales. Break bulk cargo or general cargo refers to goods that must be loaded individually, not in intermodal containers, nor in bulk, as with oil or grain. The ships that the Venezuelans use are small- or medium-sized general cargo ships. Break bulk cargo comes in bags, boxes, crates, drums, barrels and ingots, usually secured on pallets. The Venezuelans used break bulk for the simple reason that it was the most common form of transporting cargo. The traffickers like this because they can hide the contraband in the hold within the proper cargo or weld it into the superstructure of the ship for part of the journey and break it out with the rest of the goods on making port. The problem with break bulk smuggling is that it is expensive to set up, limited in load size and more likely to be detected.

Since the late 1960s, the volume of break bulk cargo has declined dramatically worldwide as containerisation has grown. Moving cargo on and off ships in containers is much more efficient and allows ships to spend less time in port. Break bulk cargo also suffers from more instances of theft and damage.

Eduardo Medina-Mora said, 'The main route for cocaine smuggling is from Colombia to Venezuela to the Caribbean, then to Spain and Portugal by boat. But what will be more important now is container-based shipping. This is already important to shipments from Mexico to the US, and it's risen in 2006, '07 and '08. Mexico moves many more containers than any other country to the US. That's because we trade more with the US. It's also because many commodities from South America are still not transported in containers. Products such as grain, soya and coffee are still transported in bulk.

'We once seized a container containing branded Ecuadorian hand soap, which had come from Buenaventura, a major Colombian port on the Pacific coast, and was going to Manzanillo, a major port in Mexico, which deals with a mountain of containers. This didn't seem right, because Mexico doesn't import soap. It's a soap exporter. I don't see a . lot of Mexican housewives using Ecuadorian soap. In addition, the cost of transportation would have been greater than the value of the products themselves. Therefore, we suspected that there were drugs inside, and we were right.

'So, it's irrational for Colombian producers to smuggle their cocaine in containers to Mexico, which are then exported to Europe. It's much more rational that they send the containers full of drugs directly to Europe.'

Medina-Mora predicts that the Colombian and Ecuadorian cartels will begin sending containerised cocaine under the stewardship of their Mexican controllers. The big problem for law enforcement is that Europe has not invested much in technology that can scan containers. Customs and Excise, police and the Border Agency largely rely on 30-year-old technology to detect drugs coming into commercial ports. They use old-fashioned 'rummaging' techniques, which involve breaking open cargoes and sifting through boxes, or drilling into sealed containers, such as metal ingots. Europe has a long way to go to catch up with Mexico, which has installed state-of-the-art, industrial-sized scanners at its super-ports. To keep one step ahead, the drug traffickers will bypass Mexico and begin their journey to Europe from less secure ports in Central America, such as Panama. The Cartel is ideally poised to take advantage of this, because Liverpool now has one of the busiest container ports in the UK. Ironically, this has not been exploited as much as it could have been by the Cartel because they prefer to send consignments to break-bulk-orientated ports – also, it is too close to home. The Cartel don't like 'crashing' Liverpool port unless it's 100 per cent safe. But the Mexican government has intelligence that suggests this is the route that will be used in the future.

Medina-Mora said, 'In Mexico, we have developed capabilities to detect consignments hidden in containers: for example, X-rays, which are costly in terms of capital investment, and gamma rays, which test the molecular structure of cargo. But even though they are expensive, they are now deployed in every major customs facility in Mexico. That's because containers are increasingly going to be used throughout the world, because of the volumes moved throughout the world. Now we have a built-in deterrent for drug smugglers. So the cocaine will go from Colombia to somewhere like Panama, then to Rotterdam and finally Liverpool. We know this from intelligence. Europe is the target market.'

The Mexican-controlled cocaine trade in South America is desperate to find new routes to Europe. Medina-Mora said, 'Submarines go from Colombia to Mexico, but they are small subs meant for local coastal waters and limited journeys, not high seas, so they cannot be used to cross the Atlantic. The route to Europe has to be different. At present, the route is mainly by boat and air from South America to the West Indies and the Caribbean, and then from there to West Africa by ship.

'If I were a drug dealer now, I would try a different route. First, I would smuggle the cocaine in containers instead of bulk. Second, instead of going to the West Indies and then to Europe, I would move the containers northwards to Central America. I would move the containers from Colombia to Panama. There, I would mix them with the crowds of other

253

containers in a consolidation area. Panama has many of these transit ports. Then I would send them to Europe. This route is much more efficient.'

The big trade has not kicked in yet, but it is likely to because of the price differences of cocaine between Colombia and Mexico. These were the prices for a kilo in Mexico for 2009/10:

Colombia: $2,000
Southern Mexico: $8,000
Central Mexico: $10,000-$12,000
Northern Border: $18,000

Therefore it's rational for the Mexican to simply control the Colombian trade and oversee direct shipments from there to Panama rather than source the cocaine in Mexico itself and send it from there. At the moment, the high price of cocaine in Mexico means trade is confined to small-time opportunists.

Medina-Mora: 'We do have some shipments from Mexico to Europe but they are carried by mules, air passengers. Those volumes are emblematic.'

Colombia became the world's number-one producer of cocaine from the 1980s to the 2000s. To keep up, Peru boosted production until in 2012 it overtook Colombia for the first time. Peru's cultivation of coca has risen for the last six years, according to UNODC. A new report showed that 625,000 hectares of land were planted with coca last year – at least 2 per cent more than in 2010. Some coca farmers had as much as doubled their crops along the borders with Brazil and Bolivia. An earlier study showed that Bolivian coca production fell by 12 per cent in 2011.

So far, the big shipments from Mexico have failed to materialise. This suggests that the Cartel have failed to forge strong links with the Mexican mafia. In fact, the only Mexicans to be caught in the UK have seemingly been freelancers with no links to either network. Medina-Mora said, 'There have been Mexicans arrested in Scotland. One was a baseball player from the US.' The mule from Mexico was later jailed for eight years after trying to smuggle more than £500,000 worth of cocaine through Glasgow Airport. Medina-Mora said,

'Seemingly he had no links to crime groups based in Mexico. He was just a mule, and the motivation for him smuggling to the UK was simply the higher purity of US cocaine and the price-differential.'

CHAPTER 49

HELL'S ANGELS

2012

In 2012, one of Britain's most notorious crime bosses became involved in a violent dispute with a foreign gang. The crime boss had very close links to the Cartel and had both supplied them with heroin and bought cocaine from them. The crime boss wasn't worried about his dispute with the foreign gang. If he followed procedure, he knew he would be OK. As usual, he would contact his protection, a very well-known Cartel enforcer, who would advise him on the best course of action and the resources available.

The crime boss expected the usual assistance. Maybe the leader of a street gang would be sent down, someone like Kallas, who would threaten the foreign gangs with hand grenades and guns. Instead, he was given the number of a third-party subcontractor that was now taking on enforcement work for the Cartel.

Who did he end up calling for help? The Hell's Angels. The smartly dressed godfather was powerful enough to call on any number of more conventional enforcers and armed street gangs to protect him. Instead he turned to a ragtag band of leather-clad musclemen from a northern chapter who sport the winged 'death's head' insignia on their patches. For one phone call to 'solve the problem', the Hell's Angels charged the convicted armed robber turned heroin baron the price of a new top-end Harley-Davidson: £10,000. The word on the street: no one messes with the Red and White, the 'colours' of the world's heaviest outlaw motorcycle crew.

The story illustrates the growing power of biker groups and their reach into the higher echelons of organised crime, particularly established ones like the Cartel. Independent crime groups such as the Hell's Angels started playing a big part in Cartel business, and more services were contracted out. Well-disciplined bikers secretly took over key areas of the Cartel's crime market. The number of Hell's Angels in the UK is estimated to have increased by almost a third in the last six years, from 200 members in 2007 to around 270 members in 2013. The threat from the Hell's Angels and their rivals, known as the Outlaws, was largely thought to have died off after a deadly feud in the 1990s that led to 11 deaths and a police clampdown.

However, both sides used their time out of the spotlight to silently move in on drugs trafficking, contract violence and debt collecting on an industrial scale. In 2012, Europol started warning the public and other police forces that the shadowy world was about to explode into a bloody turf war again as vicious foreign chapters fought for a piece of the action. Europol said that rowdier biker gangs from Australia, Canada and the US had arrived in the UK to stir up trouble. A well-known enforcer with strong connections to the Hell's Angels said, 'The Hell's Angels are like the boxing fraternity on bikes. It's a ready-made network of connections ideal for carrying out activity right across borders. If a chapter in Merseyside need to collect a debt in Holland, they contact a chapter in Amsterdam to get on it and the money is couriered back. European checkpoints are insignificant.

'They are a brotherhood; they are like marauding Vikings but with military discipline. Their efficiency has allowed the Hell's Angels to control much of the "tranny" from the Netherlands to the UK.' Tranny is gangster shorthand for contraband transport, the ever-changing fleet of lorries, vans and cars that smuggle heroin, cocaine and cannabis from Holland to the UK. The source said that biker gangs have strong connections to terrorist organisations such as the IRA and the Ulster Defence Association.

The source on the biker gangs added, 'The Hell's Angels are experts at debt recoveries and money laundering abroad, and they collect money in values of a quarter of a million pounds and upwards. A lot of the paid whacks are carried out by Hell's Angels.'

Biker gangs had the advantage over traditional Cartel members because of their complete anonymity. The police in Liverpool, Amsterdam and Spain had now identified hundreds of Cartel members, but many bikers have no fixed abode, no National Insurance number and do not use their own names. Being highly mobile, they can get in and out of the country fast. A foreign assassin can ride into the UK from a European chapter to carry out a killing. Before the hit, he can blend in seamlessly, no questions asked, with a local chapter before leaving the country promptly after the murder has been carried out. Wannabe Hell's Angels have to spend two years as a trainee, known as a 'prospect', before being initiated into the group. Prospects are ordered to carry out crimes to test their loyalty to the group.

The source added, 'Hell's Angels are not wild. They are completely rational, and every mistake is punished severely, so it runs like clockwork. They are like a well-trained army. But they are lawless, and that's why they are attracted to setting up in Eastern Europe, because that is considered a lawless place by the underworld.'

However, in recent years, both the Hell's Angels and the Outlaws have tried hard to stay off the police's radar. In a bid to legitimise the gang, the Outlaws have recruited scores of respectable members who hold down day jobs. In one case, Tory councillor Jim Mason was revealed to be an ex-Outlaw. But senior members have masked their involvement with the authorities by leading double lives.

A prominent member of the Outlaws in London is a mysterious businessman known as Phil the Hat. When not wearing his biker helmet, he sports a signature bowler hat. By day, Phil the Hat sells fuel to commercial clients and lives in a nice house. His attractive wife wears designer clothes and drives a BMW. But by night, Phil the Hat is the boss of scores of Outlaws. He rules with a rod of iron and is feared all over the world.

Europol said the number of biker gang chapters in Europe has increased significantly since 2010 and there are now more than 700 chapters across the continent. In Germany, the police have enforced a massive policy of disruption against biker gangs to stop the menace spreading east. Today, there are 230 chapters of Hell's Angels in 27 countries, with an estimated membership of between 2,000 and 3,600.

Their motto is: 'When we do right, nobody remembers. When we do wrong, nobody forgets.' The US Department of Justice classifies the gang as organised crime. The number of Hell's Angels in the UK is estimated to have increased by a third in the last six years, from 200 members in 2007 to around 270 members. But their affiliated clubs have many more members. The number of chapters in the UK has increased from fourteen to nineteen in six years.

CHAPTER 50

OPERATION RETURN AND OPERATION CAPTURA

2012

The public face of SOCA's investigations into organised crime in Holland and Spain were two high-profile campaigns led by the charity Crimestoppers. Operation Captura appealed for information regarding wanted villains believed to be in Spain. Operation Return published pictures of British criminals hiding out in Amsterdam. Wanted Cartel drug dealers almost always featured in the strips of mug shots, which invariably featured images of shaven-headed white men with scowls on their faces.

Three of the six suspects named in Operation Return II were Liverpool-based drug dealers wanted for cannabis, amphetamines and heroin. The others were two Albanians linked to a cocaine network in the UK, and a man wanted by the Metropolitan Police, in London.

In January 2012, the fifth man arrested as part of Operation Return was 41-year-old Mark McKenna. In 2005, McKenna had been sentenced to 15 years' imprisonment for conspiracy to supply Class A drugs, but he absconded from prison in June 2008. Though he was targeted in Holland, McKenna was a typical Cartel scally who flitted between Amsterdam and Spain. He was arrested at a hotel in Madrid by the Spanish National Police.

A month later, in February 2012, Operation Captura celebrated one of its biggest successes against a central Cartel figure. Dennis O'Brien was jailed for 27 years for plotting to flood the UK with £166 million of 'staggeringly high purity' cocaine, as he described it. He was told by the judge that he was likely to die in prison. Like McKenna, O'Brien had been on the run since 2005 but was picked up in Spain. O'Brien fitted the Cartel profile like a glove; he was a truly globalised criminal whose gang spanned nearly every continent. The investigation led police from Peru to England, via Rotterdam, Madrid and Amsterdam, and even saw gang members tailed to Hong Kong. The crime lord was undoubtedly at the top of Britain's drug chain. His operation looked like it had been ripped from an intelligence report in the Mexican ambassador's secret dossier of predictive crime mapping. As Peru grew in prominence over Colombia, O'Brien conspired with international smugglers to buy 1.6 metric tonnes of coke from Lima, disguised as tins of asparagus. He then had the Class A cargo, which was between 92 per cent and 93 per cent pure, shipped from Peru to Rotterdam by boat and moved in two containers to Amsterdam, where it was then intercepted by JIT tactical police before it could reach Liverpool.

The drugs were worth £83 million in their pure form, but could have been doubled in value once diluted with other chemicals. The O'Brien gang were expecting to take a quarter of it for themselves. But it wasn't to be.

O'Brien was an ageing Cartel godfather. He was 62 years old when he was finally found at a Costa del Sol bar one Saturday by SOCA and the Spanish police. O'Brien had fled the UK in 2005 before he could be put on trial for the Peruvian connection. His son, James O'Brien, had been jailed in 2007 for his part in the same trafficking plot. Before he went on the run, Dennis had bought a pub. For a laugh, he'd called it 'The Dealers'.

CHAPTER 51

THE NIGHTMARE

2012

By 2012, the young Cartel gang members still had not started dealing direct with the Mexican mafia, as had been rumoured in both the underworld and the press. There had definitely been meetings, but both sides performed a merry dance around each other. Trust was not in evidence, according to an ex-enforcer who was party to confidential information.

However, both sides settled on a compromise. As well as dealing with the Mexican's South American sales reps in Holland, members of the Cartel said they would buy more cocaine from West Africa, where the Mexican mafia was shipping direct. At least nine Mexican and Colombian drug cartels had established bases in 11 West African nations by 2012, according to the UN report 'Transnational Organized Crime in West Africa'. The Colombian and Mexican cartels had discovered that it was much easier to smuggle large loads into West Africa and then break them up into smaller shipments to Europe: mostly to Spain, the UK and Holland. The new route was proof that the Mexican ambassador Eduardo Medina-Mora was right: the Mexican cartels were targeting Europe in response to higher demand for cocaine in Western Europe and the success of North American interdiction campaigns. By 2012, nearly half of all non-US bound cocaine, or about 13 per cent of all global flow, was heading to West Africa.

In addition, reports from Italy suggested that Mexican drug cartels had joined forces with the Sicilian mafia. Italian officials unearthed information that Palermo, along with other Italian ports, were being used by Mexico's drug cartels as a conduit to bring drugs to the European market.

British and Italian gangs liked to buy together because their markets snorted a lot of cocaine and it paid to buy in bulk and get a discount – if you could trust your partner. The model had worked 15 years earlier when the Cartel and Italians had bought heroin together from a Turkish gang based in London. For now, the British-based drug gangs were keeping their powder dry and the Mexicans at arm's length. They preferred to go through middlemen in Africa, Amsterdam and Italy rather than deal direct.

In Mexico, the violence was now out of control. Mexican cartel members routinely dismembered bodies. The mausoleums built to honour 'narcos' looked like palaces equipped with flat-screen TVs, wardrobes and fully fitted kitchens. Police in Tijuana resorted to strange voodoo rituals, including animal sacrifices and spirit tattoos, amid claims they were 'running scared' of the savage trafficking gangs. Students, housewives and children were routinely killed in the crossfire between drug lords and the army. The death tally reached 60,000 in 2012 after six years of martial law. The new president, Enrique Peña Nieto, switched the focus from tackling the gangs and hunting drug barons to reducing the crime and violence that affected the lives of Mexicans. However, violence dropped markedly in places like Juarez, in which some 3,100 were killed at the height of the drug wars, in 2010. A US security firm said that Los Zetas were the biggest cartel in terms of geographic presence.

But the Mexican ambassador in London had a new way at looking at the violence. Medina-Mora said that the violence was a direct result of the pressure that was being applied to the criminals by the police and the army. He said that the number of deaths was regrettable, but violence was a signal that the authorities were winning the war, by confronting and disrupting the cartels successfully. The alternative was worse. When the drug dealers were quiet, you could be sure that they were making money. Medina-Mora said, 'Take for example what happened in Colombia. The head of Colombian National Police once said that when drug traffickers have penetrated certain parts of society, you can be sure of an absence of violence. They are carrying on their criminal activity with precisely nothing disturbing them. The fact that Mexico is facing an upsurge in violence is a reflection of the authorities' efforts to root out criminal activity. They are losing their comfort.'

For Medina-Mora, the Mexican cartels were weaker than they appeared. They were much less cohesive than previously thought. He was not intimidated by the godfathers, nor was he obsessed with tracking them down. For him, the godfathers were figureheads. Joaquín Archivaldo Guzmán Loera headed the Sinaloa cartel before he went on the run. Known as 'Shorty' Guzmán, in reference to his stature, he became Mexico's top drug kingpin in 2003 and was declared 'the most powerful drug trafficker in the world' by the US. However, Medina-Mora is unfazed. He said, 'Drugs organisations are much more fragmented than is portrayed by the media. Shorty is an emblematic figure: one of the "Emblemas"'.

The Mexican authorities introduced crime mapping to target the cartels and allocate resources efficiently. But the battle also had to be fought in Europe. Western consumers needed to understand that there was no such thing as recreational drug use; they had to understand that using drugs for pleasure had a huge hidden cost. Medina-Mora added, 'The priority is to crack down on criminal groups to stop them reproducing criminal models. Europe is now the target market for cocaine. Cocaine is destroying rainforests and funding the assassination of police officers and law-abiding citizens. There is no such thing as recreational consumption in Europe. Spain has the largest per capita consumption rate of cocaine in Europe. Along with Italy and UK, those three countries account for 65 per cent of the cocaine in Europe. In Europe, you also have problems with opiates and cannabis, but cocaine consumption has doubled in the last five years. It will double again because of the prices being paid here in Europe. That's why we must see it as a global problem. In Europe, we do not yet see organised crime as a threat to democracy, health, peace and tranquillity.'

In February 2012, United Nations drugs chief Professor Hamid Ghodse said in a report that British cities, including

Liverpool, had lawless 'no-go areas' comparable with the most dangerous parts of Brazil, Mexico and the US. Professor Hamid Ghodse claimed three cities, Birmingham, Manchester and Liverpool, were on a par with the drug and murder capitals of the world. Professor Ghodse said the police had lost control of parts of these cities and drugs gangs had taken over.

His comments were rebutted by the Establishment, but those who were on the front line, including some police officers, community workers, drug workers and researchers, and criminals, knew at least that some of his analysis was right. The Iranian-born doctor claimed that Birmingham, Liverpool and Manchester were experiencing 'a vicious cycle of social exclusion and drugs problems and fractured communities'. He continued: 'Drug traffickers, organised crime, drug users, they take over. They will get the sort of governance of those areas. Examples are in Brazil, Mexico, in the United States, in the UK, Birmingham, Liverpool, Manchester, and therefore it is no good to have only law enforcement, which always shows it does not succeed.' The UN boffin was heavily criticised by the ACPO, but his only crime had been to speak the unspeakable: to dissent against the status quo of Establishment propaganda.

CHAPTER 52

THE KING OF MARBELLA

2012

John Disley is a 46-year-old security consultant known as the 'King of Marbella'. Though Bolton born and bred, the multimillionaire businessman has been travelling to Spain for 14 years. Bullet-headed and tanned, dripping gold and with a gorgeous girlfriend, Disley knows everyone and understands the area better than anyone. Worth half a billion pounds in property and other business interests, Disley built his empire by running security on the doors of nightclubs in Manchester. He spends his time in Marbella on his £2 million yacht. Though he doesn't deal drugs, Disley's reach stretches far and he has often used his security know-how to solve disputes between rival gangs. By 2012, Disley had noticed that the Cartel was losing its grip in Spain. A democratisation of gangs was occurring, brought on by an influx of cheap criminal labour from Eastern European gangs. Instead of a few big gangs comprised of close-knit people who knew each other, they were splintered into many gangs who employed outsiders, such as Romanians, in addition to their traditional members. In a sense, the Cartel had become victims of their own success. A sophisticated market had been created by their expertise, but that market was no longer dependent on them or crime alone. Other factors were coming into play. A gang's specialty in a particular field, such as transport or security, might give it an edge. It was no longer just about being a good all-round trafficker. This meant that no gang had overall supremacy in the drugs industry.

Disley said, 'I don't think there is any power ratio in the drug job in Spain, any more. I don't think there is a struggle to control the turf. That's because there is no real turf in Spain, in the sense that there's no one making drugs in Spain itself. It's about people doing the import and export. Transport, getting it over the water. Security is a different component. Each part works in sync with the other, like parts of a clock. I don't know what part of the clock the Liverpool guys are now, but I don't think there's a power struggle. I don't think that they are greater or weaker than any other team. That's because there are new players coming into it. It's like anything – it's tuned into pure business, so you find that the better-priced person gets the job, which is not linked to how big a villain he is. So there are various players saying, "We can get it from A to B via the air; we can get it from A to B via the sea." The people who want the end product at a certain place simply use the best, cheapest and most efficient way to do it.

'Now the pay-off is this: the counties that are getting strongest, and the workforce that is coming forward to meet these new challenges, are those that can compete simply on price; the Bosnians, the Latvians, the Eastern Europeans. They are the foot soldiers that can offer that facility, because they've got the manpower.

'Liverpool has always been strong because it's always had some big players, so that has been about status. But manpower wise, it's never been that strong. They can't flood the market with workers as fast as the Romanians can. The Liverpool mob is just to do with key people that are in Liverpool: the key personnel.'

Disley dismissed the myth that the Eastern Europeans were more desperate and willing to take more risks. It wasn't even about volumes of cocaine any more; it was now about numbers of people who could process the product through the organisation. It was now a game of numbers based on attrition. Eastern European gangs were prepared to 'throw bodies' at a border until it was breached by sheer numbers.

Disley said, 'You've got a lot more people to go at it, and if you are the police, you've got a lot more people to catch, so it makes it mind-boggling. That's where the Eastern Europeans have got the edge. Today, big boys are all about:

"How can I get it from there to there?" They have rationalised a complicated business right down to first principles. They are not afraid even to admit that they are drug dealers because they see themselves as successful businessmen. Their women are actually proud to say that their fellers are drug dealers. That's the culture here in Marbella, and it's very strange. I hear young girls all the time saying, "He's a drug dealer, my boyfriend etc." – these young, beautiful birds bragging about the situation.'

The downside, says Disley, is that the new emerging networks are much more vulnerable than the old, tight cell system of the Cartel. The Liverpool mafia are now forced to work with Eastern European networks that aren't secure. He said, 'There's no control within these loose arrangements. The drug dealers are not impregnable. If an Eastern European boss is paying a forklift truck driver 300 euros to move some stuff, then that's the weak link in the chain. The Liverpool guys wouldn't choose that method, but now they've got to take a chance because they have less control. They're as strong as their weakest man.'

Ten years ago, the bars and shops of Marbella were full of ageing Cartel godfathers. Today, they are all either behind bars, dead or fleeing the threat from teenage gang members. Disley says that the Cartel is gone and only lives within the imagination of the young gang members. In addition to competition, the other big factor in the Cartel's demise has been the police's success at clawing money back from drug dealers and criminalising black money. The Analyst's work was paying off big time.

Disley said, 'You never meet the old drug dealers these days. The word "cartel" conjures up an image of the very top end of organised crime. You think of the Italian mafia, Colombians; we've all seen the films. What is imagination becomes a reality in your head, because you see it on TV. But that's as far as it goes with the younger lads. Today they can no longer make the money their dads made, because the police have become experts at asset stripping. The government and the police have choked off the profits. A lot of money has been lost in the system. There are squads of specialist police and organised agencies that are out there to get these people.'

Disley said that the only godfathers who'd been able to keep hold of their wealth were the globalised super-criminals, like those described by Dutch sociologists, who'd evolved and operated on a much higher plane. They felt at home on the trading floors of Canary Wharf, they recruited CEOs from FTSE companies to run their empires and they dealt in politics. Many were involved in think tanks that ploughed money into local council schemes. Others used ex-government ministers to lobby on issues related to their business interests.

Disley said, 'These are the cases in which the police will never get the money off certain people. That money is still there in the system, but it's hidden. In those cases, no one will ever find it. But that's the result of people who've got away with it since the 1980s and managed to keep one step ahead. In the last 30 years, the drugs job has been massive. Certainly, for them it's become so organised that it's evolved into a blue chip business. The small drug dealer invests in sunbed shops and gets caught. But these big boys have been investing in shares and blue chip companies. Using their power and knowledge, the money is sunk into the system beyond reach. It would be very naive to think that money isn't in the system. There's much of it that cannot be untangled from the legitimate economy.'

Disley is convinced that there are plenty of white-collar professionals who know that they are working for drug empires but turn a blind eye. The problem was common amongst lawyers and accountants and had become entrenched because firms have come to rely on dirty money over a long period. The influence of crime on buying justice has made it harder for law-abiding people to get good lawyers, he claimed. He said, 'The black economy keeps a sizeable proportion of middle-class professionals employed. There's an unspoken understanding that barristers, solicitors and other professional people can charge an extortionate amount of money because they know where the money comes from. I know this has become more of a problem because many barristers can no longer rely on government income. The government have realised that the legal aid system is madness and have now reduced the payments. So a barrister might have a 50,000-page court case and get 30 seconds per page to study it on a legal aid rate. So what do they do? They end up defending drug barons or the companies they front. This makes it hard for ordinary people to get justice, unless they're paying for it themselves. And so if the solicitors cannot get money from legal aid, where's it coming from? It's coming from the money they charge organised crime. If you stopped crime, there would be no business.'

Disley is convinced that drug money has had a disproportionately destructive effect on the legitimate economy because bad money has pushed out the good, particularly as the economy has become more service-based over the past 30 years and in times of recession. In the millionaire's playground of Marbella, he claims businessmen talk openly about money laundering. Disley said, 'Once there was a black and white economy. But big parts of it are now grey because of the sheer scale of organised crime. Crime is a hugely powerful sector, which plays a role in the process of pushing good money out. I've noticed that it's had a greater influence since the 1980s. When Britain used to manufacture goods, it was harder for organised crime to wash money. It all goes back to Mrs Thatcher and the failure of the normal economy over a long period. So now if you took black money out of the system, you might have a problem because it's tied up with the service sector and it's fragile. Of course, none of this is a problem in Marbella. Buying the cars, the luxuries, keeps everything afloat here. In a world recession in which three countries have gone under, you've got shops in Marbella selling £1 million Bugatti cars. Who do you think is buying them? Drug dealers by any chance?

'When it's no longer just a struggle between the lower class and the upper class, and it becomes one between the legal class and the illegal class – now you've got problems.'

CHAPTER 53

CHINA CRISIS

2012

By 2012, the Cartel knew that their future in Europe was bleak. They started looking for new markets. The only problem was that the Analyst was one step ahead. The police had identified the Cartel's next move even before the godfathers had thought about it properly. Astonishingly, the Cartel had their eye on China.

Merseyside Police's focus on Amsterdam had revealed some frightening new intelligence. First, police officers had been successful in identifying a hierarchy in Holland in so much detail that it enabled officers to track their movements over thousands of miles. This strata of criminals were drug dealers in Amsterdam who were largely seen by the Cartel as 'regional managers'. The successful candidates from this crop who had performed well in Holland were then offered other territories to work in. Merseyside Police tracked the men as they were posted to Spain. But then police discovered a secret cell that had so far eluded them, a cell that was operating under the regional managers' control, but far away from Europe. A new outpost had been opened up. Some members of the middle management had been given the task of organising a group of young gang members who set up in Thailand. So far, the group of Liverpudlians in Thailand had confined themselves to lower-level activity, such as counterfeiting. However, it was definitely a reconnaissance mission to see the lie of the land in Bangkok. But then came a worrying development. Senior members of the Cartel were sent to Thailand to expand the cell – to open up opportunities in China.

The Analyst took up the story. 'It's like discovering a new oil field. China has a growing economy and the highest population density. It's newly affluent and has strong trade links. It's an untapped source for organised-crime drugs. Of course, there are the Triads and other domestic crime groups, but so far Chinese culture, a disciplined society and communism have prevented their dominance.'

The Cartel planned to set up a regional hub in Thailand: a staging post on the way to China.

The Analyst: 'Is Thailand the new Amsterdam? It could be, because of its liberal laws; it's also a nice place to do business and it's cheap. China could go through similar heroin problems to what the UK had in 1983 and '84. At the moment, the criminal infrastructure for distribution does not exist in the same way over there. If you're thinking about smuggling heroin from Afghanistan into China, then the system that delivers to end users within China does not exist. So do our people see an opportunity there? Could they help build up that network? It's globalisation. Eastern Europe went into criminal meltdown after the collapse of the USSR. But are they organised enough now to exploit China? In effect, it would be a two-way trade from Thailand. Designer drugs and synthetic tablets coming this way into Europe, and heroin and coke going that way from Europe to Thailand to China.'

For the Cartel godfathers, access to new opportunities outside Britain couldn't come quick enough. Britain still remained a lucrative market, in some ways. In the UK in 2012, 60 million E tablets were sold to young people by criminal gangs. But that market was being eroded by new products, such as legal highs, and disrupted by violence associated with young gangs. This state of affairs was demonstrated by the fact young gang members continued to cause murder back home in Liverpool. Old scores from five or ten years earlier were still being settled, like an Albanian blood feud that had no end. By 2012, the gang war that had triggered the rise of the foot soldier had come full circle. Joe Thompson had been there when the first shot was fired nearly a decade earlier. Thompson had been leader of the Norris Green Strand Gang when they split from Croxteth during a gun fight in a pub in 2003.

Now Thompson was a balding father. Unlike some of the early pioneering gang members, such as Kallas, he had failed to make it big, partly because the shooting of Rhys Jones in 2007 had brought so much heat on his crew, stopping his rise to riches in its tracks. The Cartel drug dealers had effectively disowned him in order to keep the heat off themselves. Thompson reverted to type, going back to thieving and petty drug dealing.

One day he was walking near his Norris Green home when he was ambushed and shot dead at close range. Underworld sources say he was murdered after he kicked in a house door and stole three £800 mountain bikes. His death came days after a gun attack on a rival's house. Earlier, his brother Gerard had four fingers blasted off as he walked through the Norris Green–Croxteth border. Round and round in circles, the tit for tat went on as though it was still 2003.

In the five years between 2007 and 2012, the gang war had been raging on. A staggering 910 firearms had been seized since Rhys Jones was tragically murdered in 2007 aged just 11. Yet, despite the haul, shootings continued to take place frequently: 170 on Merseyside, 69 of which took place between spring and summer 2012. The onslaught left police fearing the next tragic cross-fire killing.

Teen gangsters still found it easy to get hold of firearms in the area. Many used to hire pieces from Steven Cardwell, a gun dealer who sold weapons smuggled into Britain from America by former US marine Steven Greenoe. The flow only stopped when the racket was smashed in 2012. Cardwell and his accomplice were sent to prison.

Meanwhile a similar cycle of events was keeping a blood feud alive in a neighbouring gang. In 2008, 16-year-old Jamie Starkey shot and wounded Daniel Gee at point-blank range during a 5 a.m. New Year's Day stand-off. Starkey had been sent to jail, but for four years Gee had been waiting for revenge. The police knew this. Officers had previously secretly recorded a conversation during which Gee had said, 'Don't worry, the little fucker is going . . . the only place he is safe is in jail and he won't be safe there . . . it'll be even worse in there

. . . than he is out. I'll slit his fucking throat.' The police did everything they could to break the cycle and prevent the threat from being carried out. In 2010, they jailed the drug dealer after catching him conspiring to buy guns to kill Starkey as soon as he was released.

However, the reach of Gee's gang remained long. In 2011, Starkey was released from prison. Within a year, he was dead. Starkey was shot dead by a hitman while walking to his car outside his home in Fazakerley. The assassin, dressed in dark clothing, cut him down in a hail of bullets before running off across a playing field, leaving Starkey to die. The killing went on.

Meanwhile, the Analyst was now in charge, having risen to a senior position in Merseyside Police. For the first time, he was in complete control of operations against the Cartel.

The Analyst said, 'I'm in the position now that I run a big department where they do what I say. It's my decision now. That's where I can influence those decisions, which is a nice position to be in. The buck stops with me. I choose the crime group that we target. And that's the way to do it.'

Operationally, the Analyst was in favour of the long game. For years he had been frustrated. Long-running operations had been sold short and stopped earlier because ambitious bosses were always under pressure from politicians to put drugs on the table.

The Analyst said, 'You can still run your big news stories, the good news stories, but if you wait a little bit longer, they'll be better. That was my take: patience pays even more dividends. It's not just about a good news story; it's about making a difference to the public.'

But just as the Analyst thought he was winning the game, some officials called for the towel to be thrown in altogether. A former MI6 chief declared that the war on drugs had failed and the world must now consider legalisation. Nigel Inkster, a former number two in the Secret Intelligence Service, called for a review of the world's narcotics laws. The report entitled 'Drugs, Insecurity and Failed States', by the International Institute of Strategic Studies, stated that the War on Drugs had led to little more than violence on Britain's streets and instability in Third World narc-economies such as Africa and

South America. The War on Drugs was marking its 50th year, but despite billions of pounds poured into the conflict, it was argued it had simply undermined international security. Britain and other countries had failed to prevent the widespread production, trafficking and consumption of drugs: end of story.

But the Analyst wasn't so sure – nor was he ready to give up now. In fact, he said that the police were now for the first time one step ahead of the Cartel.

The Analyst said, 'Law enforcement in the UK is significantly more sophisticated now. Since 1981 we've not only kept track with the criminals; we are now one step ahead. That's why so many are in jail. Our gun-crime figures are good. Matrix is so intrusive and in your face that it makes criminality difficult.'

On the ground, it certainly was a mixed picture. In the six months leading up to December 2012, there were 122 firearms discharges and an increase in 'bad-on-bad' shootings, as the Analyst put it. On the positive side, the force's elite anti-gang Matrix unit was now 300-strong. Since its inception in 2005, there had been a 33 per cent drop in the number of firearm discharges.

But critics claimed that some of the new initiatives operated by Matrix to tackle gun crime weren't working as well as they should. One new crackdown called 'gun nominals' seemed to be backfiring. Police targeted armed gang members by handing out 'gun nominal' orders. The most dangerous yobs were awarded 'gold' status, which became known on the street as 'gun ASBOs'. Gold level meant that the police had received strong intelligence that a suspect was involved in firearms activity. However, teen criminals began to sport the orders as 'badges of honour'.

Officers targeted their 'gold' nominals with intense disruption, searching the suspects' houses every day and using close surveillance. The three lower levels of risk were silver, bronze and a 'holding area' where those coming off gold were placed on file while officers assessed their behaviour. Each gang member received a hand-delivered letter from Merseyside Police notifying them of their new status. In red capitals, the letter stated: 'You are now formally advised that Merseyside

Police has identified you as a gun crime nominal. This means that there is intelligence available that links you and/or your associates to firearms. You will now be visited by police officers on a regular basis to check on your safety and that of your family, and to dissuade you from being involved in criminality involving firearms. There is a simple way to avoid this attention from Merseyside Police: have nothing to do with guns or others who use them.'

CHAPTER 54

RUSSIAN HEROIN

2013

By 2013, the Cartel was under pressure from new competitors and new circumstances. The price of heroin was soaring after the War on Terror left the Russian mafia controlling the deadly trade. One kilo of heroin rocketed in value from £15,000 to £23,000 in just a few months. The price hike sparked a mini crime wave in some cities as desperate addicts once again turned to burglary, muggings and drug-related gang violence to feed their habits. Experts feared the knock-on effects: a rise in overdoses, for instance, as users injected heroin cut with poisons as a result of dealers trying to cut corners and stretch supplies.

In the new globalised crime market, the chaos was the result of events taking place more than 3,500 miles away in war-torn Afghanistan. By 2013, the US-led forces finally managed to wrestle control of the Afghan–Pakistani border away from the Taliban following a series of killer drone strikes. The north-west frontier was not only militarily significant; it was also the main conduit for poppy paste out of Helmand Province. The knock-on effect of military success plunged the global drug trade into turmoil. The upshot was easy to predict. The Cartel lost its main supply route as the Turkish Connection ran dry of heroin. Instead, greedy Russian godfathers cashed in and upped the price of opium.

Pakistani tribal lands near the border region were the gateway linking the poppy fields of Helmand Province to mainland Europe. More than 90 per cent of the world's heroin once flowed across the north-west frontier before making its way to the West. The heroin had always followed a secret trail known to Interpol as the 'southern route', through Turkey and the Balkans and up into Western Europe. The southern route was once the safest and most profitable way to smuggle heroin for the Cartel. For 20 to 40 years they had turned over hundreds of millions of pounds because the trade was controlled by their main partners, an Istanbul-based mafia known as the 'Turkish Connection'. The huge volumes meant that the price of heroin had been kept historically low. But now the shadowy network was broke after supply lines were cut off by NATO. Instead of selling their heroin to the Turkish Connection, Afghan traffickers switched northwards and were selling to the Russian mafia. The Russian mafia made matters worse by stockpiling thousands of kilos in a bid to push up prices. A London-based heroin dealer who had for years been supplying the Cartel said, 'Two months ago I was buying a kilo of heroin for £15,000. The most I have paid was £17,000 to £17,500, maybe £18,000 in 2010. Last week I paid £23,000, which is the most I have ever paid. I had to pay that because there is a drought on. No one is selling in big amounts because no one knows if there will be any more for a while. Everybody is sitting on their stash. The people in Amsterdam, who sort the transport for my gear, said it's out of their control. They blamed the Russia mafia, saying that the Turks are no longer the main boys. Everything used to go through the Turks. The Turks looked after nearly every dealer in the UK. I used to buy off Turkish people in Green Lanes in north London. Now it's the Russians that have taken over, because no one else can get gear out of Afghanistan, because of the war. It's all to do with borders. If the grower can't get it out in the south, it means they've just gone north. It's simple supply and demand. The Russians aren't straight-shooters. They are just trying to make a monopoly so that they can make more money.'

A street dealer in Liverpool reduced the size and quality of £10 wraps on the street. He said, 'A £10 bag used to contain around 0.25 grams of heroin. I used to measure it out using a small plastic spoon from McDonald's. Now I sell between

0.1 and 0.2 grams in a tenner bag because it doesn't come up level on the spoon. It gets bashed up with more powder, because I need the punters to come back after two hours for another bag. That's how I make my money.'

TEENAGE MUTANT STREET FIRMS

By 2013, Liverpool's best-known exports were still the Beatles, football and organised crime. The future of all three, however, was far from rosy. Half of the Fab Four were now dead and the city's once-dominant football teams, especially Liverpool FC, seemed to be in decline. After 40 years of on–off growth, the Cartel still made up Britain's richest and most powerful crime syndicate, with hubs in places like Amsterdam, Spain and Portugal. But there was no doubt that over the previous decade there had been noticeable decline, mainly caused by mass police disruption and the transfer of power to younger gangs. The fate of the Cartel now hung in the balance. The big question was: how long could the graft go on for?

To find the answers, experts like the Analyst looked into the past to find out how the Cartel had coped with life-threatening shocks since its inception. Like the mainstream economy it was part of, the criminal history of the Cartel was one of troughs and peaks, booms and busts. There was, however, a thread of continuity that ran through it and could be relied upon. It was a kind of fortuitous and determined opportunism. It was an ability to cash in on unforeseen events, and even to turn a profit unexpectedly, from the changes in the social landscape that were going on around the Cartel itself.

The network had been founded in 1973 by ex-dockers who were experts at smuggling contraband. In the 1980s, the traffickers joined up with what the police called 'travelling Scousers': itinerant young urchins who were going to the Continent in search of exotic sportswear, exciting cup football and contacts in Europe's underworld. Many of them had found their future business partners while serving jail sentences in Holland, Germany and France. The formula was a recipe for success, pushing the Cartel into a strong hierarchical structure that functioned later, during the 1990s, as a de facto narco-corporation, manufacturing and distributing a wide range of drugs on an industrial scale.

By the turn of the millennium, a loose federation of CEO figures, each worth between tens and hundreds of millions of pounds, sat at the top of the tree. They formed a governing body that shouted the odds and said what went. At the bottom, a resilient layer of young gang members were still doing most of the work and generating most of the cash. However, the make-up of the Cartel would soon come full circle. During the 1980s, armies of terrace urchins and jobless scallywags had formed the Cartel's workforce. By 2013, it was the next generation's turn. They were of a similar age to those youthful scallies who had joined the Cartel in the 1980s, but had different attitudes and lifestyles. Now it was the time of the teenage killers and the armed criminals to have their go. The time had come for the superhoodies who hung around outside the off-licences and rode around on mountain bikes to come in from the cold. The generation gap was the source of difference in outlook. Attitudes had hardened. Anger had increased. Unlike their fathers, the new gang members weren't prepared to settle for less. Like their idol, Scarface, they wanted money and power. Right here. Right now.

The new gang members were unlikely bosses-in-waiting, owning little more than the black, micro-porous North Face all-weather gear they stood up in and automatic weapons, which they coveted more than anything else. The young gang members, mainly aged between 17 and 21, had more often than not been groomed for low-level jobs in the Cartel, such as street dealing and contract violence. As they got older, the more trusted ones became couriers, ferrying messages between Liverpool, Amsterdam and the Costa del Sol by word of mouth. Like the emirs of al-Qaeda, none of the Cartel godfathers would talk on the phone, so this small army of messengers went back and forth on budget flights out of John Lennon Airport and other regional centres as part of a system known as 'easy graft'.

Merseyside Police developed a number of unique systems to fight back, and, because of their success, they quickly became a 'beacon' force that led Britain's response to drug crime. Merseyside is still the only police force outside of London to have Level 3 capability: the resources to track serious villains across borders and mount complex international investigations. In addition, it has deep-seated, long-established 'protocols' with other police forces from around the world so that investigations can move seamlessly from one country to the next, sucking up evidence and building cases with machine-like efficiency.

The force's narco-intelligence system of agents, informers and James Bond-style surveillance assets is unrivalled in the UK. Some senior officers, like the Analyst, have an encyclopaedic knowledge of hundreds of key players, some of whom they have been monitoring since they were bobbies on the beat in the 1980s.

On the street, Merseyside Police have deployed their hugely successful Matrix Firearms Team, developed after the force's brightest and best officers were sent around the world in 2003–04 to study gun-control measures and best practice in other countries. The result is a self-contained, heavily armed, semi-militarised cadre that snakes through the city in counter-insurgency-style convoys of battered yellow 'shippers', striking fear into key impact players. There is no doubt that Matrix has reduced overall gun crime. Like so many Merseyside Police initiatives, the Matrix model is now being rolled out across the country.

To stop the tentacles of the Cartel spreading to other countries, Merseyside Police practised a policy of containment. If they could cut off the head of the Cartel in Liverpool, then it would seriously reduce its ability to operate in Spain and Amsterdam. This was no easy feat. Liverpool was a difficult city to police. By 2013, Merseyside Police were responsible for an area of around 647 sq km containing a population of

1.5 million people. Organisationally, the force was split into two basic command units: Liverpool North and South. Merseyside Police also covered the outlying areas of Sefton, Wirral, St Helens and Knowsley.

In 2010–11, Home Office crime figures showed that drug-related offences were still higher in Liverpool than in the rest of the country: Liverpool had a figure of 15.9 drug crimes per 1,000 people, compared to a national average of 4.2 offences. Despite this, and the upsurge in gang violence, the Home Office was convinced that Merseyside Police's response to the feud between the Croxteth Crew and the Norris Green Strand Gang was a great success: textbook modern policing. The mandarins in Whitehall liked the fact that all firearms discharges across Merseyside were dealt with by a reactive investigation arm. The force was also commended for having close links with social services and school. A multi-agency governance group had been brought together to coordinate all the government's resources in gang areas. A study found that Merseyside Police were good at propaganda, striking fear into gang members by extensively publicising the reach of the Matrix team. Not only did the force have a powerful press and communications office, but it also had a marketing department.

In overview, Merseyside Police based their response to the Cartel on two policing and criminology models. One was the 'Boston' model, which is all about the strategic use of criminal justice and linking up with lots of different agencies. In Liverpool, there is daily contact between the police, the Crown Prosecution Service and the National Probation Service. Schools, housing providers and children's services are also brought together. However, the caring side was also backed up with a strong anti-gun campaign. Gangs were constantly bombarded with Matrix team propaganda. The other, the 'Hot Spot' model, combined together the outcomes of all these partnerships, while simultaneously targeting the offenders ruthlessly by swamping gang members and their families with evictions, care proceedings, ASBOs, gun nominal orders, multiple stop-and-searches and so on. Aggressive police tactics were used to clear gangs from very bad areas.

Meanwhile, community policing was aimed at reassuring

people and restoring trust in the police. The Crime and Disorder Reduction Partnership was an umbrella organisation that brought together all of these resources but preferred to use them in the longer term to reduce gang activity.

For all of its power, the levels of violence associated with the Cartel are relatively low, and for all of their recent failings – in particular the hostile takeover by young gangs – the ruling elite is still largely rational-economic, and they understand that shooting and killing are bad for business. Even the conspirators who killed Colin Smith calmed down once they had killed the boss and his loyal associates in Liverpool, Amsterdam and Spain. Kallas, who had started out as a rapacious teenage hothead, became less volatile, relatively speaking, once he had reached a high level within the pyramid. In general, the younger generation of gang members learned that prudence was preferable to punishment once they had taken on roles of responsibility. Such is the nature of leadership. Such was their response to the threat from Merseyside Police.

The new bosses were sometimes rash, but they weren't stupid. They had learned lessons from the past. They had been taught well by their forefathers. In the mid-1990s, a series of gang wars in Toxteth disrupted sales of Class A drugs, and forced the police to clamp down. Learning from history, having an organisational memory and drawing on 40 years of organised-crime heritage: these were the benefits of being part of a cartel that had been around for a long time. The tricks of the trade were passed down from one generation to the next, like know-how in a family business.

Today, by and large, the Cartel like things to run smoothly. They have adopted the rationale of the head of the Colombian National Police, who said that when drug traffickers have penetrated certain parts of society, you can be sure of the absence of violence, as they do not want to attract attention.

Of course, there have been other setbacks. Like al-Qaeda, some of the Cartel's key personnel have been taken out. Curtis Warren, the richest criminal in British history, is wallowing in Belmarsh Prison after being jailed in Holland and Jersey almost continuously since 1996. David

Hibbs-Turner is unlikely to taste freedom for a long time, after his small army of white-van-man drivers was caught smuggling drugs instead of delivering building materials and motor parts to local businesses. In 2007, Curtis Warren's 40-year-old successor, Colin Smith, was gunned down in a Liverpool backstreet. His demise played out like the final scenes of a gangster movie. Over a thousand miles away, off the coast of Spain, a £40 million importation controlled by his gang was about to be beached – but was pulled back at the eleventh hour after news reached the smugglers' ship that Smith had been 'plugged'. Colin 'King Cocaine' Smith, drug baron and fanatical Everton fan, had lived the terrace urchin's dream. He had accumulated a £200 million fortune, but he looked like a scally that had got the bus home from Goodison Park. He was just as streetwise. Smith concealed his wealth and power by driving around in an anonymous Ford Galaxy and going to the match with the lads. According to the Analyst, he ran an enterprise as complex as a corporation and employed hundreds of people in his immediate circle.

In recent years, the younger gang members grew impatient with their bosses' highly organised set-piece plans, in which they were expected to play the part of functionaries who carried out their work without complaint. They were expected to wait patiently for the chance to move up the ranks; they took risks but didn't reap any of the rewards. Consequently, they started 'terroring' their bosses because, simply put, they had nothing to lose. For one such upstart, Kallas, the terror tactics worked and he leapfrogged to the top.

For sociologists, the power struggle was like watching an experiment in criminology live and writ large over several continents. For years, academics had tended to divide organised crime into 'street gangs' and 'crime firms'. But no one had ever studied what happened when the two groups began fighting with each other, never mind when the group perceived as the weaker decided to make a hostile takeover. Crime firms were characterised as those groups formed specifically for the purposes of committing criminal activities, such as the old-style factions that had collected around the Cartel godfathers. Street gangs, on the other hand, were formed largely for other social and psychological reasons, and crime was only a part of their lives. Up until recently, street gangs were confined to antisocial behaviour, street crime and public-safety issues. But what happened when someone like Kallas organised his gang to mutate into a kind of crime firm? Things got confused and there was no definition for this new type of enterprise. In *The Eurogang Paradox: Street Gangs and Youth Groups in the US and Europe*, sociologist Malcolm Klein said street gangs were disorganised or moderately organised. Gangs were characterised by strong identities based mainly on location, 'versatile offending patterns' and increased law-breaking behaviour over time. Crime firms, on the other hand, always had a level of organisation related to the type of crime committed, usually dealing and trafficking in drugs. Crime firms were more organised. Some did not have leaders, but they made up for it by 'specialisation' of tasks among members. Kallas's success lay in his ability to form a new kind of organisation. Revenge of the teenage mutant street firms.

No matter how they are defined, today police fear that the new generation of stripped-down Cartel bosses will inevitably take more risks than the silver-haired imperators who went before them. They fear what is known in police jargon as 'displacement'. As policing improves and the old heartlands in Europe, especially Amsterdam, become intolerable for the Cartel to do business in, forward-looking officers like the Analyst think that the crime groups will target China, via Anglophile trading hubs in South East Asia such as Thailand.

The police also fear more violence and a link-up with the Mexican crime groups that are currently being forced by drugs wars from their homelands in North America into the cocaine-producing heartlands of Venezuela and Colombia, where the 'travelling Scousers' have had good contacts for more than 25 years.

In September 2010, the Embassy of Mexico in the UK produced a report called 'The Fight Against Crime in Mexico'. The document was marked 'sensitive' and its contents were never disclosed to the public, partly to prevent scaremongering in the press and partly for security reasons. If the document fell into the wrong hands, the contents would undoubtedly help criminals here and in Mexico.

The briefing was, in effect, a call to arms for Britain and Mexico to work together in a bid to stop the Cartel, and other, lesser British crime groups, from forming a strategic alliance with the Mexican drug barons. The UK–Mexico plan had three central tenets: countering money laundering, controlling immigration and monitoring cyberspace. First, the Mexicans wanted help in countering money laundering, which they saw as key to the problem and one that Britain was in a good position to help with. The rationale was straightforward: stop the flow of cash, stop the flow of drugs. The City of London was a world centre for financial institutions. If the banks could choke off the supply of money to Mexican criminals then no one could buy or sell drugs. Specifically, several initiatives were put forward for the proposed inter-governmental alliance. First, it proposed the establishment of 'bilateral mechanisms' for cooperation, increased meetings between British and Mexican police, and lots of intelligence sharing. Second, Mexico wanted more immigration controls 'to prevent criminals from around the world using Mexico/UK as a bridge for UK/Mexico and other countries'. Third, the Mexican government also suggested putting in place 'virtual border protection' to stop the various cartels using cyberspace to communicate and trade. In short, Eduardo Medina-Mora wanted 'to make it difficult for the criminals to use both countries as "hosts" for their illegal activities.'

In return for UK cooperation, the Mexican government vowed to continue to clean up its act at home, particularly with a view to reducing the numbers of firearms and the numbers of guns in Mexico. The document said that Mexico 'promotes the strengthening of national laws and policies to control firearms, ammunition and explosive production'. For this, they would seek help from British businesses fresh back from Iraq and Afghanistan that had expertise in security and bomb detection, which they hoped would play a tactical role in defeating the Mexican cartels.

However, the solution was not that simple. The threat from Mexico would never be solved by a two-country agreement between the UK and Mexico alone. To stop the British and

Mexican criminals from joining up would require a truly international approach, and one that involved the United States. Here's where the story got tricky.

In short, Mexico blamed two countries for its massive crime epidemic: itself and the US. Failing to tackle the problem in both these countries now would inevitably lead to contagion into other countries, especially Europe, which the Mexican mafia now had its eye on.

To make them understand what might happen in the future, the Mexican government were keen to tell the Brits about the factors that had led to the current situation. Before the 1990s, the Mexican drug cartels were not dominant, because the prior regime was strong and was served by functional civic institutions. One-party rule by the Institutional Revolutionary Party (PRI) prevailed between 1929 and 2000, largely propped up by an 'economic miracle'. For instance, there were more than 2,000 police corporations in the country that kept criminals in check. However, the model ended in the 1990s during economic crises that led to more openness and more political diversity. However, the sudden regime change was not followed by strong security institutions. Though the former rulers were replaced by a vibrant democracy, many of the unwritten rules of life in Mexico stopped working. Power was decentralised, but there was often too few regional hubs with the capacity to deal with the new authority. Consequently, the Mexican cartels started as service providers for Colombia, gaining power alongside the general institutional weakening in the country. This led to widespread corruption and criminality in Mexico.

The erosion of governmental power was accompanied by a change in drug-trafficking routes – one that would eventually benefit the Cartel indirectly. During the 1970s and '80s, the quickest, most profitable and most geographically logical route was always through the Caribbean and into the USA. But towards the end of the 1980s and the beginning of the 1990s, the US was successful in closing the Caribbean route. This caused narcotics to be shifted to both Central American and Mexican territories. A by-product of the closure of the US–Caribbean smuggling route was that Colombian cartels were left with unsold cocaine that had been destined for the US. This was rerouted to Europe by the Cali cartel, a major factor that boosted the wealth and status of the Cartel. Curtis Warren personally profited from this cocaine.

The current situation in Mexico in 2013 is one of drugs, guns and violence. In 2009, the global intelligence company Stratfor identified four main smuggling routes into and through Mexico and ending up in the US. The main route was obviously for cocaine traffic, another was for huge amounts of ephedrine-based stimulants, another was for methampetamine and cannabis, and the last was a general route for everything.

The discussion between the UK and Mexican officials was not without its sensitive moments. It was clear that the Mexicans were unhappy with their closest neighbour, the United States. This was potentially difficult territory for the UK, as the US was its closest ally. The Mexicans partially blamed the US for fuelling the drugs wars in Mexico by allowing guns to be smuggled across the US–Mexican border and for creating a demand for drugs in the US for drugs from Mexico. The page in the dossier that dealt with the thorny issue was entitled 'The Demand Factor – A Sleeping Monster in the US Basement'. The text continued: 'The US has its own monster right at home, and its potential for violence should not be underestimated.' A diagram of the US and Mexican flags illustrated the fact by showing an arrow marked 'drug traffic' pointing upwards to the US, and an 'arms traffic' one going the other way, downwards to Mexico. Mexico was painting itself as a victim of US imports and exports of contraband. To back up the claims, there was a list of explosive statistics that showed US organised crime spreading like a cancer into Mexico:

- 1 million gang members, organised in 20,000 gangs, present in all 50 states.
- Distribution of drugs reaches 35 million consumers.
- Distribution networks employ more criminals than the Mexican and Colombian cartels put together.
- Great potential for violence because weapons being sold easily.

Around 90 per cent of all weapons seized in Mexico come from the US. The Mexican authorities had identified four main 'weapons routes' from the US that penetrated deep into the heart of Mexico, and even further south into Central America. The Gulf route started near the US–Mexican border town of Acuña and went down the whole western seaboard until it reached Tuxtla Gutiérrez in the far south. The other routes were called the Central, South and Pacific routes.

The Mexican government openly called for more gun control in the US and subtly asked the UK to use its special relationship to help them put pressure on Washington. More than 10 per cent of America's 110,000 gun shops were located on the Mexico–US border. In relative terms, the border region gun shops 'represent the majority of the profits of the US weapons business'. Any American citizen without a criminal record can freely acquire weapons from a .22 calibre pistol to an assault rifle. Drug-trafficking groups from Mexico acquire guns from these shops by sending in third parties to buy them. This is because there is no formal follow-up procedure in place to track weapons once they have been sold and resold again.

Despite the huge numbers of guns, in 2010 the Mexican government were claiming that levels of violence were actually falling. The ongoing war, they claimed, was largely limited to six states and was being waged for a shrinking slice of the pie. Around 90 per cent of deaths were Mexican cartel members. Between December 2006 and September 2010, 28,000 persons were killed. However, the Mexican government argued that the violence levels weren't as grim as they seemed. According to the Mexican government's report, 'Murders, high calibre weapons, beheadings all amplify the perception of the violence levels.' However, in 2009 there were fewer killings per 100,000 inhabitants than in most South American countries – and even in Washington DC. In Mexico, the rate was 11.5 killings per 100,000. In Brazil, it was 25. In Venezuela, it was 48. In New York in 1990, it was 14.5, according to figures supplied by the FBI.

The main objectives of the Mexican government were to stop the problem from being a threat to national security and take it back to the public-security sphere, to take away the 'intimidation capabilities' of the Mexican cartels and return peace to society.

The Mexican government started to do this by trying to improve the rule of law in general. However, this was not going to be easy. The government's report concluded that it was 'much harder to take the ideology out of someone's mind, than to stop the money flowing into the cartels' because 'drugs trafficking is a business'. The authorities clamped down on corruption. More than 230 former officials, including Mexico's drugs czar, went before the courts, and 3,000 police officers were sacked. In the four years up to 2010, more than 85,551 weapons were seized, of which 49,032 were high calibre. Around 8.6 million rounds of ammunition and 6,200 grenades had been captured. The list was astonishing: 34,599 land vehicles, 482 planes and 354.9 million pesos were seized, along with $416.2 million in cash. More than 63,500 drug criminals were captured, of which 378 were extradited, mainly to the US.

The drug-seizure stats were even better: 99.3 tonnes of cocaine were found, worth a billion dollars, and also discovered were 7,138 tonnes of cannabis and 59.8 tonnes of meth-related drugs. The upshot has been a total decline in the flow of drugs entering the US.

All this meant two things. Although Mexico was winning the War on Drugs, it would need the help of Britain to stop it from spreading to Europe, and it would need Britain to ask the US to do its bit as well. The War on Drugs was a very complicated business.

Back home in Liverpool, the hidden cost of the Merseyside Cartel was a graveyard of destroyed lives. In 2007, a 14-year-old junior gang leader from Page Moss called Sean Westall was being groomed for a top slot in the corporation. Sean's blond hair, baby-faced looks and rosy cheeks belied a troubled and violent life. By the age of 14, he boasted that he had fired several guns and had been involved in 30 firearms incidents of some form or other. At 15, he was caught attempting to either retrieve or bury a handgun in waste ground near his home. Sean looked up to his older brother, a well-known gang member who posed with shotguns in his firm's YouTube videos: three-minute-long DIY pop videos with a soundtrack of Biggie Smalls and Tupac. Showing off their armouries was meant to deter other gangs. Being a gang member put a lot of pressure on Sean: it involved committing acts of violence, being hunted down by rival gangs, trying not to be arrested for firearms and drugs, and undergoing relentless Section 60 stop-and-searches. To de-stress from all this, Sean smoked green skunk cannabis almost relentlessly. At the age of 17, the pressure grew too much. Sean was found hanging in his back garden.

In 2012, the Cartel had reached the status of a terrorist group. The military and intelligence publication *Jane's Defence* devoted a four-page article entitled 'Mersey Heat' to an academic study of organised crime in Liverpool. The threat level posed by the group was defined as 'active' and 'medium'. The article's author, Anna Sergi, an expert in transnational crime, wrote, 'Liverpool is regarded as the UK's major centre for organised crime outside London. UK authorities have linked criminal activities in Liverpool to Spain, Turkey and South America.' The University of Essex academic added, 'Liverpool's unique characteristics and history make it likely that the city will continue to produce major figures in organised crime. Meanwhile, its continuing social and economic poverty mean that street gangs will remain characteristic of urban life, with all the dangers that poses for community safety in the city's poorest estates.' The report also stated that the Cartel had thrived in Liverpool 'owing in part to its geographical situation and historic port, with its connections to the Americas as well as Europe.' Rightly, *Jane's Defence* noted that 'organised crime in the city comes in two parts: on the one hand, powerful individuals responsible for controlling large amounts of money and drug shipments, and on the other, street gangs made up of local youths who may become involved in drug dealing and gun crime.' The third key point was that 'Despite significant victories for police, the underlying threat from organised crime in Liverpool remains substantial, as the socio-economic situation continues to tempt teenagers into joining gangs, and powerful criminal individuals remain at large.'

Many experts feared that the existence of the Cartel, and widespread organised crime in general, was a ticking time bomb in British cities. The empowerment of young gangs, militarised police and the effects of economic recession was a dangerous cocktail, one that could lead to a nightmare scenario in which there would be repeat riots, like those of August 2011, but this time there would be widespread use of guns. Thirty years on, a businessman was standing at the exact spot where he started the Toxteth riots in 1981. Back in the recession-hit '80s, he was angry at government cuts that had led to massive deprivation. The crisis had been made worse by heavy-handed policing. Today, the 53-year-old ex-gangster, who cannot be named for legal reasons, predicts that Britain will go up in flames again – for exactly the same reasons. However, this time he warns there will be a serious difference. Instead of bricks and petrol bombs, today's rioters will be armed with automatic weapons, handguns and IEDs.

'It's like history repeating itself,' says the businessman, who escaped the grinding poverty of riot-torn Liverpool 8 to become a successful Cartel drug dealer turned entrepreneur, 'except now the angry young men are either armed or have access to guns. That's a tricky situation on both sides of the barricades. Even jobless brickies know how to get hold of a gun these days, because, simply put, they are out there in large numbers. Gang culture is deep rooted on these estates – and the unemployed are swelling their ranks. What's different is that people today are not afraid to use serious violence, especially against a system they blame for obliterating their future.'

The businessman, who has ploughed some of his fortune into projects to help teenagers in poor areas, is not alone in his apocalyptic vision: it is shared by politicians, experts in public order and urban security, and even police officers. Some observers believe that the disproportionate power of organised crime combined with over-armed police and increased poverty is too much for communities to take. They say it is threatening to provoke Britain's poorest areas into more rioting. Tensions are rising between police and unemployed youths on a scale not seen since the disturbances in 2011 and, before that, in Toxteth, Brixton and Handsworth.

The police are also gearing up for the threat. In London, the Metropolitan Police have bought 13 Jankel Guardian armoured personnel carriers weighing six tonnes each and equipped with sniper platforms and 'reactive intervention systems'. Merseyside Police have acquired two army-style

Snatch Land Rovers – called Ballistically Protected Vehicles – like those used in Northern Ireland and Iraq. Kent Police are leading a consortium of law-enforcement agencies to buy military-standard aerial drones built by BAE and used in Afghanistan. New police paramilitary squads have also been formed, armed with German Heckler & Koch G36 machine guns with a range of half a mile and capable of firing 750 rounds a minute. SAS-trained police units are based at Manchester, Leeds, Birmingham and London. The squads are under the control of Police Chief Constables, except if there is a major incident, in which case a senior officer from Scotland Yard will take charge. Police officers have also been photographed wearing civilian clothes with blue caps marked 'Police', and carrying a specially modified Heckler & Koch G3K rifle with a shortened barrel and a butt from a PSG-1 sniper rifle fitted to it: a combination used by the SAS. Others wearing T-shirts, jeans and trainers have been identified carrying Heckler & Koch G36C with new target illuminators purchased as an 'urgent operational requirement' for UK special forces.

Forces around the country have updated their training, and now have many more armed officers and specialist weapons, such as those carried by the police hunting Raoul Moat, the armed fugitive who went on the run in Northumberland in July 2010. But experts warn that this 'militarisation' of the police is leading to an arms race between officers and disillusioned pockets of society. Speaking to this author, Professor Stephen Graham, an expert in cities and society at Newcastle University, said: 'Military ideas of counter-insurgency that have been learned in Iraq and Afghanistan relate increasingly closely to domestic policing. Examples include the deployment of drone systems, anti-terror surveillance and the barricading of whole city centres for sports events and political summits. Armed response units are increasingly called out for relatively minor offences. Cities are being increasingly viewed by the authorities as threatening spaces where everyone is seen as a target.'

In 1981, the former Cartel drug dealer turned businessman was one of three young black men who tried to stop a pal being arrested by what they believed were heavy-handed policemen. The dispute sparked the Toxteth riots that raged for nine days and later the man became a hero in parts of his community. 'The information coming back to me this time,' he says, 'tells me that the disturbances will be more widespread and won't just be confined to the ghetto. It'll be the poor white suburbs as well, because those places were already on the breadline even before the cuts. I've spoken to the lads about it in these places. Places like Toxteth in the inner city have become gentrified and even Islamified. The youngsters have more money. It's still as fragile as it was back then, but it's just that there are many more tinderboxes around. Back in my day, black people were angry with the suss laws. Today it's the white kids who see themselves as oppressed by the anti-terror legislation, such as section 44 of the Terrorism Act. Then there are section 60s, pre-crime laws. It goes on. There's a tension, a real hatred now of the police anti-gang units, which is similar to what we had in our day. But it's not just Toxteth; it's Croxteth too.'

He is referring to the sprawling housing estates in the North End of Liverpool. Black people jokingly call it 'the Snow' because of its overwhelmingly white population. In neighbouring Norris Green, which falls under the same postcode, the gang members agree.

'It's breaking point,' said 18-year-old Liam. 'I used to work part-time as a labourer and a roofer, but that's gone. I used to go to day-release at college, but there's no funding now. There's anger, and it will go off. I'm not a gang member, but what else is there to do? There's shootings all the time round here now. Can you imagine what it will be like when it kicks off? There will be more shooting.'

The youths said that tension had been building up since around 2005, when the gangs started to ascend the Cartel hierarchy, but that the recession, gang warfare and problems with the police had accelerated the feeling of despair. On another estate, the language is similar.

'Would I shoot at the police?' asked a teenager from a notorious estate. 'It's not a case of "if" but "when". The police are going to get a very hard time around here when it goes off.'

The 19-year-old isn't a gang member. He's an unemployed car valet worker.

'It's wolf season round here. Everything is tightening up. People are stealing even small things to make money. I heard a girl saying that she might not have a job because the Sure Start centre might be going. Another woman was in tears because her benefits had been stopped. They are stopping people's Jobseeker's Allowance for small things, like not turning up or postponing a meeting at the job centre, whereas you used to be able to phone up and rearrange it. That all adds up to pressure.'

His 40-year-old friend added, 'I remember there were riots in the 1980s. But I've seen clips on YouTube of the riots in LA in 1993, and I think it will be like that over here. There's going to be people running about with guns, mayhem, people getting hurt.'

Speaking to this author, Dr Mike Rowe, a criminologist at Northumbria University, said: 'Public disturbances in the future will look very different from those in the 1980s. Footage from the riots then show police officers hiding behind dust-bin lids. Rapid changes in policing have led to police looking and behaving in a much more militaristic way. Legal powers, technology, CS gas, Tasers and guns are just a few examples. The police have access to much more varied and more powerful weaponry these days. It will be very different. If there are shots, the police these days can do so much more than withdraw or practise containment. Before a disturbance, there's much more emphasis on gathering intelligence. There is close monitoring of the use of weapons on estates. There is pre-emptive use of community intelligence, which is sophisticated, and social indicators to gauge whether a community is at risk of disturbance. And afterwards there's much more effort in treating riot areas as crime scenes with a view to gathering evidence for conviction. It's no longer seen as a no-man's-land. Firearms haven't been used in great numbers in a public disturbance on the British mainland for 150 years. But we do seem to have more weapons in society in general, and the effect of criminal groups on urban unrest is not yet fully known. That factor, combined with rioters' use of technology, makes the situation much more unpredictable. For instance, in 2005 rioters and protesters in Birmingham used mobile phones and social networks, making the disturbances much more unpredictable from the police perspective.'

Following the 1980s riots, the police have been trained to deal with a small number of gunshots being fired during a riot. During the Tottenham unrest in 1985, two shots, believed to be from a shotgun, were discharged from a tower block while riot police clashed with crowds in the streets down below. In 2011, several shots were fired at police in London and Birmingham. Using Broadwater as a blueprint, the police developed a make-believe British town called Sandford, in which senior officers modelled their decision-making in riot situations under ACPO-guideline conditions. However, police officers say that this training is now seen as obsolete because of the unrealistically low levels of gun threat and the huge changes in armed police protocols.

One police firearms officer in Liverpool told this author how police officers feared a 'worst-case scenario' of multiple gunshot attacks on a crowded, riot-torn street at a time when the police's capability has been cut. He said, 'There's a high probability of riots involving more shooting, more people. You only have to look at what happens in Northern Ireland now: even if it's just a gang of kids, they bring their weapons out. And let me be clear on this point: we can no longer just write that off as a Northern Ireland phenomenon that's got more to do with gangs and hoodies than sectarian violence. No matter what the situation, it's the same training and tactics to deal with a firearms incident. We train for every eventuality. The threat level is extremely high in a public-order situation. We have trained to deploy with a BPV, which has 360-degree armour plating. Normal armed-response cars are only armoured at the front. We can now use ballistic shields to enter a hostile area and can use tactics such as mobile containment and stop. The likely scenario is this: there's a disturbance on an estate and unarmed staff are sent to deal with it. A "bandit" call goes out. That's when an officer calls out "bandit, bandit, bandit" over the radio to say that shots have been fired. Their job is to seek hard cover behind, say, a wall, a substantial tree or an engine block. At this point it's vital that the unarmed staff at the scene start to secure the area. Obviously they cannot approach the gunmen: they have to wait for the specialist officers to get there. But they can clear a perimeter area of people, thus making the job easier for us. This is called an "outer containment area". It's essentially a "sterile" area: one that does not contain civilians, rioters or suspects and is under our control. It's an area into which we can be brought. It's a place we can operate from. Then, say, two cars per shooter are sent in. Contain and neutralise the threat. The problems come if the sterile area is overrun. There's a high chance of being attacked and disarmed. We're trained to watch for people coming up from behind and trying to knock us out. That's why we each have a Taser and a baton. But if there's a riot going on, it makes it very risky. It would be difficult to deal with a sterile area suddenly filling up with civilians, hostile or otherwise, and then you come under attack from several shooters. I wouldn't like to be in that situation.'

The social distortions caused by the presence of organised crime are the hidden cost of the drugs problem and all-powerful groups such as the Cartel. However, the overt costs are just as high. Globally, for more than 40 years, the War on Drugs has accounted for 45 million arrests, cost more than $1 trillion, made America the world's largest jailer and damaged poor communities at home and abroad. Yet for all that, drugs are more available today than ever before according to filmmaker Eugene Jarecki, who made a documentary called *The House I Live In*, which investigated the poor rationale behind the War on Drugs and explored its systematic failures. David Simon, creator of *The Wire*, who became an authority on inner-city policing after spending years as a reporter covering crime in Baltimore, believes that drug investigations have zombified large sections of the police force, because concentrating on the easy arrests of non-violent drug offenders has left many police officers unable to solve proper crimes, such as murder. The big question is: will Britain go the same way?

Today, the Cartel is both a victim of the War on Drugs and one of its unintended successes: a victim in the sense that today the Cartel is more vulnerable than it has ever been, and a success in that it is undoubtedly stronger in sales and reach than at any time in the past 40 years, with plenty of potential for growth in new overseas territories and in new alliances with foreign gangs. Today, the Cartel stands at a crossroads. Undoubtedly, the police have the capability to take it down. But the Cartel also has the means to outmanoeuvre the police. For the time being, it's a stalemate. Only time will tell who will win and who will lose.

For those who were involved, the picture is clearer. The Analyst has now retired from Merseyside Police after 30 years of service. He said, 'I can leave the force knowing that I did my best and that we have had many successes against the drug dealers.'

Yael Feeney was released from jail in January 2013 and now runs a legitimate business abroad. He said, 'The Cartel is still going, but today it's run by kids, teenage gang members who behave like scum. My guess is that they will kill each other and the multimillion-pound operation we had will be destroyed.'

Bubbley Shalson is also out of prison but has gone back to dealing drugs. He said, 'The drugs cartel I work for will always be there. Today I sell less drugs, but I do a kilo every two weeks between me and a couple of contacts. I have branched out into other forms of crime. Some of us are moving into the manufacture and distribution of legal highs.'

Kallas is believed to be in Spain running a high-level drugs operation. David Hibbs-Turner and Curtis Warren are still in prison.

Terence Riley, the drug dealer who found the body of James Bulger when he was a child, is also behind bars.

No one has been charged or convicted for the murder of Colin 'King Cocaine' Smith, and police are still pursuing the main suspects.